Courage in Adversity

Michael Forsyth-Grant

Courage in Adversity

The Pentland Press Ltd
Edinburgh

Typeset by IPEK Origination Ltd.
Printed and bound by Billing and Sons Ltd
Jacket design by Janet Dalgarno

ISBN 0 946270 81 3

To

Sub-Lieutenant I.B. Galbreath
R.N.V.R. of H.M. Motor Gunboat 118
H.H. Motor Torpedo Boat 437

Killed in Action 23.12.43

Contents

		Page
Foreword		viii
Acknowledgements		xii
Part I	**My Early Life**	
1	Genesis	3
2	Exodus	9
3	War is Declared	16
Part II	**From Coastal Drifter to Destroyer**	
4	H.M. Drifter Shower	27
5	H.M.S. Tynedale	38
6	Further Adventures in Tynedale	53
Part III	**Coastal Force**	
7	Coastal Forces (I)	65
8	Coastal Forces (II)	78
9	Gaining Experience of Motor Gunboats at Dover and Ramsgate	88
10	Further Adventures and Some Misadventures with M.G.Bs.	97
Part IV	**In an Escort Destroyer on the Russian Convoys**	
11	Musketeer	111
12	Gun Control Officer and Correspondence Officer in Musketeer	118
Part V	**Shore-based at Freetown**	
13	Fresh Experiences in West Africa	129
14	My New Post as Naval Transport Officer	138
15	Further Experiences in Sierra Leone after VJ Day	145

16	Hunting for Elephant in the Wilds	155
17	The Voyage Home	159
Part VI	Return to the Peacetime R.N.V.R.	
18	Back to the R.N.V.R. in Dundee	167
19	Cruises Farther Afield and a Sojourn in Portsmouth	173
20	Further Adventures in the R.N.V.R. during the Fifties	180
Part VII	Business and an Excursion into Politics	
21	Early Struggles to Establish Myself in Business	191
22	Two Salmon Wars	201
23	Excursion into Politics	211
Envoi		221
Index		226

Foreword

by
Surgeon Vice-Admiral Sir John Rawlins, K.B.E.

It was during my third term at Wellington College that I first became aware of Michael Forsyth Grant. He was 4 years senior to me and seniority at Wellington in those days was taken every bit as seriously as seniority in the Navy. My elder brother, Sam, was 5 terms senior to me and he had made it crystal clear that I was not to be seen talking to him in any circumstances.

What brought Michael to my notice was his performance in House and School debates. He invariably spoke from the floor and took on all and sundry. Like many boys in the middle 1930's, particularly those from military families, he was an ardent supporter of the National Socialist movement in Germany, which he perceived as a bulwark against the threat of world Communism and against economic domination of Europe by the great Jewish finance houses. He was indeed obsessively anti-Semitic and whatever the subject of the debate lost no opportunity to deliver waspish attacks on certain seniors whose accident of birth, commercial background and evident affluence he regarded as an affront to public duty. I had no particular sympathy for his views – indeed my sympathies were rather with his opponents who seemed nonplussed by these onslaughts. What impressed me was that this rather small, lightly-built Junior had no hesitation in berating and not infrequently insulting Seniors, including House prefects, who appeared to me to be almost on par with the Staff.

Having two older brothers I was accustomed to standing up for myself, for we had fought amongst ourselves as long as I could remember, and with an inborn love of wrestling (I was later President of the Oxford University Judo Club and taught unarmed combat) I had physically dominated my prep-school comtemporaries at Wellington. But seniority was sacrosact and masters, whom my brothers and I regarded as the enemy for we hated school, were to be outwitted if possible but never confronted: for they were on a totally different plant and armed, not only with absolute authority but with the cane! For all masters at Wellington were entitled to use the cane as were House Prefects, and there were a number of notorious and terrifying sadists whose displeasure was to be avoided at all costs. Worse still were the School Prefects, athletes for the most part, who took a pride in the technique of beating and literally took great strides to maximise the effect.

I soon found that Michael had no qualms about confronting any and all of these superior beings if he had the least cause to suppose that he was the victim of an injustice. He would threaten to report a prefect to the House Tutor or the Tutor to the Master himself, and to my astonishment emerged from these encounters unscathed, frequently having obtained an apology.

Until then I had associated mainly with my immediate contemporaries, all excellent games-players which I was not and from a very different background. Michael had not then assembled the Mafia-like gang which would later indulge in criminal activities that were unprecedented at Wellington. However he already had his henchman, Conn Hackett, a charming and romantic Irishman who educated me in the facts of life which until then I had been entirely ignorant, my brothers, who were undoubtedly well-informed on the subject, having never bothered to enlighten me.

Conn introduced me to Michael and we at once discovered a common interest in field sports. I loved shooting, albeit on a scale far inferior to Michael's battues in Scotland, and I kept ferrets. I was also an accomplished poacher, instructed by the son of the village carpender and by reference to a small library of books including the incomparable "I Walked by Night", "The Keeper's Book" by P.I. Mackie and the works of Richard Jefferies, and I knew thing or two about animals. My brother Sam kept a menagerie of snakes, lizards, birds and mammals which we brought back to Wellington each term and kept in the garden of one of the masters: in addition we kept bees in primitive but effective hives in the woods at the bottom of the House garden.

It was, I imagine, this familiarity with country matters – all too rare amongst our College contemporaries – that induced Michael to take an interest in me. I became the third of his entourage and as he recounts, followed him blindly on all manner of escapades. We assembled a considerable armament comprising a .22 Webley air pistol, a "garden gun" which fired small shot cartridges, and eventually a .410 double-barrelled pistol, a marvellous weapon for ferreting and for keeping the ferrets supplied with fresh meat.

Such firearms were unheard of at Wellington and were concealed as Michael relates. Our rooms were repeatedly and fruitlessly searched by Ian Husband, the House Prefect with whom Michael had such sport years later in Sierra Leone, and Michael became so confident that for a bet he shot a starling on the House roof with the .410, out of a window, in broad daylight!

Discovery would have been calamitous – a severe beating all round and almost certain expulsion, and we came close to it when Michael forgot to hide the barrel of the garden gun from which the stock and bolt had been disassembled. Ian Husband walked in unexpectedly, found the barrel and conveyed it triumphantly to Tutor. Michael was summoned and we waited with bated breath for the inevitable: but he returned, grinning all over his face. Obviously the barrel and trigger mechanism were unusable by themselves and he had succeded in persuading Mr Tancock that it was broken antique which he was polishing up!

When I was fifteen Michael invited me to Ecclesgreig. It was magical! The castle itself was beautiful, with its witch's hat tower. The great hall was festooned with displays of spears and claymores. The gardens with their clipped hedges and statuary, the splendid gunroom, and my bedroom which, like all the guest bedrooms, bore a pub sign and had appropriate chinaware and decor, (mine was The Green Dragon, with The Rose and Crown next door), and last but never least the loo, where on sat enthroned upon a dais in a small room wall-papered with entertaining family photographs and appropriate cut-outs – all were a delight. Both my parents were dead and Colonel and Mrs Forsyth Grant treated me almost like another son. I could never forget their kindness and many years later I spent happy hours with Evelyn Forsyth Grant, then more or less confined to her bed, chatting about those far-off days and about Portsmouth which she had so loved as a girl and missed so much as she looked out of her bedroom window over the austere east coast landscape.

Most people, I suspect, can count on the fingers of one hand those people who have made a recognisable contribution to their characters. For me there were the headmaster of my prep-school, two masters at Wellington, the surgeon for whom I first worked and Michael Forsyth Grant. From Michael I learned never to be scared of authority, and that loyalty, like gratitude, had to be earned: they were principles which carried me through a career in the Navy and led me into many a conflict with senior officers. But I maintained my course unswervingly, never found it necessary to kowtow to anyone, and always did my duty as I saw it to the best of my ability. Promotion never ceased to surprise me and, I suspect, surprised my colleagues a good deal more! But I eventually emerged on top of the naval medical pile as Medical Director-General of the Navy, and it was just prior to that final promotion that Michael and I made contact again after a 40 year gap.

Not long afterwards I took the family to Ecclesgreig en route to a holiday in Orkney, insisting that they brought a change of clothing suitable for a stay in a Scottish castle: only to find the castle converted into a grain store and Michael living in the adjacent cottage. The boy had grown into an affable bull of a man but I knew him at once from his characteristic walk and the twisting movement of his hand as he strode along.

We talked into the wee small hours that night and have remained in close contact ever since. He has an amazing memory – his story illustrates his near total recall – and he makes great efforts to keep up with his old friends. He and I and Ian Husband foregathered not long ago, and most happily.

I have fished the South Esk and 'Loch Ecclesgreig' and shot again with Michael last year, two marvellous days. The man is still the boy I knew, in spite of physical changes and a wealth of experience. He is a robust and highly entertaining companion, a man's man with a strong taste for the ladies, but a formidable adversary: if you want to trace the history of those belligerent genes you have only to read the story of his Uncle Osbert in the book "An Arctic Adventure – Grant and the Seduisante" by Fraser and Rannie.

The fact is that Michael has always seemed a trifle larger than life and in some respects something of an anachronism, a throwback to his Highland ancestors. A man of courage and decisive to the point of ruthlessness he is nevertheless a most kind, generous and loyal friend. His story is racy, frank, often ribald, and withal highly entertaining. There is no false modesty, but then you would not expect that in a man who has enjoyed such a rich and varied life and has lived it to the full.

The motto of the College which he evidently holds in high regard could well be his watchword – VIRTUTIS FORTUNA COMES – fortune favours the brave.

John Rawlins
June 13th, 1990

Acknowledgements

In writing this book I have had a lot of help from many people, reviving memories of things that happened long ago, and I thank them all for their efforts in producing the text and the illustrations.

The Imperial War Museum in London was most kind in allowing me to re-produce various photographs and to check various dates, and I particularly wish to thank Mr Roderick Suddaby, Keeper of the Department of Documents and Mr Paul Kemp of the Photographic Section for their time on my behalf.

I am indebted to Admiral Philippe de Gaulle for sending me his photograph as a midshipman aboard a Free French Motor Torpedo Boat in Dartmouth, where we served together, and to ex Ambassador Harry Jorissen for details of the battle shown on the Frontispiece, and to my son Maurice who painted the scene from these details, and also the battle scenes of other actions; and to Ronnie Barge, DSC., who painted Motor Gunboat 118 off South Foreland.

It would also be impossible for me not to express my sincere appreciation to Surgeon Vice Admiral Sir John Rawlins K.B.E. for having written such a good Foreword to the book.

I am most gratefully to my Secretary, Mrs Jean Paton, who has patiently typed and retyped my many ramblings on the subject until the final edition was agreed.

Finally, I would like to thank Douglas Law, the Publisher for his help and guidance in getting this book off the ground!

Michael Forsyth-Grant
Ecclesgreig
May 1990

PART 1

My Early Life

CHAPTER 1

Few people, I imagine, remember much of their lives before they were four years old. The earliest event that I can remember is the day my nanny left our home, Ecclesgreig Castle, near Montrose, and a certain Miss Cassidy came as governess in her place. I was the youngest of three children, my sister Fenella being six years older, and my brother Maurice four years older than I. It may be that all three of us were spoilt and unruly, but the fact remains that Miss Cassidy was somewhat irascible and took a dislike to all three of us right from the outset. She only lasted a month, to be replaced by a magnificent specimen of that now defunct breed, the upper-crust governess.

All this was in the 1920s, and in those days no family of standing could do without an army of servants, including cook, butler, housemaids, pantrymaids, and so on. In the houses of the exceptionally rich these had their quarters in the servants' hall. The governess was superior in status to all the staff, and held an exalted social position between the parents and the servants' hall, even drawing respect from the chauffeur and the butler. Miss H.E. Knight had previously been governess to a number of distinguished patrician families. She knew her place and how to wield authority without ever being overbearing. "Knight". as we used to call her, remained my governess for five years, teaching me the rudiments until I was sent to prep. school. Far more than that, however, she became a lifelong friend for over fifty years, and right up to her death I used to travel 500 miles every year to visit her.

The first time I was ever entirely on my own was the occasion when, at the age of eight, I was sent to Aberdeen to have my tonsils and adenoids removed. The experience of being anaesthetized was one that I shall never forget to my dying day. It was simply appalling. A sheet was placed over my face and ether was dropped onto it until I felt that I was being suffocated; people have died less painfully. When I awoke without my tonsils, I straightway vomited

The Author (standing) with his mother, brother and sister, 1926

blood violently all over the bed. In doing so I felt that I had repaid, at least in part, the sadists who had inflicted the vile operation upon me.

That was the first nasty experience I remember, but it was soon followed by another, no less nasty. At the age of nine I was wrenched from my home and sent away to prep. school at Malvern. I was miserably homesick, even though I found some consolation in the presence of my elder brother, whose companionship I was lucky to have for two terms. Once he had left for Wellington, however, the bullying began in earnest. The ensuing year was one of the most miserable that I can ever remember. All the bigger boys set about me, and I was bullied, kicked and beaten from morning to night.

Life was made still worse by a disaster which befell my parents at this time. Up to 1931 they had been rich and influential. But my father had invested heavily in companies directed by the two well-known financiers, Kruger and Staviski, including the Swedish match company, of which Kruger was chairman. Then the news broke that Kruger had committed suicide. It triggered off one of the worst share crashes ever known between the wars, and its repercussions were felt not only in Britain but throughout Europe, where it rocked established institutions and even brought down

Ecclesgreig Castle

governments. In recent times, there have been certain city scandals which have been considered grave. Those who think so never experienced the effects of the Kruger and Staviski crash.

The impact of all this upon our family was devastating. In a single night my father had lost £45,000, the equivalent, in contemporary terms, of several millions. Drastic economies became inevitable. Keepers and gardeners were paid off wholesale, to say nothing of the indoor staff. My parents thought of abandoning Ecclesgreig Castle altogether and building a smaller house nearby – still with a servants' hall of course! Not all families would have been as badly hit as we were, I suppose, but for us, at any rate, the days of affluence had ended. From that point on and for most of my life I was to know what it was to count the pennies.

As a matter of interest, it was about this time too that the great Dartmoor Prison mutiny took place. At ten years old, I was already an avid reader of the papers, and I regularly pored over the pages of the Daily Sketch, one of the most sedate of the tabloids of the period. Splashed across the front page one day was a picture of Dartmoor Prison on fire and enveloped in flames and smoke. There was also a photograph of the prison governor, whom the mutineers had abducted and taken hostage with a knife at his throat. As it turned out, this was by far the worst prison mutiny between the wars, and the governor was lucky to escape with his life. He owed his survival to the immense courage shown by one convict, who shielded him from the violence of the rest. After the riot was over, the outstanding bravery shown by this man earned him a pardon.

Even as our family fortunes were taking such a terrible turn for the worse, my personal life was beginning to take a more hopeful shape. By this time, although rather puny for my age and still the victim of constant mobbing on the part of the bigger boys, I was nearly eleven. Yet this was the point at which my whole life changed suddenly and permanently for the better. I can remember it as if it were yesterday.

I was in a dormitory of sixteen boys, and the bane of my existence was a twelve year-old bully named Yeatman. As usual, he had begun to kick and cuff me, and in my struggles to protect myself both of us fell onto a bed. Then some instinct made me grab his throat and I began to throttle him. His aggressiveness deserted him, his struggles grew weaker, and the habitual expression of predatory sadism which he wore gave way to a look of increasing terror. Never for one instant releasing the pressure on his throat, I jumped on top of him. Now I knew, and so did he, that I had the upper hand. Other little boys gathered round in astonishment and awe. For the first time in my life I experienced the exhilaration of power. It was a sensation which I was neither to forget myself, nor allow others to forget of me. At last, with a final contemptuous shake of Yeatman's head, I allowed him to get up and slink away. I was never bullied again.

The headmaster and his wife happened to be my uncle and aunt (she ranked one above the matron), and my elder brother had been quite popular with them. In my case, however, the bullying I had experienced had somehow left a chip on my shoulder, and I never got on with either of them.

From this point onwards my attitude changed radically. At that particular school the upper age limit was thirteen and a half, and by the time I was twelve I was slowly but surely becoming a dictator. I hope I was not a bully; I do not believe I was. I just wanted my own way. My attitude at that time could be summed up as: "If the headmaster and his wife don't like it, to hell with them!" Naturally, it was not long before I was at loggerheads with them both. It was no longer a case of the bullied little Forsyth-Grant against the mob (by which, of course, I mean the other boys!); now it was I who was being "bolshie" towards authority.

Although, as I say, I now found myself exercising an almost

dictatorial control over the other boys, I was in reality an individualist. The conventional aims of scholastic achievement and prowess in school games held little real interest for me, with the exception of tennis, at which I was fairly proficient. Both my father and the headmaster had excelled at all organized games, cricket in particular, but I found it utterly boring. As for the boxing classes which were held in the winter evenings, despite the headmaster's angry railings against my anarchy, I ignored them. Thus I incurred his fixed disapproval. In spite of this, I occupied the time that I might otherwise have spent at those boxing classes in designing and building a magnificent model of a battle cruiser. It was powered by electric batteries, which I encased in candlewax so as to make them waterproof. For armoured plating I hammered out sheets from a McVitie and Price biscuit tin. When it was finished it proved to be virtually unsinkable and became my pride and joy.

Though the headmaster so thoroughly disapproved of me, in two instances in particular he was proved wrong. First, goaded on by his strictures, I rose triumphantly to his challenge and won a much coveted prize by becoming form dux. Then in my final term I passed into Wellington 18th of 65, even though in that particular year about two hundred failed to obtain a place at all. Among them was my best chum, whose papers were sent on to Bradfield. It is a measure of the severity of the exam. that he sailed in there high on the list.

After this good pass into Wellington, I found myself relatively at a loose end for my final three weeks at prep. school. For some time I had been interested in explosives, and also in certain dubious forms of fishing and poaching. Running through the school grounds was a magnificent spring-fed stream (it was the one from which Malvern Water was bottled), and it was brimming with trout. These, then, were my quarry, and while others played soccer or cricket, I used to poach them. I devised a method of catching them by means of dams. I would first dam up a section of the stream and then release water, catching the trout that were left stranded in the process. Thus I and the gang I led became dam-builders.

For our dams we needed clay, and clay had to be quarried. This was where the explosives came in. I decided on an experiment in quarry-blasting on a miniature scale. My materials were a shotgun cartridge, a quantity of petrol which I stole from the cricket pitch lawnmower, and a slow match, also stolen from the store of fireworks set aside for Guy Fawkes night. I laid a trail of petrol, connected the cartridge to it, lit the slow match, and ran. At that moment the headmaster blew his whistle and shouted "time", signifying that in twenty minutes we would have to be in class. Just before we entered the class building, I heard a distant boom. Never shall I forget my triumph – I had fired my first explosive charge! Later that same day the results were such as to delight me.

The heartfelt thanks I felt as I took my leave of my uncle and aunt and their prep. school were no less heartily reciprocated by them. They were as glad to see the last of me as I of them.

CHAPTER 2

Exodus

The holidays following upon my final term at prep. school were full of interest. I had always been keen on field sports, fishing, shooting and riding, and in August 1934 I was lucky enough to be invited to shoot driven grouse on the Fetteresso Castle moors near Stonehaven.

Fetteresso Castle had been rented by a Mr Herbert Pratt, one of the richest oil tycoons in the United States. How my father had come to make his acquaintance I do not know, but here I was, a boy of thirteen, invited for a couple of days on his moors! I had shot grouse before, but only doing it the hard way, and carrying all my equipment; this was to be quite different. On arriving at the castle, I was introduced to Mr Pratt's guests, comprising a gallery of his fellow millionaires and including such names as Hutton of Woolworths and Kellog of cornflakes fame. Off we set in a fleet of Rolls Royces, all supplied by Harrods. On arriving at the Stonehaven-Banchory road, we were met by a troop of ponies, the object being to save us from having to walk a single yard. Further pack ponies brought up the rear, carrying all the gear.

When I arrived at my grouse butt, which had been provided with a camp seat, it proved too high for me to see over the edge. Forthwith a host of retainers gathered round and commenced rebuilding it round me, pulling down the high bits and reducing it to a height more suited to my thirteen year-old stature. Meanwhile the Americans read novels and financial papers until the driven grouse arrived in sufficient numbers to justify them in opening fire.

Lunch, spread out on trestle tables in the heather, was a magnificent four-course affair, all of it supplied daily by Harrods and Fortnum and Mason. The Chicago butler, however, whom the Pratts had brought over with them, rather spoilt the Edwardian splendour of the occasion. I was the only guest under fifty, and as he was handing round cigars he addressed me in the following terms: "Say, little guy, how about a smoke for you?" Politely I declined. I doubt whether those Americans had ever seen a typical Scottish laird's son of thirteen opening up on the grouse as though he had been doing it all his life, even though his accuracy was no better than theirs. However, they kept a close eye on my activities, and soon decided that if I did miss a few grouse, "he sure is a dead-eyed Dick at them blue hares!"

By mid-September our holidays were over, and Maurice, Fenella and I set off together for our respective schools in England. Our London rendezvous was the fabulous grill-room on Platform 10 at King's Cross. For many years it was presided over by the famous John Cobb, the head waiter. He was a splendid old Victorian character, complete with wing collar and long tails, and he organized all our expenses and arranged taxis for us. No doubt he was suitably rewarded by our grateful parents. In after years John Cobb was to continue to be a staunch supporter of our family. Sadly, during the blitz the grill-room at King's Cross suffered a direct hit, but he survived and became head waiter at the Great Eastern Hotel in Liverpool Street. All through those war years, when hotel rooms in London were like gold dust, he was to continue to look after our family superbly. On the only occasion when the Great Eastern could not provide me with a room, he took me to his own magnificent house at Acton to be looked after by his wife!

Although not all of its pupils took up military careers, Wellington College was unquestionably the foremost military school in the United Kingdom. It was divided into a main block and four outlying houses. My father and many of our relatives had been in the main block, yet he refused to allow me to enter there. The reason was that in the previous year its reputation had been darkened by a great scandal; the nephew of Winston Churchill had been expelled for distributing Communist propaganda! Accordingly, I was assigned to one of the outlying houses, Wellesley House.

I settled in fairly easily. Once again it was pleasant to have my elder brother in the offing. He was in a distant part of the college, and in a school of this type age distinctions were rather rigidly observed even between brothers. The result was that we seldom met. Even so, he still managed to keep an eye on me for my first two terms. One of Maurice's friends, I remember, was a decidedly unmilitary-looking character, who wore his hair unconventionally long at a time when "short back and sides" was de rigueur. He also used to make thoroughly unsoldierly remarks about the establishment in general. In the end, however, all this seemed to make very little difference, for some thirty years later he was to achieve distinction as General Sir Harry Tuzo, commanding the British Army of the Rhine.

My first two years at Wellington were relatively uneventful. In my class work I was just coasting along, neither outstandingly good nor startlingly bad. I still showed little enthusiasm for organized cricket or rugger, and this may be one reason why my relations with my tutor or housemaster were always strained. Instead of these more orthodox interests, I kept a large number of animals – it almost amounted to a menagerie – at the house of another master, who was more sympathetic in outlook, and not a housemaster. Amongst other creatures, I kept ferrets and bantams, while another chum had a mongoose.

I took carpentry and gardening classes, but shone at neither. However, I did devise a magnificent window-box for my room, which overlooked a council road leading from Crowthorne to Sandhurst. It was much admired and commented on by school staff and outsiders alike. Little did they know that that window-box had a false bottom stuffed with guns, pistols, and ammunition galore! We used them to shoot rabbits, rats, pheasants, squirrels and starlings, most of which were fed to the ferrets and the mongoose. I joined the Natural History Society, membership of which carried with it the privilege of keeping a bicycle. This, of course, greatly enlarged my field of activities, and I was able to range far and wide smuggling liquor and cigarettes from Camberley for some of the bigger boys. It was hardly surprising, in view of the profits I made from these expeditions, that I did not need any extra pocket money from my father.

In defiance of the school rules, I joined the Farnham and District Angling Club, and thought nothing of cycling forty-five miles on Saturdays and Sundays to fish Frensham Pond or the River Loddon. In this I was joined by two friends, Alastair Telfer Smollett and John Rawlins. The first-named was destined for the army; he was unfortunately killed just before Dunkirk. The second was a scrawny youth, one year younger than I. As he followed me blindly on our highly illegal forays through the countryside, I could never have imagined that he would one day become Surgeon Vice-Admiral Sir John Rawlins, Medical Director-General of the Navy. Sitting next to me in class for several terms was another friend, who was later to achieve a tragic fame. This was Christopher Ewart Biggs, who years later was assassinated by the I.R.A. while British Ambassador in Dublin.

On certain Saturday nights in winter we had a cinema show in the Old Hall of the main college block. With 700 boys and others all thronging in, it used to become jam-packed, and there was always a terrible scramble for seats. Wellesley House was nearly half a mile from the main block, and to counteract this disadvantage we were allowed to queue at the Great Gate. The gates were unlocked at seven-thirty p.m., and then all hell would be let loose, as five hundred boys rushed in simultaneously to grab seats.

Now lurking within me there have always been the instincts of the explorer, and it was not long before I discovered that beneath the college there was a network of underground passages running to boiler-rooms, water- and sewage-pipes, and so forth. Access to them was by means of manholes placed at strategic points both inside and outside the Great Block. It was not long before I had discovered an underground route which enabled me to avoid queueing at Great Gate altogether. All I had to do was to jump down one manhole outside, come up another inside a quadrangle in the Green Quad, and from there move quietly into the Old Hall. I and my friends used to carry in cushions with which to reserve seats for older boys, who paid us handsomely for the service. In this way too I added appreciably to my pocket money. One evening, however, I had a narrow escape. I was discovered by a fireman and chased along the catacombs, very nearly being caught. I decided to teach him a lesson, and this led me to devise my first rocket-launcher. Next time he chased me I opened fire. Back down the length of the brick tunnel the rocket crashed and spluttered, while the terrified man ran for his life. It was the last time anyone tried to intercept me!

Up to this point my scholastic progress, meagre as it was, had seemed to be even further in decline. Now, however, I came under the care of a new form master, who was intriguingly strange and different from any I had met before. To begin with, unlike his colleagues, who were notoriously badly off, he was relatively affluent, having inherited from a distant relative a small factory engaged in the production of corsets. Yet instead of retiring from teaching, he chose to put others in charge of the factory and continue in his chosen calling. So far as I was concerned, this man's history teaching was, academically speaking, the catalyst I had been waiting for. I was absolutely inspired, and my work was suddenly transformed. Relying entirely on history and english – for I took little interest in other subjects – I became dux of my class. Three times in one term I was presented to the headmaster for meritorious work. This was F.B. Malim, who ranked fairly high among the great public school headmasters. I came to know him quite well. Few pupils liked him, but he was always thoroughly pleasant to me, and even admired my gardening efforts, which, it will be remembered, served as camouflage for the criminal firearm offences which I was committing almost daily!

When I took my School Certificate, the then equivalent of "O" Levels, I flabbergasted both myself and my parents by gaining far greater honours than I had ever expected. As things turned out, however, it was of less value than appeared at the time, for I was never destined for an academic career.

I entered with a fair degree of enthusiasm into the activities of the O.T.C. (later superceded by the Army Cadet Force), and for one fortnight attended an O.T.C. camp at Strensall near York. In those days the army marched in fours, but the growing threat of war with Germany had made the authorities very conscious of the need to modernize. Wellington had a whole battalion of cadets, and the manoeuvres held at Strensall were realistic to a degree. In our fours we marched along country roads where, by way of exercise, we were constantly being strafed by low-flying bi-planes. Instead of diving for cover, as the modern practice would be, we remained packed like sardines in our fours in the narrow road. As the planes dived to attack, ranks one and three would fire a volley of blank cartridge at it on command, and as it passed overhead, ranks two and four would do the same. Six hundred .303 rifles all firing blanks in unison made a fairly awe-inspiring noise!

Within a matter of months, however, the army had changed from the four- to the three-rank formation, and the anti-aircraft drill was changed. No longer were we required to stay packed in our ranks on the roads when an enemy aircraft attacked, or to blaze off at it rank by rank. That particular form of response was consigned to oblivion. More regrettably, perhaps, the magnificent sight of troops marching and changing direction left and right in fours on the parade ground was likewise lost for ever.

At Strensall I saw some magnificent spectacles, notably an attack by tanks which had taken part in the Battle of Cambrai twenty years earlier. The Bren gun had just been introduced from Czechoslovakia. Its name was made up by combining two different place-names: the first two letters of "Brno", its Czech town of origin, were joined to the first two letters of "Enfield", the English town where it was manufactured. In demonstrating the various types of machine gun, the instructors blazed away first with heavy Vickers Maxim guns, then with Lewis guns, and finally introduced the new Bren. It was said never to jam, but on this occasion, much to the instructors' embarrassment, it promptly proceeded to do so.

At these O.T.C. camps there was always rivalry, and often some bad feeling too, between the various schools attending. Insults were traded between schools. Hostility might arise, for instance, between ourselves and Hymers, Liverpool Grammar School, or some other rival. One night we decided to hold a pogrom, at least to the extent of letting down the guy ropes of some hated rival's tents. However, the Military Intelligence proved to be unexpectedly on the alert, and got wind of the plot. The upshot was that we were sent with full packs, side-arms and all equipment on a fifteen miles route-march. By the time we returned, we were too dog-tired to do anything, and the whole nefarious operation was cancelled.

We had endured two weeks under canvas. The food had been indescribably awful, the washing facilities primitive, and the latrines thoroughly insanitary. Now it was time to pack up and go home – in my case to Montrose. Accordingly, I caught a train at York. I cannot now remember the name of the train on that London-Edinburgh service – perhaps, since it was the anniversary of George V's accession, it was the Silver Jubilee. At all events, it was by far the most luxurious train journey I have ever made. I was able to take a bath, have my hair cut, and visit a cinema, all on the train!

That summer holidays of 1937 seemed to be packed with fun and enjoyment. At a local poultry show I gained a gold medal with my bantams, and also won the junior mixed doubles at Montrose Tennis Tournament – all on the same day! There were endless shoots, some provided by very famous people. One such was Sir James Caird, the shipping millionaire, who, incidentally gave the money for the naval museum at Greenwich. Another was Sir James Macdonald, who had once gone barefoot in Glasgow selling newspapers, yet had risen to become a millionaire and chief-of-staff to Cecil Rhodes. To meet and talk with such famous people was a wonderful experience.

All too soon the holidays came to an end, and I found myself returning to Wellington feeling at a loose end. So far as my studies were concerned, I had got as far as I could. I was not interested in going on to university, although, with my London matriculation, that road lay open before me. My father wanted me to go to Assam, and there join the firm of Matheson Jardine, in which the family had powerful connections. Alternatively, he was fully prepared to buy a share in a quarry in Wales, and put me in as a trainee. As it turned out, this would have been far the most profitable course. The quarry was later to prove a great money-spinner. It had its own harbour, and produced ballast for ships and for road metal. My godfather, Sir Robert Pearson, was Chairman of the Stock Exchange, and it was even suggested that I might try that as a career. When my tutor heard of it, however, he became quite apopleptic. "Then you will be no more than a parasite!" he exploded. With hindsight, I fully agree with him. Next, I wanted to be a barrister. My father told me that I talked too much already. Then I would be a farmer, but he would have none of this idea either. "No money in farming," he said.

Meanwhile I was making a nuisance of myself at Wellington, and none of my elders knew what to do with me. In desperation my father wrote to me to say that I could become an apprentice with a local fishing company. I would start at a very low wage, but if, after training, I made the grade, I might rise in that. As a prospect it was better than nothing, and faced with the threat of getting into serious trouble if I remained at Wellington, I decided to accept.

From January 1938 onwards I installed myself in a bed-sitter in Edinburgh, and embarked on a further course of studies as a preliminary to joining the firm. In the mornings I learnt to type and do book-keeping, and in the afternoons I used to work at the Fishery Board for Scotland, Salmon Fishing Inspectorate.

Having the status of independent student opened up a quite new world to me. I was studying fairly hard, and did not have much social life, although I did do some skating. However, friends and relations in Edinburgh were very good to me. For instance, the Second-in-Command of the Gordon Highlanders, stationed at Redford Barracks, was a friend of my parents, and gave me permission to use the regimental squash courts there. Thus squash became one of my principal means of keeping fit. It was during this period too that, for the first time, I felt myself strongly attracted to a girl, and I shall never forget it. The outlook was certainly not propitious; she was a gorgeous twenty year-old, whereas I was only seventeen. I never actually had sex with her, though it was not for want of trying. Sadly, the opportunity was lost, and it was not until two years later, in the course of my naval training, that this part of my life finally took wing.

I duly qualified in my Royal Society of Arts exams, and, in October 1938, just after the Munich crisis, I started my professional life as an apprentice with Joseph Johnston and Sons Ltd., Salmon Fishers, Montrose, at a wage of £1 a week. In the morning I learnt to weave nets, and in the afternoon I studied accountancy and the history of the firm. I was to continue in this calling for the next 48 years, interrupted only by my wartime service in the Navy.

CHAPTER 3

War is Declared

Despite the temporary lull following upon Chamberlain's famous "Peace in our time" speech in the latter part of 1938, throughout most of that year and up to September of the year following, the threat of war with Germany hung heavy in the air. Everywhere the nation was preparing for it, with the older generation leading the way. The veterans of World War I, for instance, were practising air raid precautions and counter-measures against possible attacks by poisonous gas, that being considered likely to be the first weapon which the enemy would use against us.

I was keen to do my bit by joining the Territorial Army, but when I approached my employers, they were anything but enthusiastic. I was very much an apprentice trainee, and since T.A. camps were always held in the summer, I would be away just when I was most wanted. Many of our men belonged to the Naval Reserves, and they suggested that I should join these, which would entail doing my training in the winter instead. It was even suggested that I might be a good candidate for the position of paymaster midshipman. However, I was very lucky. After some energetic lobbying by my family and certain influential friends, I was offered a vacancy as an executive midshipman in the Royal Naval Volunteer Reserve, East Scottish Division, at Dundee.

It was one evening in April 1939 that I received my first instructions. I was to report to H.M.S. Unicorn at Dundee. It was decided that I should make the journey by car, but my own car was unreliable, and my driving still far from perfect. Accordingly, to make sure that I actually arrived, my father sent his chauffeur with me. It was fortunate that he did so, for the Vauxhall broke down, and the damage was such as to require far more than the efforts of a tyro like me to put right. Nevertheless I managed to arrive in time for the drill.

Once having joined the gunroom of H.M.S. Unicorn, I found that training was fairly intensive, and everyone involved thoroughly enthusiastic. At first I found such experiences as walking out on booms, and climbing jacob's ladders somewhat terrifying, and I was in constant fear of falling into the water below. Gradually, however, I managed to master the necessary techniques. Then a day came when the latest type of heavy naval anti-aircraft guns were installed in Unicorn. They were twin-barrelled 4 (inch) Mark 16s, and we were all very flattered.

The citizens of Dundee used to gather in East Dock Street to watch our boat-handling in the Earl Grey Dock, sometimes admiring, but more often sneering at it. On my first stint in handling a cutter, powered only by oars, I gave the wrong orders, and the oar blades, which at that moment were pointing skywards, collapsed on the crew like a pack of cards, bruising most of them. Meanwhile the cutter hit the dock wall with a resounding crash, to the accompaniment of hoots of laughter from the two hundred or so civilian bystanders, and the fury of the captain and commander, who had witnessed the entire disaster. However, in the end this was another of the skills which I mastered.

By mid-July, the senior officers had decided that it was time for the midshipmen to show their metal. It was arranged that five of the most junior should take charge of three whalers manned by a score of fairly junior ratings. We midshipmen were eighteen years old apiece, while the ratings were aged up to twenty-four, and far more men of the world than we; they were already well accustomed to frequenting pubs, whereas some of us had never yet so much as entered such places! The plan was, then, with these somewhat ill-assorted crews, to row and sail the whalers across the Tay.

As we set off, we happened to pass the Dundee-Newport car ferry, and our manifest inexperience evoked howls of derision from the passengers who were watching us. At last we made Woodhaven on the other side. A very green rating leapt ashore and tied our painter (bow rope) onto another rope, unfortunately with a very slippery hitch. Shortly afterwards, as we were unloading, a second rating was in the act of transferring a huge crate of tea to the pier, when the slippery hitch began to slide down the main rope, and the boat drifted out from the pier. Transfixed with horror, I looked on helplessly as the sailor who was unloading the crate changed posture from the upright to the horizontal. "Help, save me!" he screamed. "Fuck him – save the tea!" retorted a callous voice. At that moment, with a stupendous splash, both sailor and tea were hurled into the water. Both of them were fished out, the latter drenched, furious, but otherwise uninjured.

Once ashore at Woodhaven, we pitched tents for the night and proceeded to scrape up some kind of meal. We had been instructed to set a good example, and so refrained from visiting the local pubs – not so the sailors! Some of them returned from their forays thoroughly drunk and truculent. By this time the rain was pouring down and, as we struggled to restore order, it became increasingly obvious that our efforts were pretty futile. Finally, soaked, dispirited and miserable, we retired to our tents and tried to get some sleep. From such initially poor material as we then were, are forged many of our best officers and ratings.

I was the most junior midshipman, and was also pretty slow in the uptake, and I was very conscious of both facts. Nevertheless I made great efforts to improve. I used to watch all activities with the utmost attention and, in case I had any trouble with my transport, took care always to arrive at drill twenty minutes early. Finally in August, I and a fellow midshipman, Eric Thomson by name (he was, by this time my immediate junior), were told it had been arranged for us to join the Fleet flagship for a month's training.

Alas, it was not to be! One night as I arrived for drill, I found that, as usual, I had twenty minutes to wait, so to kill time I strolled into the old L.M.S. station at Dundee to buy a newspaper. Before I had even opened it, the bill-boards all round the station told the tale: "Russia and Germany sign pact". I knew then that war was inevitable, and that it was most unlikely that Thomson and I would ever be sent to H.M.S. Nelson. So, in fact, it proved; within a matter of days we were at war.

Personally, I found the experience of going to war for the first time a fairly traumatic one. At that time, even though in theory the rank of midshipman in the navy was equivalent to that of second lieutenant in the army, or pilot officer in the R.A.F., in practice the senior service regarded midshipmen as neither officers nor ratings, but somewhere in between, and, as such, "the lowest form of life in the Royal Navy". Sometimes they were treated with the same disdain as they had suffered under in the pre-Nelson days of Captain Bligh of Bounty fame.

My orders were, after getting all my kit together, to report to H.M.S. Unicorn at Dundee, pick up Midshipman Thomson there, and proceed to Hove for a short course prior to joining a ship. Having boarded the train for Dundee, resplendent in my wartime plumage as a midshipman, I made my way to the restaurant car for a cup of tea. I was promptly assailed by an able seaman, Royal Navy, who was unmistakably drunk. I was highly embarrassed;

Joining the pre-war Naval Reserves, 1939

Off to the War, 1939

what on earth should I do? Luckily the train reached Dundee without further incident, but that was the first and last encounter with a drunken sailor in which I was at a loss what to do.

I duly reported to H.M.S. Unicorn and, after picking up Midshipman Thomson, and being bidden a kind farewell by the captain and commander, I joined the night train for London, on which we had first-class sleepers. It was the first time I had ever travelled first-class.

Since my encounter with the drunken sailor, my self-esteem had been sufficiently restored for me to decide that Eric Thomson and I had sufficient funds to buy dinner in the restaurant car. The menu and service were superb, certainly of a standard undreamt of by those who have only known British Rail. There were six courses: hors d'oeuvres, soup, fish, meat, sweet, and savoury. After ploughing through these, we felt distinctly replete.

As we were finishing, I espied some very senior R.A.F. officers at the other end of the car, and recognized them as old friends of my family. One was Air Vice Marshal Champion de Crespigny, who three years previously had been in command of R.A.F. Montrose; in former days my sister and I had often played tennis with him. The other was his A.D.C., Flight Lieutenant Milton, who had also been a shooting and tennis friend of mine. Now, however, the gulf in rank between us seemed to yawn so wide that I dared not introduce myself. Just as we were rising to go, the Air Vice Marshal recognized me and asked us to join them for coffee. To be on such terms with these two high-ranking officers put some real dynamite into our self-esteem.

Subsequently I was to take great interest in the career of Hugh Champion de Crespigny, whom I greatly admired. He had already distinguished himself in World War I, winning several decorations. Furthermore, under his command R.A.F. Montrose never suffered a single fatality, even though at No. 8 Flying School innumerable trainee pilots must have passed through his hands. By the outbreak of World War II he had already achieved very high rank. Yet in spite of this, and of his distinguished record, he was only appointed Inspector-General of Flying Training, whereas his friend Sir Arthur Longmore became a well-known Commander-in-chief.

Hugh had his problems of course. He was a firm disciplinarian, and very outspoken. After the war he offered himself as Tory candidate for the constituency of Kincardineshire, but was turned down. Then he joined the Labour Party, and in the 1945 election stood for an English constituency. However, in spite of the vituperative efforts of Harold Laski in his support, he was defeated. (Subsequently this campaign of Laski's led to one of the most celebrated libel actions of the century). Then Attlee sought to reward his efforts by making him governor of Schleswig-Holstein. Hugh, however, was not of the Laski-Bevan mould, and it was not long before he was at loggerheads with his masters. He resigned, and eventually went to South Africa, where he died in obscurity. It was a sad end to a great flying career.

However, I disgress; it is time to return to the story of my own early career. On arriving at H.M.S. King Alfred at Hove, I met another tennis-playing chum from Montrose, namely Alan Rothnie, who had also become a midshipman. Eric Thomson and I soon found that among our fellow midshipmen we belonged to a rather rare breed. Unlike the hundreds of others there (a much better description of their attitudes and experiences is to be found in Ludovic Kennedy's autobiography), our status as midshipmen was neither Temporary (i.e. for the war) nor Probationary (for three months), but Regular – and we were very conscious of the fact. It meant that we were rated high above the "war only" intake, and this was borne out by the kind of duties assigned to us.

One character in particular from that draft stands out vividly in my mind to this day. In appearance he was tall and highly arresting, partly because he wore an ear-ring, an almost unheard-of adornment for men in those days, and utterly alien to the Navy. I took note of his name, Ronald Chesney (though this, as was discovered later, was an alias; his real name appears to have been George Merritt), but at the time I felt quite sure that his was a wasted journey, and that among the probationary intake he would turn out to be one of those who were returned to their original units as "unsuitable".

In this, however, he proved me wrong. Chesney did actually become sub lieutenant. Much later I discovered that he had a most lurid past. At an earlier stage in his career he had been charged with having murdered his mother in Edinburgh, and had actually spent several years in prison, although the murder charge had been reduced. Next he had joined the Navy under a false name, eventually rising to the rank of lieutenant commander. In 1941 he did good work in running supplies to beleaguered Tobruk, and he was Midshipman Thomson's C.O. in Motor Torpedo Boats. In 1945, after the war ended, he became an officer in the Control Commission in Hamburg, but was court-martialled for stealing the most sought-after Mercedes in all Europe, the one which had belonged to Admiral Doenitz. Subsequently, he landed up in Tangier, and spent some time in running illegal Jewish immigrants from there to Tel Aviv.

Ronald Chesney, alias Donald Merritt

Before the war, his wife had stood by him and done much to rehabilitate him, after the murder charge against him had been found "not proven". Now, however, having made a large sum of illegal money, he decided to get rid of her, for by this time he had fallen in love with a German girl, Gerda Schaller by name, whom he had met in his Hamburg days. Accordingly, he worked out a most ingenious plan for the murder of his wife. Flying entirely incognito from Amsterdam to Ealing in London, he carried out the murder and was just leaving her home when his mother-in-law caught him. Without hesitation he murdered her too. However, his plans had been upset, and within a week he had been tracked down to Düsseldorf, only escaping justice by committing suicide in a cemetery there. The whole story has been brilliantly told, and of course in much greater detail, in a book entitled "Portrait of a Bad Man" by Tom Tullett, the chief crime reporter of the Daily Mirror. Again, however, I find myself digressing. Back to my own war!

The first sea-going ship to which I was appointed was H.M.S. Hood, then the largest warship in the world. However, my whole desire was to go to small ships, for which the experience I had gained in my civilian occupation should be of considerable help. To the consternation of my colleagues, therefore, I tried to get the appointment changed. The upshot was that I was sent to join H.M.S. Iron Duke, once the flagship at the Battle of Jutland, but now being used as a depot ship in Scapa Flow.

While in Scapa, Iron Duke had recently been bombed, and had actually had to be temporarily beached. Those of us who joined her spent a short time sleeping in makeshift bunks made from packing cases in what had once been Admiral Jellicoe's cabin. Before long, however, we were detailed to join the Auxiliary Patrol, which was made up of steam drifters. This was, in fact, only just after the disaster in which an enemy submarine had actually penetrated the Flow and sunk the battleship H.M.S. Royal Oak with great loss of life. The main job of the drifters, therefore, was to steam up and down the boom defences ready to drop depth-charges on any intruding submarines. I was introduced to Lieutenant D.B. Somers R.N.V.R., who was my C.O., and we were both told to go to Inverness and thence to Loch Ewe, where Somers was to assume command of H.M. Drifter Shower.

As we were crossing the Bay of Scrabster in the Pentland Firth, I came face to face with my first Germans. They were a Luftwaffe crew who had been shot down somewhere over Scapa and were now on their way to a P.O.W. camp under escort.

On arriving at Inverness, we reported to the naval railway transport officer, who, I discovered, was none other than Commander Lord Colville of Culross R.N. (Retired). He was a near neighbour of ours whom I had often met out shooting. Somers and I spent the night at the Station Hotel, and next morning, carrying all our extremely heavy kit, we caught first a train to Achnasheen, and then a bus to Aultbea.

Achnasheen is a place that I shall never forget; it was just like a frontier post in Texas a hundred years ago – not that it has changed much today! As for our trip on the mail bus, that was unforgettable too; for me it had the aura of dreamland! It was the only form of public transport to Aultbea. There were six pubs on the way, and the driver got out for a welcome dram at every one of them. Meanwhile two schoolgirls who were travelling on the bus were sick.

Finally we arrived at the Aultbea Hotel, where we and our luggage were dumped. The hotel housed the naval officer in charge and his staff, and shortly afterwards Barrie Somers and I found ourselves installed in H.M. Drifter Shower, with Somers in command and myself as his first lieutenant or Number One.

PART II

FROM COASTAL DRIFTER
TO DESTROYER

CHAPTER 4

H.M. Drifter Shower

H.M. Drifter Shower was a coal burner with steam reciprocating engines. Being constantly covered in coal dust, she was always pretty filthy. The lavatories were simply buckets with ropes attached to the handles in evil-smelling coops. After use they were emptied into the sea. Then the bucket would be lowered into the water by its ropes, and by these-rough-and-ready means swilled clean (more or less!). Except in the galley, the ship had no running water whatever, and no waste pipes into the sea. We washed in crude cabinets with a bucket below, into which the dirty water was emptied before being tipped over the side. To say that conditions were radically different from those at the Station Hotel, Inverness, or at my home at Ecclesgreig, would be an understatement. Yet I loved every minute of my time with Shower.

The day after installing ourselves aboard, Somers and I were introduced to the captain N.O.I.C. and to his staff. Captain H.D. Briggs R.N. (Retired) was a fiery old gentleman, who in 1919 had commanded the battleship Resolution in the Black Sea. Paymaster Commander Watson R.N. (Retired) was a charming old boy who spent all his time fishing. The boom defence officer had risen from the lower deck. The captain's executive officer was a certain Sub-Lieutenant W.R. Grieve R.N.V.R., two years older than I, who was later to become one of Scotland's best known law lords.

The crew of Shower was decidedly mixed. It consisted mainly of Royal Naval Patrol Servicemen who had formerly been fishermen. There were also merchant seamen and men who had been discharged from the Royal Navy without honours (?), as well as two Borstal Boys and a Union Castle steward. They were a pretty tough and undisciplined bunch, and I liked them all without exception.

When I first joined Shower, I was virtually teetotal and hardly ever smoked. However, on one occasion I was travelling from Perth to Thurso on the Jellicoe troop train to join H.M.S. Iron Duke. A group of us were sitting up all night, and an army captain passed round a bottle of whisky, inviting everyone in the compartment to have a swig. For fear of showing my virginity, I dared not refuse. The swig nearly killed me on the spot, but from then on my teetotal existence went into shattering reverse,

Somers was a very pleasant fellow. Five bottles of duty-free whisky costing £1 and cigarettes at 400 for £1 (old money) were just too much for him, as also for me. It was not long before I was drinking half a bottle of spirits and smoking 40 cigarettes a day, a practice which I was to continue for the next thirty years.

Loch Ewe had been a highly secret anchorage for the Home Fleet, and after the Royal Oak disaster, some ships had left Scapa Flow for its safety. However, the security of the Loch had been seriously compromised when H.M.S. Nelson, the fleet flagship, had been mined at the entrance with very severe damage and heavy casualties. In consequence, during those early days of 1940, H.M. Drifter Shower and four "armed yachts" were the only regular occupants. Nevertheless, a boom had now been constructed, a high-powered minesweeper was shortly due, and, once it had been made U boat-proof, great things were being prophesied for this huge sea anchorage. These prophecies were to prove quite accurate. It was to Loch Ewe that H.M.S. King George retired after sinking the German super-battleship Bismarck, and it was from here that the Russian convoys were to sail.

However, I am moving too quickly into the future. After the Nelson tragedy, the Loch was left in peace and solitude for a while, and our main job was to protect the boom against U boats by patrolling it with our three armed yachts. Then a point came when the Admiralty decided to build a large naval shore barracks there. One day Captain Briggs sent for me and told me that I was to muster all available labour, both Naval and Navy civilian and including two fisher crews, and lay the first sewer. With picks and shovels, as well as with some demolition charges which I had obtained, we dug and blasted the county council-owned tarmac road leading to the pier, put in huge sections of concrete sewer pipe, and were just getting the job consolidated, when along came a county council workman with a road roller, demanding immediate access. I refused. He declared that the Navy had no right to dig up the road, and proceeded to drive straight over our work, breaking the sewer we had just laid. There was nothing to do but dig the shattered sections out and replace them. Then the road roller returned, threatening to shatter it all over again. This time I ordered a Bren gun to be fired over the driver's head. He stopped his vehicle and came storming up to me, but I stood my ground, and he went off uttering dire threats. Afterwards he laid a complaint with Captain Briggs. However, he found no support in that quarter. Even though it led to a political row later, at the time Captain Briggs stood up for me and praised my action.

In those dark days of 1940, in the aftermath of Dunkirk, it was amazing what energy the country displayed. It was no time before several acres of barren land round Aultbea Pier had been transformed, with an extensive barracks, a large canteen, and naval stores standing upon them. It had all begun with my sewer!

Most of our stores had to be brought in by sea, but although MacBraynes, Island Ferries carried most of them, when it came to coal, we had to ship in our own from Stornaway. This was Shower's task. One Sunday we coaled early and sailed for Aultbea before noon. We had a rough passage in the Minch, and coal dust was washed everywhere, until the ship was dirtier than any coastal collier. We arrived about 10 p.m. and started to unload the coal onto the pier. Within ten minutes we received orders from the captain to stop immediately, and wait until one minute past midnight before completing our task. However dire the emergency after Dunkirk, the threat from the Germans, or any other consideration of wartime needs, the local minister and elders had absolutely refused to allow the work to proceed on the Sabbath! How we blasphemed against the Free Presbyterian Church of Scotland!

The local practitioner was a Dr. Hunter. He played the bagpipes quite beautifully, and he was a boon companion for my skipper. One evening he arrived in a state of great depression. He had delivered a child dead, and blamed the disaster on the fact that a small screw had been broken in the forceps he had been using. He showed it to me and asked to discuss the matter with the skipper. First, however, he wanted to consult our chief engineer, to see whether metal fatigue could be the cause of the breakage.

Now Petty Officer Engineer Charlie Coleman was a drifter engineer, an expert indeed on crude coal fire boilers, capstans, steam winches and the like. When it came to fatigue, however, the only form of this complaint he was likely to be capable of diagnosing was that arising from sweat and alcohol. I explained to the doctor that the skipper was ashore at the moment, but would be returning, and then, as a matter of courtesy, poured him a drink. Two hours later he had finished one bottle of Haig's Dimple, and I would give him no more. He tried to down some of the Isle of Ewe Mist (presumably an illegal potion), but I coaxed him ashore. He climbed unsteadily into his car, and had considerable trouble in starting the engine and putting it into gear. Now in terms of sound and speed, Dr. Hunter's car resembled a dive bomber. As he set off, I hastily telephoned the sentry from the pierhead to warn him that a madman was about to crash into the barrier – that he was to keep it open, not shoot, and ignore him. He would be harmless so long as no attempt was made to stop him. The doctor lived only about half a mile away round the semi-circle of the loch, and I was able to watch his progress. I was thankful when I saw him arrive – or so I judged from the headlights. Next day when I met his wife at the local store, she frostily refused to acknowledge my greeting. Apparently Dr. Hunter had stopped at his house, but then taken the wrong direction. He had been nearly up to his chest in the loch when his wife had rushed out in her night-dress and rescued him. It seemed unfortunate that it should be I who got the blame.

Being very much of the old school, Captain Briggs was a tremendous snob. He had a poor opinion of the less than upper-crust staff appointed to serve him, but my pedigree was well-known to him; in fact my brother-in-law was the tenant of a house of his in Suffolk, where he was commanding a bomber wing. Thus, whenever there was any upper-crust visiting to be done on the local lairds, I became his unofficial flag lieutenant or flag midshipman. It was in this capacity that I was often paraded when the captain went to tea with Mrs Sawyer at Inverewe, a house that is now the showpiece of the National Trust in West Scotland. On other occasions he took me to dine with a Mrs Mathews, and there I used to meet her daughter Susan. Sue used to be slightly embarrassed. She knew that I had seen her cavorting in an air raid shelter with a very tough stoker of ours from Lowestoft. I was not in the least embarrassed.

The man on the beat at Aultbea was Police Constable Bob Sinclair, and he had one of the better habitations in the hamlet. I came to know him well, for he was forever having to sort out the standing problem of "Navy versus civilians" in the Aultbea Hotel bar. We became firm friends, and he introduced me to his cousin, Police Constable Willie Sinclair, who had the next patch at Gairloch. Willie was a great fisher and shooter, and we had much in common. This included his daughter May, whom I courted vigorously, and who was kind enough to return my attentions. One way and another, I spent most of my time off in the vicinity of the Gairloch police station.

In September 1940, Willie organized a stalk for me after red deer. It took place on Flowerdale Forest, and was my first stalk ever, but alas, I missed an easy stag! I was mortified and inconsolable. Bob Sinclair had loaned me the police car for the day, and as I left in it I was almost in tears. Once back at Aultbea, I invited Bob to a drink – he too enjoyed the "duty free" – and before long I was well and truly in my cups as I explained to him how I had come to miss my first chance at a stag. Bob wound me up (I am sure it was because he needed the whisky), and in twenty minutes we had finished the bottle, at which point he departed. Then the skipper, D.B. Somers, arrived, and I had to tell my story all over again over a second bottle of whisky. By the time that was finished, I had passed clean out. I woke up in my bunk with handcuffs on. On losing consciousness, I had been duly fettered, lest I did damage to myself or, worse still, to somebody else. It was the first time I was ever completely drunk, and I was thoroughly ashamed of myself.

Dr Knox, the medic at Gairloch, had recently died, and I was able to buy his mahogany dinghy and outboard motor. I used it for fishing from Shower, and with great success. Nearly all our crew were expert fishermen, with the result that I was able to provide us all with fresh fish.

The great problem was petrol, for in wartime it was very strictly rationed and obtainable only on licence. However, the N.O.I.C. Stornoway, from whose command we obtained our stores, granted me a very small ration on the grounds that I was using it to provide fresh fish for the crew. The ration itself was miniscule, but then a strange thing happened. While on anti-submarine patrol, a huge Sunderland flying boat based at Invergordon ran out of fuel, landed in the Minch at Loch Ewe, and sent out an S.O.S. We towed the flying boat to a safe anchorage off Aultbea Pier, and the R.A.F. sent lorry-loads of fifty-gallon drums by road to re-fuel the monster. The drums had to be ferried out by small boat, and the petrol had to be pumped by semi-rotary into the Sunderland's tanks. The whole operation took several days, and meanwhile the crew of the flying boat was being looked after by us with plenty of "duty free". As for the petrol, the lorries simply dumped their barrels in a lay-by, and departed empty for Invergordon. Just before taking off for Invergordon on his return. the Squadron Leader skipper, who had greatly enjoyed our fishing trips, asked if I would like some petrol for my outboard. He told me that there were four barrels "buckshee", containing in all two hundred gallons of pure octane. They were mine so long as I removed them quickly. Acting like greased lightning, I soon had the stuff in hiding. Then I approached Bob Sinclair. "You have a car but no petrol", I said, "I have petrol but no car." "Deal!" replied Bob, and so it was sealed. I actually used to drive his car, with its sign of "Police" on the windscreen, from Gairloch to Montrose. Many were the surprised looks which I received from the Blue Caps, or

Military Police, but I bluffed my way through the lot of them. I was becoming educated, and thereafter, for the duration of my stay at Loch Ewe, motor transport was the least of my problems.

By this time Loch Ewe had a large naval presence, and on one occasion the famous actress Evelyn Laye came with an ENSA party to give a show at the Sailor's Canteen. At the end of the performance, Captain Briggs had just mounted the stage to thank her, when a loud voice rang out: "Sit down you old bastard, we've seen enough of you!" To my horror, I realised that it was Davis, our stoker, who, twenty-one years before, had been on the Resolution in the Black Sea, when Briggs had been captain. Davis was promptly arrested and did ninety days detention before being returned, well pleased with himself, to H.M. Drifter Shower.

In Shower the food was as filthy as the ship herself, but Steward Osborne, late Union Castle, used to cook tasty snacks for me from food of my own, which I produced from my father's estate, such as grouse, salmon, trout, and other delicacies. The ship's cook, however, was a disaster, and was speedily sacked. His replacement was a certain leading cook Royal Navy Patrol Service, but within three days he had gone back with acute V.D. and scabies. He in turn was replaced by Ordinary Cook Wilf Smith, who was eighteen and straight out of Borstal. He was a good-looking lad, and cooked quite well so long as he could escape from the lecherous, sex-starved gropers, of whom we had more than a fair share in our crew.

We had about four pleasure yachts, now called H.M. Yachts, which had been fitted with depth-charges, and assisted us in patrolling the booms. They had a single lieutenant R.N.V.R. and no other officer, and their crews included some strange characters. A certain lieutenant, for instance, seemed to me an austere figure, who had little time for youngsters like me, and I never really came to know him. Rather to my surprise, he later ended disgraced and in prison. His offence had been selling pornography involving WRENS. Lieutenant Gradwell R.N.V.R., on the other hand, though he was twenty years my elder and had served as a midshipman in World War I, was particularly kind. At that time he was courting a Laurencekirk girl whose family I knew, and whom he later married. We became great friends. There were disagreements between him and Captain Briggs, and eventually he left us, allegedly because of drink problems. Notwithstanding this setback, when disaster struck on the famous P.Q.17 convoy to Russia, he showed himself a hero in the truest sense. The part he played in this episode, and the decorations he won, have been very well documented. Subsequently he became a very celebrated magistrate in London, and I am deeply proud to have his autographed memoirs in the book entitled *The Destruction of P.Q.17* by David Irving.

One of the armed yachts, together with a motor drifter called Dundarg, needed a re-fit on the Clyde, and Captain Briggs ordered me to take over Dundarg for the passage. It was my first "acting command", and I was very proud. All went well, and I delivered the drifter to Bowling. Then, before rejoining my ship, I spent the night in Glasgow's Central Hotel. The first train for Inverness left about seven a.m., so in order to be in time for it I asked the hall porter to call me at six. It was the night porter who called me – and as he did so he dropped an entire tea tray on my bed before falling on it himself. He was hopelessly drunk. I kicked him out, went without tea, and caught my train.

On arriving at Inverness, I met my old friend Commander Lord Colville, the R.T.O. He told me that since in my absence Shower had sailed for Stornoway, I could have three days leave to go to Montrose. I thanked him most gratefully, but replied that to get to Montrose and back would take too long, and that I would be quite happy to join Shower in Stornoway. It was not long before I was on my way to Kyle of Lochalsh, and thence by Macbrayne Mail Boat to Stornoway, where I arrived in the late evening but in full daylight. Just as I was about to board Shower, I was accosted by Lieutenant-Commander Hughes-Onslow R.N. (Retired), who greeted me with a barrage of abuse. I was dumbfounded.

He told me that Shower had arrived in Stornoway at short notice for some unknown reason, and that Somers had asked for leave. Since Shower was to be in Stornoway for four days, and since the Naval Base assumed that as second-in-command I would take control, this had been granted. They were quite unaware of the fact that I had been sent to the Clyde with Dundarg. Meanwhile Somers had left Stornoway on the night mail boat for leave in Glasgow.

Officerless, the entire crew of Shower had broached the rum, and had got drunk practically to a man. Many, so it was alleged, had tried to interfere with the virgins of Stornoway, though I knew that these were rarer than ospreys! The entire crew, barked Onslow, had been confined to the ship, and he would see me in the morning. With a final growl of "Goodnight", he stormed off.

With some trepidation, I boarded the soul-less Shower, which reminded me of the Marie-Celeste. I descended to the Wardroom, so-called, off which were two bunks normally occupied by Somers and myself. On this occasion, I discovered, my bunk was occupied by Telegraphist Williams, and not unnaturally I asked him what the hell he thought he was doing there. Now Williams was a superior young man from the London R.N.V.R., a clerk in peace-time, well-bred, and never truculent. He asked me to view the state of his own bunk, next to the Wardroom, which he shared with Chief Engineman Coleman, and which also served as the wireless office. The whole thing was just about the size of a second-class sleeping berth in a night train.

I stepped into the wireless cabin. Charlie Coleman was asleep, as he had been for about the previous thirty hours. During that time he had evacuated his bowels as frequently as he had urinated. He had also been sick. The combined effluent was steadily dripping onto Telegraphist Williams' bunk below. After contemplating the scene, I decided to sort the whole sorry mess out in the morning, and meanwhile told Williams to remain where he was while I slept in the skipper's bunk.

Next morning at ten a.m. I was ushered into the presence of Captain Wauchope R.N. (Retired), N.O.I.C. Stornoway. In the course of a decidedly frosty interview, I received the impression that his idea of the Navy was somewhat out-of-date. I told him that I completely disclaimed any responsibility for what had happened, and that I had been on duty elsewhere. On this note our interview ended. When I returned to Shower, the entire crew was still drunk, and twenty-four hours later I was still having no small difficulty in sobering them up. I was engaged in this task when, on going on deck, I found to my horror that Captain Wauchope was scowling out of the dining-room window of the County Hotel, where he stayed, at this dreadful 1940 version of "The Bounty". Meanwhile, the crew on our fo'c'sle had trained the gun on his head and were standing by. It was lucky that they did not have any ammunition; I had the key! I dispersed this unruly mob, and peace reigned again, until Somers arrived the next morning off the MacBrayne steamer.

Once we arrived back at Loch Ewe, of course, there was a terrible row. Courts martial were threatened, and all leave was stopped for officers and crew alike. In those days, however, I was immoderately brash and forward. Storming up to the captain's secretary (Pay-master Lieutenant Robinson), I demanded to know why MY leave had been stopped. At the time of the disturbance, I protested, I had been on duty elsewhere. I demanded reasons in writing – this to a full captain R.N. from a nineteen year-old midshipman! Within hours we had been sent back to Stornoway for another load of coal, and I had been given a sealed letter to deliver personally to Captain Wauchope.

When we arrived at Stornoway, an armed guard with bayonets

Vice Admiral Sir Thomas Binney with Premier Churchill

fixed was placed around Shower. No one except Midshipman Forsyth-Grant was allowed to leave the ship under any pretext whatever. I landed and delivered the letter from Captain Briggs to Captain Wauchope. It simply stated that all leave had been stopped for a week for the captain and crew of Drifter Shower, with the sole exception of Midshipman Forsyth-Grant, to whom this did not apply. I had won my argument.

Not long afterwards, Admiral Sir Hugh Thomas Binney, Admiral Commanding Orkneys and Shetlands, came to visit outposts of his command. Having signed my sponsorship with the Navy, he knew all about me, and now he sent for me for a private talk. It turned out to be a thoroughly pleasant talk, as between father and son, and he even told me the real facts about the sinking of Royal Oak, much of which were secret at the time. However, when it came to my period of service in Drifter Shower, he seemed very dissatisfied. This interview gave me forebodings of change which, as it turned out, were later to prove all too well founded.

In late September 1940, news came that Shower was to refit in Aberdeen. Our first overnight stop was at Mallaig, and Skipper Somers asked me if I would accompany him to the local pub for a drink. On our return to the ship we passed some goods wagons on the quay, which were used for transporting sulphuric acid in great glass carboys wrapped in straw. One of them had its centre door open, and some decidedly sexy noises were emanating from the straw. Somers peered inside, and discovered to his horror that one of our able seamen was having sex there with a soldier. He proceeded to upbraid the sailor, but the latter simply turned on his side and retorted: "Fuck Off, skipper! This ain't your ship – it's mine!" Somers withdrew his head, and launched into a sermon for my benefit on the downturn in modern morals. It was all I could do not to burst out laughing.

The next night found us at Fort Augustus on the Caledonian Canal. While I went foraging for some fresh milk, Somers met two lay brothers from the huge monastery, probably in the pub. On my return to Shower all three of them, hopelessly drunk, were singing every bawdy song known on land and sea. Being scarcely able to stand, Somers asked me to escort the brothers back to their monastery, and eventually I managed to do so, though not without a considerable expenditure of muscular effort. When we arrived at the monastery door, they hammered at it, and as they entered they were in full song, giving a lusty rendering of "The Hoor of Kirriemuir". Before the abbot could knobble me, I beat a hasty retreat!

From Fort Augustus we sailed to Buckie, and thence to Aberdeen. Off Rattray Head, we ran into a fearsome storm. Enormous waves were cascading over the fo'c'sle and flooding the crew space, and we were in grave danger of sinking. Faced with such conditions, we decided to turn back to the Moray Firth. The minutes and even seconds that followed upon this decision were absolutely crucial. Could we turn the ship before she capsized in the storm, and thereafter got "pooped" down the engine-room by the stern-following sea? Those ten minutes seemed like as many hours, but at length we did make the shelter behind Rattray Head, and nosed our way into Fraserburgh with all our nerves on edge. Afterwards we found that the convoy just ahead of us had run into the same conditions, and four ships, including the commodore's, had run aground off Rattray Head. While aground they had been heavily bombed and subsequently abandoned.

While Barrie Somers went ashore, I stayed on board, probably reflecting on the disaster from which providence had plucked us. We were still sheltering in Fraserburgh when Sabine, an Ocean Rescue Tug, joined us. She had managed to put men aboard the stranded ships for a short time in order to try and salvage them. Suddenly the Wardroom door burst open, and in came our coxswain, very drunk, with the lieutenant (E) from Sabine. Each of them was armed with a bottle, or bottles, of brandy, which they offered to me. However, I shooed them both out. By this time I had discovered that the salvage men had spent more time in looting the ships than in preparing them for their recovery!

The following day we made Aberdeen, and I lunched with the Inspector of Coastguards, who was a family friend. He quizzed me about the convoy, saying that there had been awful stories of looting and piracy. I kept a very discreet silence.

Leaving me to deal with the re-fit, Skipper Somers went off on leave to Glasgow. I was to get my leave three weeks later when he returned. The Aberdeen Dockyard people were most helpful. They even provided flush lavatories and running water in the ship, and gave me my own hot water running off the capstan steam pipes. All was going splendidly when, two days before my leave was due, a signal arrived ordering me to report for a new appointment. Admiral Binney had struck!

CHAPTER 5

H.M.S. Tynedale

Having received the shock news that I was to join H.M.S. Tynedale in Glasgow, I was in a great hurry to pack my kit. In those days, identity cards had to be carried at all times, and it was not until I was standing on Montrose Station that I realised that on this occasion I had mislaid mine. However, I caught the train, while my father promised to return home and search for the missing card. It was vital not to be late in reporting at Glasgow, and I sweated no end as I wondered what would be said about the card. Then as I was changing trains at North Queensferry, an agitated station master came rushing up to me, the only uniformed passenger on the platform. He asked whether I was Midshipman Forsyth-Grant, and when I replied in the affirmative, hurried me to his office to take a most urgent telephone call. It was my dear father, who had found the missing document, and would send it to me care of F.O.I.C. (Navy Headquarters) in Glasgow.

In a great lather, I arrived at St Enoch Hotel in Glasgow, sought out the duty officer, and explained my mission. By this time it was 10 p.m.; he told me that everyone had gone home, and that I had better come back in the morning. Now came the problem of where to spend the night. At that late hour in wartime it was nearly impossible to get a hotel room. I was discussing the matter with the hall porter, who was surreptitiously drinking with a civilian behind his desk. The civilian intervened, explaining that he was a commercial traveller and kindly offering to let me share his room in the Adelphi Hotel nearby. Eagerly, and perhaps somewhat innocently, I accepted.

The Adelphi was well supplied with liquor, and by the time we went upstairs to his bedroom, my companion and I were fairly well oiled. Without further ado we both piled into the single bed. Hardly was the light out, before he started "touching me up"! Now I was far from innocent, but after life in H.M. Drifter Shower I was fairly tough, and far more powerfully built than he. I told him in no uncertain terms that if he tried it again I would belt him, whereupon, somewhat grumpily, he went to sleep. Next morning we had quite a pleasant breakfast together, and at 10 a.m. I returned to Naval H.Q.

A very agreeable captain, who had commanded the Clyde Division of the R.N.V.R. before the war, gave me the necessary "gen", informing me that I was to report on board H.M.S. Tynedale at Stephen's Yard at Govan. Here I duly arrived in a taxi with all my kit. As I mounted the gangway, saluted the officer of the day, and reported for duty, I was feeling overawed – possibly even terrified – at the prospect of this new adventure. It was not long before I had been introduced to the captain and the rest of the officers, all of whom were senior to me. Then I was allocated a double cabin all by itself off the tiller flat, access to it being through No. 2 seamens' mess deck. A leading sick berth attendant, Richards by name, introduced himself, and told me that he had been detailed to look after me.

H.M.S. Tynedale was a new Type I Hunt Class destroyer armed with two twin mark 4 inch guns, a four-barrel pompom firing two pound shells, several machine guns, and complete depth-charge kit. She was an ideal coastal escort destroyer for convoys. When I joined her she was already overdue to sail for Scapa Flow to work up her efficiency, but all the electricians in the yard had gone on strike for more pay. As a result, much to the disgust of the ship's company, we were waiting for them to finish the electrical fittings before we could leave, and they would take at least another week.

To me the delay was a godsend. I asked my mother if she would care to spend a few days in Glasgow. Never daunted, and always knowing the right people, she was quickly installed in the Central Hotel, and I was able to visit her when I was off duty.

In those days Glasgow was a pretty rough sort of town; this in spite of the high reputation of its no-nonsense chief constable, Percy Sillitoe. I received a pep talk on the subject from the first lieutenant. He warned me that muggings, robberies and even worse were taking place all round us; if I should ever witness any crime or disturbance ashore, I was on no account to become involved in any way. I rather thought that he was exaggerating until, on one of my afternoons off, as I was walking down the Dumbarton road at about two p.m., I witnessed an appalling stabbing, man to man, right opposite me in the street. My immediate instinct was to rush to the victim's aid, but the words of admonition I had received rang clearly in my ears. Transfixed with indecision, for about ten seconds I froze; meanwhile a large crowd gathered round the pair. I strode rapidly off towards the Central Hotel.

At last Tynedale was ready to sail. One cold winter's morning I was "fallen in" on the fo'c'sle with the "forepart", and we steamed down to Greenock. A mighty cold passage it was too!

After that it was off to Scapa Flow to work up the efficiency of the ship before going to war in earnest. I had several friends in Scapa. One, a fellow midshipman in the destroyer depot ship, H.M.S. Maidstone, seemed to have influence well beyond his rank. Another was a petty officer in a boom vessel, who before the war had been a fishing skipper in our company. Then of course there was my old ship, Shower, now patrolling the boom defences of the Fleet's great anchorage.

Our own activities in Scapa were of a fairly routine sort: firing our guns, letting off depth-charges, conducting practice attacks on real submarines, and so forth. Nevertheless, there were some amusing episodes.

One evening I was given leave to visit my old ship, Shower, in her berth alongside the battleship Iron Duke, now being used as a depot ship. Barry Somers had not changed and neither had most of his crew. They were still an amusing lot and still seemed to drink as much as ever. I was engaged with Somers in some heavy drinking when a sailor arrived to say that Commander Shillington R.N.V.R., Commander of the Auxiliary Patrol, Scapa Flow, would like to see me over a drink in Iron Duke's Wardroom. When I arrived there, the Wardroom was very quiet and uncrowded, but Shillington took me into a corner and told me that he had received very bad reports about my undisciplined conduct while at Loch Ewe. He went on to say that the admiral had demanded that I should go to a ship with better discipline. We left on good terms, and I returned to Shower, where Barry was about to go on patrol. It was arranged that in the course of Shower's patrol of the boom, I would be picked up by Tynedale's motor boat.

Once on station at the boom, Barry handed over the ship to my successor.

All at once we heard an awful noise of screeching along the hull accompanied by shouts and convulsive throbbings of the engine. A deathly silence followed, broken only by the pattering of boots along the deck above. Next an excited crewman announced breathlessly that the drifter had run into the boom and was inextricably entangled with it, held fast by her propeller. Barry was quite unperturbed. He said that the ship could just stay as she was until we had finished our meal. This was just coming to an end when Tynedale's motor boat arrived to take me back. As I left, Shower was still firmly anchored to the boom.

Eventually she must somehow or other have been freed, for next day we saw her sailing close under Tynedale's stern, where I stood resplendent in immaculate uniform, white collar, black tie, and with a telescope under my arm. As she passed, Shower's loud hailer boomed forth: "Nice to see a well-dressed midshipman, who knows his place!" I pretended not to hear, but the bosun's mate stared in bewilderment first at me, and then at the coal-spattered drifter. The look of astonishment on his face is something I shall never forget.

On another occasion, the captain sent for me in much agitation and showed me the following signal: "Tynedale – from (A)dmiral (C)ommanding (O)rkney and (S)hetland. (R)equest (P)leasure (C)ompany Midshipman Forsyth-Grant 1300 Lyness Pier. Car Waiting." Lieutenant Commander H.E.T. Tweedie, himself the son of an admiral, asked how I knew Admiral Sir Thomas Hugh Binney. I replied that he had sponsored my application to join the R.N.V.R.

I duly lunched with the admiral at Melsetter House – a very grand occasion for me. Better still, however, a certain V.A.D., Blair Imrie, who was a close friend and neighbour of our family, had also been invited. Little did I know that the admiral had fallen for her, and that within a short time she would be Lady Binney! The admiral was very kind, and after lunch I returned to my ship, my prestige slightly enhanced by this social occasion. Now, however, my real war service was about to begin.

On 24th December we were just on the point of sitting down to our Christmas dinner (for which someone had found a turkey), when we were ordered to sea at very short notice. A scratch group of destroyers commanded by Lord Louis Mountbatten set out for Muckle Flugger off the Shetlands, and we spent all that Christmas day plastering the ocean with depth-charges. None of us, I believe, had any luck, but this was our baptism into real action. Whether on account of the rough seas or of the dropping of depth-charges, in the course of all this a major fire broke out in our paint store, from which choking fumes were emitted. I was one of the party sent to extinguish it, which we finally achieved, though not without much excitement and trepidation. I had a feeling at the time that for me this was the real beginning of the war.

A few days later we sailed for Portsmouth, classed as a fully operational destroyer, to join the First Destroyer Flotilla based there. We had heard all about the Battle of Britain, and how badly certain towns had suffered from the blitz, and knew that it was likely to prove a very tough spot.

For the actual passage to Portsmouth we were on our own, but it was devoid of incident and unexciting. My mother had spent

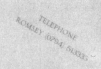

BROADLANDS
ROMSEY,
HAMPSHIRE,
SO5 9ZD.

14th November 1978

Dear Forsyth-Grant,

Thank you so much for your letter
of the 9th November.

I am so glad you enjoyed the shoot
at Broadlands. I enjoyed having you.

I was interested to hear you had met
your cousin, Malcolm, whom I passed into the
Royal Navy at the Interview Board in 1938.

Thank you for asking your friend,
John Forrester, to send me a copy of
"The Mountbattens. From Battenberg to
Windsor". I made immediate enquiries after
you told me about this and found that a man
called Liversidge makes a profession of
writing about the Royal Family without their
permission or concurrence. He has written
books about the Queen, the Queen Mother and
the Prince of Wales, and in every case it is
a re-hash of what he has read from other
sources, without going near them or their
staff.

This really is highly unsatisfactory
but apparently there is nothing we can do
about it. However, I am looking forward to
getting the book when your friend sends it.
Thank you so much for arranging this.

Yours sincerely

Mountbatten of Burma

Private letter from Earl Mountbatten to the Author

much of her childhood at Portsmouth, so on arriving I hastened ashore for a quick look at the place. At the time it seemed quite undamaged, and I quickly penned a note to tell her so. Barely had I put the letter in the Wardroom box, when action stations sounded, and I rushed to the signal bridge to man my Hotchkiss machine gun. The air raid alarm for Civil Defence was blaring out, and already guns were firing. Out of the gloom roared a bomber, and with a massive roar a stick of bombs went off not far ahead of us. I believe a tug was sunk. As I let off a good half belt of my machine gun, I felt that it was all great fun and thoroughly exciting. The date was the 9th January 1941, and little did I know then what the morrow held in store for us.

We passed our first day in Portsmouth trying to familiarise ourselves with the port, for we were a Devonport-based ship's company, and for many of us this was our first visit to the dockyard there. After tea I asked the ship's barber, a stoker, if he would give me a haircut, and he arranged to do this in the officers' bathroom. Just as he began, the civil air raid sirens started, but taking no notice, he continued to cut my hair. A few moments later we heard an appalling shriek of bombs, followed by a colossal explosion. The blast blew me off the chair into the bath, while the stoker crashed across the deck and hit his head against the bulkhead. I suppose he had really finished, but whether he had or not, this certainly put an end to our haircutting session, and we rushed out into the open air to see what had happened.

It was not easy to make the situation out, for there was dust and smoke everywhere, but what astounded me was that the otherwise dark night had been transformed into day by the light of the descending flares. We immediately went to action stations, but were forbidden to fire our main armament for fear of giving away the ship's position. However, we were allowed to shoot at the flares in the hope of extinguishing them, and with my loading number on my machine guns, I belted away for all I was worth. Stick after stick, the bombs were raining down, until soon all Portsmouth and Gosport seemed on fire. About 11 p.m., with the whole area ablaze, the bombers appeared to have gone, the all clear sounded, and I made my way to my solitary cabin aft. I was not to be there long!

In no time the air raid sirens were sounding again, and more bombs were falling. If we were hit, I felt, it would be a long way from my cabin to the deck. Feeling very lonely and vulnerable, I made my way to the Wardroom, where I found that even the captain had left his cabin, one deck above, either for company or for the relative safety of the deck below. Shrapnel from anti-aircraft guns was coming down on deck like rain, and out in the open it was highly unsafe. While the captain dozed fitfully in an armchair, I stretched out on a nearby settee. I must have dozed off, when I was awoken by the shriek of a bomb, but even as I moved, it burst with a shattering roar, and everywhere we could hear splinters of masonry flying. The captain dived under the table. This particular stick did, in fact, do serious damage to a destroyer lying alongside the jetty just ahead of us. At last, about two a.m., the Luftwaffe went home.

The following day the city was ablaze, and so was Gosport. It had probably been the worst air raid Portsmouth ever experienced, and the damage was the greatest, for, as I have already said, up till then the city had barely been scratched. The burning tower of the Guildhall is one of the more celebrated photographs of civil damage in the whole war period.

However, our job was at sea, and in no time we were shepherding a convoy round "Hell's Corner" into the Straits of Dover. At the time this was, in the whole of Britain, the worst shipping trouble spot, and the most heavily under attack. The Luftwaffe, E Boats, and the huge coastal guns which the Germans had recently installed were all concentrating their ferocity upon it, to say nothing of the mines laid in the Thames. It would be repetitious and wearisome to attempt a detailed description of the constant onslaughts from all of these to which we were subjected. Suffice it to say that we were incessantly under attack. At the time we were convoying from Portsmouth to Sheerness, after which we would hand over care of the merchantmen to smaller escorts and to the Royal Air Force. One convoy in particular does stand out in my mind.

During a late afternoon in January, we were alongside at Sheerness, preparing to join convoy off the Thames. Already we could hear an artillery duel in progress, as the British heavy guns around Dover answered those of the Germans at Calais and Boulogne. The prospects for the convoy were looking decidedly bleak, when at that moment a B.B.C. crew arrived to record the latest battle in the Dover Straits. The key figure was none other than Richard Dimbleby, and as they proceeded to rig up their apparatus, he seemed far more enthusiastic than we were! Soon we were escorting the convoy out of the Thames and on to the west, round Dungeness. By this time it was about midnight and pitch dark. We were between Dover and Folkestone, and so far nothing had happened. Sub Lieutenant Stogdon R.N.V.R. was officer of the watch, and I was his understudy. The captain was below in the chartroom studying plans.

Rain in tropical density was pouring down upon us on the open bridge, and occasionally a flash of lightning lit up the convoy for a second, so that we could see how it was spread. Then suddenly three bright flares blazed out, lighting up the entire convoy, as they slowly and majestically parascended seaward. Stogdon called the captain, while I pressed every emergency button I could find on the compass platform. People were running everywhere, gun crews closing up, orders being shouted. We were standing by to repel the worst that the Germans could do. Yet nothing happened! Not a shot was fired, no E Boats or aircraft appeared, no roar of railway guns broke out from the direction of Boulogne. I do not know what Dimbleby was doing at that moment, but in my case, I confess, such was my state of excitement that I was almost using the compass platform as an open lavatory!

Silently the flares disappeared into the sea; darkness and silence reigned once more. The only sound that could be heard was the water swishing against the ship's sides. At the time, it seemed inexplicable that we were not attacked, but later the solution turned out to be quite simple. It was the custom in those days for Naval escorting trawlers, and indeed some merchant ships, to carry barrage balloons, so as to snag low flying aircraft. Three of these had been struck by the lightning and set on fire. Afterwards we had a good laugh over it, but at the time it was no joke.

By the spring of 1941, it seemed likely that Sheerness and Portsmouth were destined to become the counterpart in Naval terms of what Flanders had been for the army during the operations of 1917. Enormously outnumbered and outgunned by German forces as we were, having only four small Hunt destroyers as our major deterrent at sea, how could we escape from having our defences overwhelmed? I had actually seen secret plans to go on using our little destroyer force until – and this was anticipated – it was finally annihilated by superior German might. The outlook was glum. One afternoon that January, I was detailed to land all our secret books in the Flotilla Office in the dockyard, as that night we were to undertake a highly dangerous mission – so dangerous that the books must be landed, in case we were sunk or captured. After completing my task, I went to my cabin and made out my will. I left all my worldly goods, amounting to less than £100, to my dear parents. Then I posted it to my Montrose bank. I was resigned to my fate!

It was not until we sailed that I was told what our mission was. It was at a time when a full-scale invasion of the country seemed imminent. To deflect the invading force, or at least to hold it up for a time, and so give some warning of its approach, it had been decided to lay a mine barrage close to the French coast. For this purpose three I Class destroyers had secretly been sent to Portsmouth, and we three Hunt Class destroyers were to escort them on their task of laying a major minefield. To complete this operation took us several successive nights, and although on one a huge German destroyer ploughed straight through our line of ships just as we were preparing to drop the mines, no shots were fired, nor any other action taken to prevent us. We hoped the Germans had not seen us, and it is quite possible that this was the case. Alternatively, they may have considered that they were outnumbered. It is a mystery which we shall never solve. At all events, the minefield was laid without any casualties on our part, and presumably it served as an effective barrier against invasion in those critical days.

One way or another, in the spring of 1941, Portsmouth was anything but a fun spot. The time we spent in port was hardly less taxing than our spells at sea, for every single night we were bombed. One night in particular, when bombs were raining down in the usual small-scale blitz, the captain decreed that dinner was to go ahead at 2000 hours regardless. At 19.45 hours drinks were served, just as though we were under peace-time conditions, and then, in the splendid old naval tradition, at 2000 hours the chief petty officer steward announced to the senior of the assembled officers – all eight of us, "Soup is on the table, Sir." The captain, Lieutenant Commander Tweedie, took the head of the table; I sat opposite him at the bottom, the most senior facing the most junior across its length.

As we took our soup, the bombs came down like hail. Already, only nine months previously, our captain had been most seriously wounded at Dunkirk. He had been first lieutenant of the destroyer Greyhound when she was sunk. Most of the officers and ship's company of Tynedale were survivors of the destroyer Brazen, which had also been sunk at Dunkirk. They knew all about death, wounds, and surviving. I was just a tenderfoot. Our captain's demeanour was marvellous. As I stared at him from one end of the table to the other, I knew that he was re-living the horrors of Greyhound. Beads of sweat were pouring off his forehead and falling into his soup. Yet he never wavered in carrying on a natural and quite unforced conversation with the officers on either side of him. I admired him immensely for what he was doing. It was a magnificent display of leadership and courage, and an example to junior officers.

Of course even in the midst of all this heavy bombing there were great moments of hilarity. On one occasion Tynedale was swarming with civilian "dockyard mateys" and scientific boffins – I think they were fitting our R.D.F., Type 286, and it was, if I remember rightly, the first radar ever installed in a British destroyer. As they were hurrying to complete this installation, the bombs were raining down on the dockyard incessantly, and to avoid them, Tynedale raced out into the Solent and beyond. Once out of danger, we sat down to dinner again as though it were peacetime, and two scientists, being given V.I.P status, were guests of the captain. They were certainly strangers to straight-backed formal naval dinners, and in no time they were discussing subjects that were really taboo at dinner – probably lavatory seats, V.D., and brothels. The most senior officers were appalled, and there were some awkward silences. The irreverent Stogdon, puce in the face with mirth, kicked out at me under the table. He missed, and his foot upset the silver cruets at our end of the table. There was a deathly hush. Angrily the captain warned me: "Snotty, if you can't keep your feet to yourself, kindly keep them on deck!" It was a splendid admonition, but I was amazed that it was not addressed to Stogdon. By then, however, I was too well trained to make any reply.

On March 10th, two months to the day after the previous large-scale raid, came another. It was now that Portsmouth experienced its second major blitz of the war, and it was every bit as bad as the one on January 10th. When the first bombs fell, we were moored at Southern Railway Jetty, and we were forbidden to open fire. However we were instructed to land shore parties to put out incendiaries. In one stick of four bombs which fell, three failed to explode, although they did much damage to the dockyard surface, and numbers three and four straddled us. Number four exploded in the water just off our fo'c'sle, and did us very considerable damage fortunately without any casualties. Our "breakwater" was blown right out of the dockyard, and we were peppered with shrapnel.

At the height of the blitz I was a member of a group extinguishing fire bombs. The bow of H.M.S. Victory had already been hit, and was in danger from two other incendiaries nearby. I raced along to the one nearest to Victory herself, but a voice yelled: "I've got that one, tackle the other one, mate!" Even as I rushed to do so, my colleague was blown to pieces in the act of extinguishing his. The Germans had fitted high explosives to one incendiary in ten, so as to deter the fire-fighters from putting them out.

Half an hour later, I was told that a traitor was signalling to the enemy bombers with a torch, and that I was to extinguish him. I identified the man concerned, and as I came up to him I prodded him with the muzzle of my tommy gun. He fell dead at my feet. He turned out to be one of the firemen. His whole face had been blown away by a bomb, and his torch must have been lit by the same blast. Thank God, within a few days we had been sent to join the 5th Destroyer Flotilla at Plymouth. Tynedale was a Devonport-manned ship, and the ship's company, some members of which would have had their homes in the area, was looking forward to being based at the home port. Furthermore, in contrast to Portsmouth and the South East, there had been no reports of heavy bombing in the West Country. However, as we steamed up Plymouth Sound, we received a rude awakening. The fires of the previous night's raid were still burning, and this turned out to be the beginning of "Plymouth Week", when that city had to endure several consecutive nights of such intense bombing, that it was reduced from a once thriving city to a smoking ruin.

It was late afternoon as we entered Devonport Dockyard, and I was sent by our motor boat to Flagstaff Steps with a bag of papers, which I was to deliver to the office of Captain (D), Fifth Destroyer Flotilla. Shortly after dark, the familiar air raid sirens blew, and soon afterwards bombs began to fall. The raid was intense, yet not quite so bad as the two major raids on Portsmouth. It was not long before the city was well ablaze, but we remained in the dockyard, which suffered less.

Next day we saw the extent of the devastation, and quite a few of the crew were given urgent daylight compassionate leave to look after their families. Apparently, a high-level decision was then taken to the effect that, should another major raid develop that night, all ships were to proceed to sea, so as to minimise the risk of being hit while in the dockyard area, for it was anticipated that the attacks would be concentrated most heavily here.

True to form, the Luftwaffe struck again soon after dark, and this time the main target seemed to be the waterfront. We were quickly under way and steaming out of the Sound into the open sea. As we came about opposite the Hoe, I looked back and counted twenty-two consecutive flashes, as stick after stick of bombs fell into the commercial harbour known as the Catwater. Devonport Dockyard was a sea of flame. The roof of a huge shed or warehouse had collapsed, and about ten firemen were standing on the high wall, playing their hoses onto the inferno below. Suddenly the whole wall fell inwards, launching the firemen into the blaze. Not one of them could have survived.

Even in the Sound we were far from safe. All round us bombs were plunging into the water and exploding. One stick fell between us and the destroyer ahead, but without causing any casualties. Immediately outside the breakwater we hit a rough sea and swell. At this, several people on the compass platform were violently sick, so that the small cramped space was covered in vomit. At one stage, my feet slipped as the ship heaved, and I fell hard on my backside into the vomit, and toboganned to the back of the bridge like a bobsleigh on the Cresta run. It was a scene the like of which I have never witnessed before or since throughout the entire war – not even in the appalling weather of the Barents and Greenland Seas. Why everybody was so sick, and so quickly, I shall never understand. For the next twenty minutes, keeping one's feet was a most difficult task, but finally the situation was brought under control, and the mess was cleared up.

The blitz continued in full intensity for several days. One detail that struck me as particularly poignant was the sight of all the civilian population leaving the city an hour before dusk – to sleep in the countryside, I was told. During the same period, we were escorting a convoy about ten miles off the coast on a fairly clear night, when suddenly we were engulfed in a huge cloud of smoke. It came from burning oil tanks many miles away at Torpoint, Plymouth. The huge oil storage depot there must, I imagine, have been completely burnt out.

Although we belonged to the 5th Destroyer Flotilla at Plymouth, our main task at this time was to escort convoys from Dartmouth to Falmouth, and Falmouth to Milford Haven. During an afternoon ashore at Falmouth, I found a shop with a particularly fine tea set, which I thought would cheer my parents up. Accordingly, I bought it and sent it off to them. Two weeks later, after thinking the matter over, I decided to add a few spares, so as to cover the breakages. When I arrived at the shop, however, it was to find that it no longer existed. All that remained to show where it had once stood was a huge bomb crater.

Our convoys were still being heavily bombed, and we lost several ships. Then we were told that from now on we could expect Whirlwind fighters to patrol over the convoys. These had just been re-formed and re-trained after a bad patch in Norway. One morning we saw two planes approaching from the coast, and a shout went up, "Look at the Whirlwinds!". As they circled the convoy about a mile off, we watched them with interest. Then one of them made a run to pass a couple of hundred yards astern of us, and right over the centre of the convoy. Suddenly there was another shout: "Look at the black crosses!". I suppose our aircraft recognition at that time left much to be desired. I stared in horror. The planes passed so close astern that the heads of the pilot and another airman were clearly visible. As if I were watching a newsreel, I looked on as the bomb doors opened, and the bombs fell out in the direction of one of the ships. It was lucky that all four missed, and that, so far as I know, there were no casualties or damage, for all this time not a single gun had fired. Then, however, all hell was let loose. Although by this time it was far too late, the Messerschmidt 110 – for that was what is was – had won only a temporary reprieve. It crossed the convoy and raced back to seaward, but apparently a group of Spitfires had been on the alert. Just short of the horizon, they shot it down. I believe that was the first and last I ever saw of the Whirlwinds.

About this time, I discovered that the Spitfires at Portreath were controlled by my cousin, Gavin Anderson, who had become a squadron leader. With the approval of my superiors, I asked him and his wife to dinner in Tynedale. I introduced him to the captain, and they soon became firm friends. Meanwhile, I and the more junior of my colleagues, as befitted our lowly station, retired after dinner to chatter with his wife, Pam. The outcome of this liaison between Tynedale and the Spitfires at Portreath was a massive step forward in air defence. Apart from having been instrumental in bringing Squadron Leader Gavin Anderson and Lieutenant Commander H.E.F. Tweedie together at dinner, I claim no credit for this. The fact remains that in no time the two of them had fitted a four-button V.H.F. set on the bridge of Tynedale, with the result that we could now call Portreath from the bridge. More valuable even than that, we could actually tell the fighters where the enemy were while they were in the air. I have no doubt that before long an improved version of this system became general. Nevertheless, if two individuals ever deserved an award, these two officers did. Together, they were certainly the first to plan this form of intercommunication in the front line battle zone in which we were engaged.

Although I had always been the junior of the eight officers in Tynedale, I had first had my own cabin aft, and then shared it with a newly appointed wartime sub lieutenant. Now, however, my quarters were to change for the worse – or so it seemed. Another wartime sub lieutenant joined, and I had to leave my cabin and sling a hammock. My fellow officers did their best for me, but there was simply no cabin available. However, Alan Milner, the surgeon-lieutenant, was not going to see me stuck! He invited me to share the sick bay with him; he would sleep in the cot, while I had the operating table! So it was arranged. The only condition was that I had to promise to vacate my bunk when he had to operate! That tower of strength, Leading Sick Berth Attendant

Richards, looked after us both as before. Although, on promotion to acting sub lieutenant, I might have returned to a proper cabin, in fact I never wanted to move from the sick bay, and stayed there until I left Tynedale for Coastal Forces.

We had now set up a system of intercommunication with our day fighters, but it did not extend to our night escort of Blenheim fighter-bombers based at Carew Cheriton in Pembroke. It was off Trevose Head at midnight that the Luftwaffe always used to look for us, for it was at that time, and close to that spot, that the North and South Convoys used to pass one another – just off St Eval Airfield, to be exact. The lighthouse used obligingly to shine its light just at that hour, and the airfield, with its runway lights, could easily be identified. Many a ship perished in these waters, including an armed yacht, the Viva II, which did gallant escort service. Some of Viva's crew were septuagenarians; others were famous industrialists who had retired from their lucrative posts to do this lowly crewing job. When they were all killed, we mourned their loss.

Meanwhile, the air crews at Carew Cheriton accused us of being a trigger-happy shower of bastards, who were for ever peppering them instead of the Luftwaffe. They said that unless things improved, they would refuse to escort us. Then, to ensure that things did improve, they sent a senior pilot to liaise with us for one trip. He went by the odd name of "Pongo" Russell and had a magnificent handlebar moustache. At dusk on his first day, a "hostile" plane roared over us as usual, and, with Pongo Russell's full approval, we opened up with all the machine guns and pompoms we could muster. I remember firing about a hundred rounds, but I appeared to miss – or at least not to wound. Shortly after this episode, there was another fearful row, and we were asked why we had yet again shot up a Blenheim. Luckily, this time we had Pongo Russell to support us in our argument as to the extreme difficulty of identifying such planes. The difficulty was still unsolved when I left Tynedale. It arose largely because we had no ship-to-plane V.H.F., as we had with the Spitfires.

Our R.D.F. (Radar) Type 286 was, of course, very primitive. Though not without its value, it was a far cry from the highly accurate image-identifying sets of 1989. By this time, in the spring of 1941, we were expecting to be attacked at any moment by German battle cruisers, cruisers and destroyers, for at this period the German Navy enjoyed massive numerical superiority in the Channel. One night, while we were escorting a convoy between Dartmouth and Falmouth, the radar operator detected a huge image to seaward, and our experts decided that it was either the

Scharnhorst or the Gneisenau. We diverted the convoy towards Plymouth, while we increased to full speed to engage the enemy. As the range decreased to within three miles, the captain ordered: "Fire starshell!", and seconds later: "Illuminate by searchlight!". Night became day, and revealed us charging at breakneck speed straight for the Eddystone Rock Lighthouse!

To our indescribable relief, we had seen it in time, though I suspect that the lighthouse keepers were relieving themselves in quite a different sense. All the same, there were a lot of red faces. We retreated rapidly, and, without much further discussion, busied ourselves in shepherding the convoy back onto its course for Falmouth.

Admiral of the Fleet Earl Mountbatten of Burma

CHAPTER 6

Further Adventures in Tynedale

From the perspective of fifty years later, and in the conditions of relative softness and luxury which we now enjoy, it is not easy to recapture or convey what life was like on those coastal convoys in the early part of 1941. To begin with, there was the sheer fatigue; we were exhausted almost beyond endurance. During one of our short rest periods, we were ordered to sea at short notice to rescue a Sunderland flying boat, which had run out of fuel and landed on the sea near the coast of Brittany. There was no question of refuelling it – only of rescuing the crew and preventing the flying boat from falling into the hands of the enemy. We had reached within a few miles of the search area, and I had been on watch. It was a relief to hand over, and I wearily returned to my "bunk" in the sick bay. Then, in a half doze, I heard shouts and the sound of running feet. Shortly afterwards that miniature Chicago piano of a four-barrel pompom began to play. The crew of the flying boat had been safely brought aboard Tynedale, and now we were sending shells into their craft to sink it. It is a sign of how exhausted we all were, that I was too weary even to watch the operation.

By this time our base in Devonport Dockyard was little more than a heap of smoke-blackened rubble. Somehow, however, the dockyard was continuing to function, and we were due for a boiler clean. This meant that half the officers and crew could go on leave for four or five days. However, it was not my turn, and I remained on board. Plymouth and Devonport were so badly wrecked that now, for the most part, the Luftwaffe used simply to fly over us and on to Cardiff or Bristol, for it was their turn to receive the lion's share of the bombing.

While in port, therefore, we were instructed to use our main armament to augment the anti-aircraft defence. This was co-ordinated from ashore, and while alongside the quay or at a buoy, we had a dockyard telephone installed. When the air raid Double Red Alert was sounded, therefore, we stood by the telephone ready to loose off our fused four-inch shells into a specified sector of the sky. I was also in charge of the ship's office, where I was assisted by an officer-candidate seaman. One evening we were both in the office, organising the pay for the crew for the current period, and surrounded by pound notes and envelopes. In the midst of all this, came the air raid Double Red, which meant that, as duty officer of the day, I had to drop everything and rush to the wheelhouse, pick up the 'phone, and direct our guns in the general barrage. I was not alarmed – merely annoyed that my work in the ship's office should have been so rudely disturbed. At all events, for the next few hours I was fully engaged in directing the fire of our guns, and in making sure that their fused A.A. shells reached their allotted sectors of the sky. About midnight, the Germans went home, and I, feeling thoroughly fed up, went to the Wardroom for a drink. Too tired to continue, I went to bed, remaining full clothed, since I was liable to be summoned to instant action on deck.

About 8 a.m., all hell was let loose. It was then that I found that I had lost the keys to the ship's office, where I had left all that loose cash lying about the night before. To add to the list of disasters, two ratings, who were under close arrest, had broken out of the ship, and as officer of the day, that too was my responsibility.

When all this was reported to the first lieutenant, now acting as C.O. of the ship, he told me that I was to consider myself under open arrest for gross negligence. He sent for assistance from the dockyard to break open the door to the ship's office, where it was discovered that the cash at least was still intact. Shortly afterwards, in the course of dusting the wheelhouse, a signalman found the missing keys where I had abandoned them the night before. They were behind the board on which was mounted the telephone used to direct the gunfire. However, even though two of the disasters had been eliminated, I was still under open arrest for letting the prisoners escape.

The following day, my brother Maurice, who was a pilot officer in the R.A.F., Torquay, rang me up to invite me to spend a night away from Devonport with him, and enjoy a cruise over Dartmoor on his motorcycle. Somewhat sourly, the first lieutenant released me from open arrest, and gave me the O.K.. Accordingly, Maurice arrived alongside Tynedale on his magnificent Ariel Square 4, and off we zoomed through the superb countryside to Dartmoor. Amongst other things, I remember, we inspected the gates of Princetown Jail. Then Maurice asked me whether I would like to learn to ride a motor bike, without a licence, outside H.M. Prison. There and then, I received my first lesson in motorcycling. After this we retired to Torquay, where he was in a civilian billet and on friendly terms with his landlord. We decided to do Torquay in style, and to take the landlord along too. At that time, the most fashionable watering spot in all Torquay was "Gibbons", and it was there that the three of us went. In such an ambience, surrounded as we were by squadron leaders and majors, our low rank rendered Maurice and myself highly conspicuous. I even spotted an air commodore! Certainly there were no "other ranks". Suddenly in walked the two sailors from Tynedale who had broken ship while under close arrest. They were in ordinary uniform, and accompanied by a civilian. For a moment I believed I was dreaming. After all, Devonport was about thirty miles away.

Recovering my composure, I whispered to Maurice who they were, and we left the bar. We went straight to a telephone box just outside the entrance, where I rang the Devonport Dockyard Royal Marine Police. They told me that I must be joking, and to get lost. Then I rang Torquay C.I.D.. They promised to come, and sure enough within a few minutes they had arrived.

Just as I was explaining the whole position, I spotted the two A.B.s darting into the gents' lavatory. In I rushed, with the two C.I.D. men at my heels. I tapped the two delinquents on the shoulder, and addressed them by name: "You know who I am," I said, "and you are under arrest – we will wait for you outside." I walked out to the internal corridor to wait with the two C.I.D. men, but suddenly one of them rushed off like a scalded cat. I asked the other what the disappearing man was doing, but he merely replied that he probably knew his job.

Five minutes passed, but the two A.B.s still failed to appear, so we re-entered the gents'. No sign of them! I was furious, but the C.I.D. man seemed unperturbed. He merely told me to return to the bar, where he would contact me. After half an hour he telephoned to say that a police car would collect me outside the bar and take me to police H.Q. On arriving there, I found them in the cells. The vanishing C.I.D. man had known that the gents' had a direct street exit, and when the sailors made a run for it, he had rugger-tackled them in the main street.

Apparently, while they were being kept in the cells, the police had overheard them say that I would not be alive to take them back to Devonport. Moreover, no civil arrest warrant had been issued – such things take time. It was arguable whether the police even had the power to arrest these men. However, all this was soon resolved. The police said that I should hire a taxi, which they would arrange, and they would send an off-duty constable with me. They also saw to it that the two sailors were handcuffed for the journey. Back we drove to Plymouth, therefore, to arrive in the midst of yet another blitz. I handed the sailors over to the Marine Police, paid off the taxi, and returned to my ship. This is how I spent what had been intended to be my evening of peace and relaxation! The two sailors were duly sentenced and imprisoned.

Two weeks later, to recompense me for my lost night, I was given another night and a day off. Back I went to Torquay, where I had an excellent dinner, before retiring to my brother's most comfortable digs. The air raid warning went and then a single heavy bomb fell. It killed the fire chief of Torquay.

The episode of the recapture of the ship-breaking sailors had an unexpected sequel. Some time later, the Secretary of the Admiralty wrote to the officer commanding H.M.S. Tynedale, requesting information as to why Sub Lieutenant Forsyth-Grant had failed to return his prisoners to Plymouth by rail with a third-class ticket, instead of causing great expense to their Lordships by taking a taxi! The captain wrote a devastating reply, saying that if their Lordships could not see their way to pay for this, he would pay for it himself. There was no further reply, and I was paid my expenses.

Spring gave way to early summer, and still the German effort to obliterate the convoys from Milford Haven to Dartmouth continued unrelentingly. Although heavily attacked, we managed to get one large tanker through, and left her with other escorts off Start Point, for it was with these that she was to continue her hazardous journey further eastwards. Darkness was gathering, and I was quietly chatting across the guard rails to a colleague in the destroyer Brocklesby, when the sky was lit up by an almighty flash. It was our tanker all right – blown up off Barry Head. There were few survivors. The officer I was chatting to that evening was Michael Tuffnel, a lieutenant, and one of the youngest destroyer captains of the war.

In his attacks upon us, the enemy did not confine himself solely to using E Boats and aircraft. Right across the entrance to Milford Haven, an enormous minefield was laid, which was the cause of great numbers of ships, as well as of individual lives, being lost. The mines were of the new acoustic type, and were laid by aircraft. We were one of the first destroyers to be fitted with an acoustic minesweep. It was a large pear-shaped steel canister, in which an electric hammer struck a plate, giving off a noise something like a pneumatic drill. The contraption was fitted to the stem of the destroyer, and was operated from the bridge by an electric switch. When required for use, it was lowered by wires from the fo'c'sle, and operated in several feet of water below the bow. It was supposed to detonate the mines well ahead of the ship. When not in use, it stood supported on the rails about four feet above the fo'c'sle. Although we tried it out several times, and followed the exact procedure laid down, it had never exploded a mine. On one particular occasion, after several hours of peaceful sailing in broad daylight, we were entering Milford Haven ahead of the convoy, when a seagull alighted on the square top of the contraption. Simply to relieve the boredom, the captain told me to switch the hammer on so as to give the seagull a fright. I did so, and the seagull flew off, screeching with rage but quite unharmed. Before I could switch the hammer off, however, there was an almighty explosion just ahead, and a vast column of water erupted, equivalent to that thrown up by about three depth-charges. We had indeed exploded a mine according to schedule, even though the gear had not been in the correct operating position. I was told to switch off at once, and we all felt rather foolish. This trick was never tried again. Thenceforward, we confined ourselves to using the apparatus in accordance with the authorized instructions.

We were not only engaged in convoying merchantmen. On one occasion we had to assist in escorting a badly damaged battleship back for repair. The battleship was H.M.S. Resolution. She had taken part in the abortive effort to neutralise the French fleet in Dakar, where she had been torpedoed by a French Submarine. From there she had limped into Gibraltar, where she had been very temporarily patched up, before being sent back to Britain for a better repair. The Germans were determined that she would never make Portsmouth, and we were detailed to join a destroyer screen well out in the Atlantic, with the aim of bringing her home despite the worst that the Luftwaffe could do. Tynedale was a small coastal destroyer, quite unfit for the raging seas of the Atlantic, and did not possess the sea-keeping qualities of a corvette or an Atlantic trawler. At all events, in company with another Hunt Class destroyer, we set out into the Atlantic to help to form the destroyer screen, which was under the command of Lord Louis Mountbatten.

On our first night, we saw flashes of gunfire, and knew that they could only come from a U Boat sinking a merchantman. To refrain from going to her rescue was indescribably frustrating, but we had our orders and could only look helplessly on. By dawn, the wind had increased, and soon a huge swell was buffeting the little ship like a cork. Before long, the forward "ready use" ammunition locker, full of four-inch shells and weighing about a ton, was torn from its mountings by a colossal wave that crashed down on the fo'c'sle. Once freed, it started to shift about on the steel deck, and was in danger of tearing a hole in the plate. If that happened, it might let in sea water by the ton and flood the ship. It was imperative, therefore, to lash the huge locker so as to prevent it from opening up the deck like a can-opener. I was one of a party sent forward under the direction of a petty officer to secure the monster which had broken loose. Petty Officer Squires was a veteran of the pre-war navy. About eight of us were working away at securing the locker, when he suddenly roared: "Look out – hold on for your lives, lads!". He was only just in time. A wall of water several feet deep swept over us with terrifying force, and smashed against the bridge superstructure. Then, as it subsided, it threatened to suck us with it over the side.

Although we were all drenched to the skin, no one, thank God, actually went overboard, but it was a terrifying experience. After much trouble, we finally managed to lash the locker securely enough to render it immovable. Then we rushed off below, thankful to have cover over our heads, and to be able to change out of our drenched and freezing clothes. Still the seas did not subside, and it took us a day and a night of steaming into the Atlantic before we found Lord Mountbatten with Resolution.

The destroyer screen we were about to join numbered between ten and sixteen vessels, and many of them, like Tynedale, were Hunt Class destroyers. These were specially built for anti-aircraft defence, and armed with excellent twin Mark 16 guns, which could keep up a rapid fire of four-inch shells. Though the very best anti-aircraft destroyers in the game, they were quite unsuitable for ocean convoys. How Lord Louis, at that time a captain (D), managed to have so many destroyers under his command, I shall never understand. Suffice it to say that even then this officer exercised a power and authority well above his rank!

It was about eight in the morning when we sighted first the battleship and then the other destroyers, which seemed like dots on the ocean. We turned under heavy rudder and increased speed to join them. At that moment an enormous sea crashed across the quarterdeck and up went the cry, "Man overboard!" I was on the bridge beside the captain when it happened, and now, nearly fifty years on, I still have the most graphic remembrance of it.

Lieutenant Commander Tweedie was a brilliant destroyer captain and, but for his temper, should have gone very high in the service. In a crisis like this he was in his element. A smoke candle was burning in the sea at the point where the man had been washed overboard, and before long, as the destroyer turned, we could see him bobbing in his lifebelt in the storm-tossed ocean. In such a howling wind and raging sea, it would have been

H.M.S. Tynedale off St. Nazaire

impossible to pick him up alongside without bashing him against the ship's side, even assuming that we could have manoeuvred close enough to attempt it.

The decision was therefore made to lower the whaler. In the conditions it was risky in the extreme, but, I suppose, justifiable. The alternative would surely have been that the man would have been drowned. Now to lower a whaler in such a sea as this is a highly skilled job. On this occasion something went seriously wrong. Somehow, part of the Robinson Disengaging Gear seized, and the stern of the whaler crashed into the sea, while the bow was held for seconds high in the air. How the crew kept their hold I shall never understand, but seconds later the bow fell into the sea with a crash, and the whaler was swamped.

In this crisis, the seven men manning the boat proved themselves both brave and competent. They baled furiously, and soon had it under oar power and were making for the drowning man. It took a highly creditable feat of seamanship to rescue him, and another to recover the whaler safely. Both the captain and the leading seaman and crew who carried out the rescue are worthy of the highest praise. After a day or two in his bunk, the man recovered completely. Meanwhile, after this excitement, we sailed on to join Lord Louis, and to be allocated our position in the escort. Then we steamed home for Britain.

All this time, of course, the Luftwaffe had not been idle. They had been shadowing us for some time, and about dusk on 2nd March 1941, while we were off Start Point, they launched their long-awaited attack. Despite their utmost efforts to destroy us, we managed to drive them off. I was manning my Hotchkiss machine gun and had just emptied my belts of ammunition, when I saw tracer flying towards us from one of the enemy planes. I told my chum, a signalman of New Zealand origin, to dive for the deck, and I quickly followed suit. As it turned out, he would have been safer if he had remained standing. The Luftwaffe tail-gunner hit the wheelhouse just three inches below our heads! We did suffer some casualties, but none of them were fatal. Eventually, the Luftwaffe was defeated, and the battleship sailed on, to be safely docked in Portsmouth.

After this excitement, we resumed our convoy duties between Milford and Dartmouth, and by this stage in the war we had no hesitation in chatting up our R.A.F. colleagues at Portreath. We used to ask them to dinner at Falmouth, while they used to reciprocate at Portreath. We were on the best of terms, and made some very good friends.

By this time, I was a fairly seasoned acting sub lieutenant with a

Fleet Watch-Keeping Certificate. Even so, I still shared the sick bay with Surgeon Lieutenant Alan Milner, who was probably my greatest friend in that destroyer. He was later to become a senior consultant in the Midlands Hospital Group, but sadly he died prematurely from overwork. My "contract" with Alan had been that I was to vacate the operating table whenever he needed it professionally. Occasionally this had to be implemented, notably when he amputated the leg of a badly bombed Dutch Merchant Seaman. He also had to amputate the foot of one of our own crew, who had got into difficulties while swimming in the Dart. A motor boat had gone to his rescue, but unfortunately the coxswain had failed to realise that even when a motor boat is idling out of gear, the propeller is often still turning. The result was that it had almost severed the man's foot.

The bombing continued unrelentingly, of towns and convoys alike. We heard of a massive raid on London on 12th May, in the course of which several well-known war leaders were killed, including Sir Josiah Stamp, the chairman of the L.M.S. Railway and one of the great railroad pioneers. The plight of Britain at this time seemed dire. All the same, we kept our spirits up, or perhaps it was the other way round; the "spirits" buoyed us up! For my part, I was spending all my pay on food and drink, and we had some splendid evenings ashore in Dartmouth and Falmouth, although Milford was decidedly drab.

After one convoy we arrived at Falmouth and I telephoned its best hotel restaurant to book a dinner for myself and several of my Wardroom chums. I also arranged for a taxi to take us there. Finally, however, when we were all ready and waiting for the taxi on the quayside, it was discovered that Doc. Milner was missing. When I chased him up, he told me that he could not come until he had examined a certain rating who was about to be escorted to Exeter Prison to undergo a sentence of hard labour. Before he was taken there, he had to be certified free from infectious diseases. With people dying all round us, this struck me as a particularly stupid and quibbling piece of red tape. "Get your sick berth attendant to see to it," I told him, "Hurry up and sign the blank form, and then get in the taxi!"

The night that followed was a hell of a good one, but next morning the following ominous signal arrived from the Commander-in-Chief, Plymouth: "State name and rank of medical officer who certified A.B. -- as free from infectious diseases. This man was suffering from venereal disease and scabies." Poor Doc.! His reward was to be appointed shortly afterwards to the 64th General Hospital near Cairo!

At 8 a.m. on the 22nd June, having just finished my morning watch, I entered the Wardroom for breakfast. As usual at that hour, I was absolutely starving, yet on that particular morning I was quite unable to eat anything. The reason was the exciting – indeed staggering – news which I had just heard. Three hours before, at 5 a.m., while I was still on watch, the Germans had invaded Russia. I felt even then that the pressure on us might at last be reduced. We might yet survive, though by the skin of our teeth. Though I did not know it at the time, my time of service in Tynedale was drawing to a close. Yet from this date onwards, enemy pressure upon us started to fall like the pressure in a burst tyre, as the full weight of the Luftwaffe's resources was diverted to the new eastern front. Attacks on our coastal convoys and on the West Country towns dwindled to a trickle of what they had formerly been.

Those of us who were already directly involved in the armed struggle in August 1939, might remember the part played by Russia in promoting World War II. If Stalin and Molotov had not signed the Non-Aggression Pact, there would have been no World War II – at least not in September 1939. I had hated Stalin and his henchmen then, and I hated them even more intensely in June 1941, holding them responsible in part for all that we had suffered in the intervening period. Indeed, so deep had my hatred of Stalin and his clique become, that it was greater than my hatred of the Germans, with whom I had been in such close contact.

Such being my attitude, my reaction to one pronouncement, very widely reported on the radio (this was, of course, years before television), should cause no great surprise. It came within a few days of the opening of hostilities between Germany and Russia, and the speaker was the then Minister of War Transport, Colonel Moore-Brabazon. He made a public statement to the effect that now that Russia and Germany were at war, he hoped that Britain would withdraw from that conflict and let the real aggressors fight it out. That, at any rate, was the gist of his message, though it may not have been expressed in those exact words. At all events, within a matter of hours he had been dismissed from office.

Yet in my view Moore-Brabazon was almost the only truly well-informed, intelligent figure in the British government, and I found myself agreeing with every word he said. As for the other members of the wartime government, I had time for hardly any of them – least of all, perhaps, for Herbert Morrison, the Home Secretary. In World War I this Minister had actually been cited as a traitor, yet now here he was imprisoning without trial men who had shown themselves heroes in that conflict, including a vice admiral and former Chief of Naval Intelligence! Moore-Brabazon's advice was rejected and forgotten. Yet for some strange reason he, who had been so much vilified, was later ennobled as Lord Brabazon of Tara, and honoured by having the largest air liner of its day called after him. To me this remains one of the many mysteries of World War II.

I must return, however, to my naval career. My time in Tynedale was coming to an end. Service in her was not always tranquil; often it was thoroughly uncomfortable. Yet it is with deep admiration that I remember her captain, her officers, and her splendid crew, for their skill and their courage, often in adversity. I am also deeply indebted to them for teaching a brash, ill-disciplined, and under-developed young officer to become battle-trained, and for giving him the sort of formation that would equip him to become his own commanding officer in a much shorter time than he could possibly have expected.

Apart from this, the officers and ship's company of Tynedale were quite the most agreeable bunch one could ever hope to meet. Although I made many friends in other ships and shore stations, never before or since have I been on such close terms with my colleagues.

Tynedale went on to serve with great distinction at St. Nazaire and other momentous battles, until she was finally torpedoed, with great loss of life, in January, 1944 in the Mediterranean. With her perished a great many of my close friends. Among those lost was a nephew of Admiral Binney's, and also Lieutenant Congreve, who had taught me so much about gunnery control and running the ship's office. On the lower deck, I lost too many friends to mention here, and now, as I look at the casualty list forty years later, I still remember everything about them.

PART III

Coastal Forces

CHAPTER 7

Coastal Forces (I)

Dartmouth was the most easterly of the ports to which we convoyed, and when we entered the river in late July, 1941, there was the usual flurry of excitement as the mail was distributed. Some of it might be days, or even weeks, late. I was reading my own mail, when a messenger arrived to tell me that the captain wanted to see me at once. What on earth could it be? In some trepidation I entered his cabin, and found him engrossed in wave after wave of paper. Pulling one sheaf out from the rest, he told me that this was an Admiralty C.W. list notifying me that I was appointed to H.M.S. St. Christopher for Coastal Force training. He added that the list was already two weeks old. I was to pack up, leave the ship the next day, and make my way to Fort William.

On the whole, I had enjoyed Tynedale, and particularly liked my fellow officers, as well as the crew. As for the captain, I had the very highest respect for him. Nevertheless, I was pleased at the prospect of a change. Tynedale's complement of officers was about ten, of whom I was the junior. Under such circumstances, I would have had to wait several years before I had the slightest chance of achieving any really responsible job in destroyers. I would be far better off, I concluded, in small ships.

Since I had the running of the ship's office, I was able to make out my own travel warrant. Seizing the opportunity, I took care to route myself from Dartmouth to Fort William via London and Montrose. The Confidential Book Officer warned me that I must return without fail C.B.4000, The Conduct of Anti-U Boat Operations. It was a book that I had been studying, on and off, for the past fortnight, but now I searched for it everywhere in vain. Now to lose a book of this sort was a court martial offence, and I wondered what on earth the captain would say when he heard that I had lost it. Luckily I found it in my small brief case, and was able to hand it in. It was in the nick of time – only just before I said goodbye to the captain.

On my final night at Dartmouth, the officers gave me a

marvellous party, attended by the captain and several of our trawler officers. We all got extremely drunk. One incident in particular still seems quite unforgettable. One of the trawler captains possessed an accordion of a very cheap type, on which, in a thoroughly drunken manner, he was playing some lively air. Our captain was urging him on with shouts to play louder and faster. Suddenly, as the noise swelled to a crescendo, the squeeze box parted in the middle. The look of utter stupefaction on the face of the musician, as he held the two sundered parts one in either hand, is something which I shall never forget.

The following day, as I left Kingswear Station for Paddington, I was suffering from an appalling hangover. It was now Thursday, and I decided to go home to Montrose, and report to Fort William on Monday. On the way, I had to fend off several officious railway inspectors, who wanted to know why I was routed by Montrose; it was, they pointed out, miles off the direct route. However, I told them shortly that these were my orders, and that it was not for either me or them to question them!

When I finally arrived at H.M.S. St. Christopher, the training base at Fort William, I reported to a duty officer, who forthwith enquired why I was three weeks late. However, once I had explained the vagaries and delays to which mail for destroyers was subject, no one seemed to worry too much, and I was allotted to a class.

At this point I have an admission to make. The fact is that my behaviour for the next six weeks or so was deplorable and irresponsible to a degree. This was despite the fact that I knew I had been very lucky to have been given such a charge, with the possibility of a command to follow in the near future. Yet now, as I reflect on my conduct during that period, I am surprised that I was not sent to a battleship to improve my sense of discipline! Although many of my fellow students had seen service and action afloat, in anything from big ships to trawlers, nearly all of them had only just been commissioned, and had come here straight from H.M.S. King Alfred. As an officer of two years' standing, therefore, and the holder of a Fleet Watch-Keeping ticket, I was accorded considerable respect for my seniority. Under the circumstances, I might and should have acted more responsibly.

I had been assigned quarters in the Grand Hotel, and our H.Q. was the Highland Hotel, a vast pile, which in pre-war days had catered for the relatively affluent. We used to be woken up about 6.30 a.m., and at seven were due to report in running clothes at the Highland for P.T. and a run to make us fit. I took the gravest exception to this, and found three others of like mind. We were determined to avoid having to endure such a burden every day. Accordingly, we formed a syndicate. Each morning when we mustered for P.T., only one of us would actually be present, and he would answer "here" to the names of the two others as well as to his own. Unfortunately, the very first time I tried this, I was caught. A chief petty officer came up to me furious and red-faced, and bawled straight in my face: "How many names have you got – Sir?" I was duly reported, and collected my first black mark.

Towards the end of my first week, the training officer told me that the first four weeks' programme of the training schedule was not designed for officers of my seniority. The outcome of all this was that at the end of that first week I was sent to H.M.S. Seahawk at Ardrishaig. There I was to undergo a three weeks anti-submarine course, before returning to St. Christopher to complete the main part of my training. On the Saturday, therefore, about twelve of us joined a naval bus for Ardrishaig. On arrival, we were billeted nearby at a guest house in Lochgilphead.

On Sunday morning, having attended church parade, I was walking back the two miles from Ardrishaig to my digs, when two delightful sisters, unmistakably upper-crust, offered me a lift in their car. They then invited me to sherry with their aunt, a Mrs Campbell, who lived in a beautiful old mill house named Drum-na-Voulin on the outskirts of the town – or rather, big village, for at the time that was all it was. After an hour or so, when I had told them, in vague terms, what I was doing, they asked me whether my mother could come to join me. She could stay with Mrs Campbell at Drum-na-Voulin, so that I could see her during my free time. My mother accepted this very kind invitation, arriving about a week later.

Once I had settled in, it was no time before I had found some good salmon and sea trout fishing. A certain Sir Ian Malcolm of Poltalloch was good enough to allow me to fish the lower reaches of the River Add, which enters the sea at Crinan. The difficulty was that it was about eight miles away, and at that time none of us students possessed a car. To journey to and fro from Lochgilphead to Ardrishaig, we used bicycles. However, the instructor of my class, a Lieutenant Bell R.N., did have a car and was also a fisherman. Before long, therefore, we were both spending most of our evenings on the Add near Crinan. Our work on this anti-submarine course consisted of classes ashore on the care and maintenance of asdic sets and on attack procedures, and also in practical work out on Loch Fyne in anti-submarine motor boats (M.A./S.B.'s) based at the port. For my own part, Ardrishaig was a marvellous holiday, and I never seemed to do a stroke of work. To the horror of my colleagues, most of whom had just become officers, I simply fooled about.

After the three weeks were up, we had to sit exams. Now, I felt, retribution was at last about to catch up with me, and I would surely pay for my sins. The day of reckoning came when Commander Vaux, a stern and unbending figure, came to announce the results. "These results", he began, "include the best and the worst I have ever seen." There was a deathly hush. "Sub Lieutenant Forsyth-Grant," he continued... I went numb. I wished I had worked harder. "May I congratulate you on an excellent result – the best we have ever had!" I could not believe my ears. Even at this distance in time, forty-seven years later, I still cannot explain it. Whether it was because my fellow students were inexperienced or dumb, or whether my instructor did something to help me, I shall never now know. Even the other members of my class were all disquieted.

I returned to Fort William via Montrose (again!), and picked up my car. Meanwhile my mother was making her way to Fort William independently, and was to meet me there next day. She too had been employing her time to advantage, and having had some distant acquaintanceship with Lochiel, had got me an invitation to shoot over some of the vast Achnacarry estates close to Fort William.

Once back at St. Christopher, the staff still seemed uncertain as to what courses I should take. All that was decided was that I should stay there for two weeks before assessing my future, and at the same time undergo some training in the sea-going craft attached to the base at Loch Linnhe. Needless, to say, I spent most of my time shooting grouse on the flats between Inverlochy and Corpach, and stalking deer on Tor Castle.

On one of these forays, I lay in pouring rain on a high slate face in the mountains, waiting for some stags to move to a better position. When finally a chance came for an easy shot, I missed, and my fingers were too cold to re-load the rifle! I returned to the base with an appalling cold, and thinking that I was in for 'flu, decided to kill or cure it with whisky. I was well under the weather when I spotted another officer in the bar, in the act of throwing a dart right through the window. It smashed the glass pane and came to rest in Fort William's main street. I went over and congratulated him on his appalling act of vandalism, and after a few drinks discovered that his name was Philip Wayre. Later he was to become a well-known writer on wild life and a T.V. personality. He also created the Norfolk Wildlife Park, and another sanctuary in Sussex. More of him anon.

At the end of my period of training at Fort William, I was due for my final assessment. I was summoned for an interview by the commanding officer, Commander Wellman D.S.O., a veteran of the Coastal Force attack on the Bolshevik Fleet at Kronstadt at the end of the First World War. This interview was the very opposite of the one I had had with Commander Vaux. He told me that I was the worst officer they had ever had to suffer at St. Christopher. Puce in the face with rage, he also informed me that the Admiralty had appointed me to command H.M.L. 292, but that if there was anything that he could do to prevent this, he would not hesitate to do it. From this it will apparent that Wellman and I thoroughly disliked each other. At all events, once this was over, I found that I had been assigned to Brixham, and set out to report to the captain of the base there.

Brixham turned out to be, in reality, only an administrative centre for the fitting out of convoy-escort M.L.s. The captain's secretary introduced me to him, whereupon this charming old man told me that I had arrived with the worst report on an officer he had ever seen! Thereafter, we got on extremely well. The captain's secretary was a very pleasant paymaster lieutenant, who introduced me to my second-in-command to be. After that, he took me round to the Berry Head Hotel, which also served as an officers' mess. Although by this time the worst of the blitz was over, there was insufficient black-out material for all the windows in the hotel. After dark, therefore, we had to creep about in pitch darkness. In view of this, I tried to do a reconnaissance before nightfall, and particularly to memorise the way to the bar and the gentlemen's loo!

That evening we had a splendid carousel in the bar, in the course of which I went to find the loo. I groped in the dark, thought I was in the correct room, but was unable to find any pan or urinal. At last I could wait no longer. I let everything go, and was disappointed to find that the sounds were not such as to reassure me. Next day, the housemaid's pantry was awash, and a search for the culprit was launched. I must have had an innocent face, for no one suspected me.

My first lieutenant was a Midshipman Dowrick. He and I set off for Plymouth, and thence over Plymouth Sound to Cremyll, where our craft was being built at Mashford Brothers. (This was the firm that was later to build the yacht in which Sir Francis Chichester made the first solo circumnavigation of the world.) The fitting out of M.L. 292, we found, would take another fortnight, so, as by this time it was getting dark, we returned to Plymouth to look for digs. I decided that we would have to use the Grand, Plymouth's premier hotel, and I asked for two single rooms. To my astonishment, the receptionist told me that we could have a luxury suite for the same price, so I settled for this. Apart from the fact that some plaster had fallen from the ceiling, that suite was the best I have ever stayed in. When we went down to dinner, we found that we two were the only guests in the whole of that vast dining-room. The explanation was that after the blitz everyone had fled Plymouth. The following day, deciding to move to something with more life, we found a delightful guest house at Cawsand in Cornwall, and were just in time to book ourselves the last two rooms. It was packed with the senior officers of H.M.S. Trinidad, a cruiser commissioning in Devonport Dockyard, and we made great friends with them. She was soon to be lost on a Russian convoy in the Barents Sea.

Mashfords was a splendid boatyard, and we all got on famously. Tynedale was still based at Devonport, and I gave a party one night for the officers. The next night I followed this up with another, this time for some of the ratings, all of whom had been close comrades in the destroyer. After a night's roistering in a pub called the Edgcumbe Arms, which was only fifty yards from the boatyard, one rating was reported missing. It was Signalman Wheeler, a New Zealander. In the course of a midnight search, he was discovered asleep in a bomb crater three hundred yards from the pub. Since that night I have never set eyes on Jim Wheeler, but since the war we have never failed to exchange Christmas cards. He now lives in Auckland, New Zealand, and we live in hopes of soon meeting again.

While we were getting stores on M.L. 292 from Plymouth, I had occasion to visit the French battleship Paris, then a headquarters ship, commanded by a Captain R.N. (Retired) – a very formidable person. My mission was to get him to countersign my form, Customs and Excise 90, authorising me to purchase duty free drink for the ship. Regrettably, I forgot that I was no longer in the drifter Shower, on which my astronomic list was based. When he read the list, the captain gasped in horror and then burst forth: "Young man, do you think you are running a ship or a public house?" Forthwith, he reduced my list by seventy-five percent!

At last M.L. 292 was launched and commissioned, but she still remained contractor's responsibility until after trials at Brixham, when the captain M.L. would sign for her. M.L. 292 was 112 feet in length, and powered by two 650 H.P. Hall Scott supercharged petrol engines, giving her a top speed of 21 knots. She had a three-pounder gun on the fo'c'sle and a two-pounder Rolls gun aft, a 20mm. Twin Oerlikon gun, and four machine guns. She was fitted with depth charge chute and throwers, and carried a good supply of 400 lb depth charges. She had asdic (sonar), wireless, echo sounder, but no radar. She was primarily designed for convoy protection against submarines, aircraft, and E Boats.. In the course of the war about five hundred of these craft were built, with minor changes of role. When it came to the greatest raid of all, that of St. Nazaire, they were the backbone of it.

To take the ship from Cremyll to Brixham, Fairmile, the contractors appointed their own man, a gnarled old fisherman, who was said to be a local pilot. As we were just off Plymouth, I discovered that the course he was taking would lead us right into a British minefield, and I told him we were on the wrong course. He replied with a withering dose of abuse, informing me that he had been navigating ships when I was in nappies! However, once I had explained tactfully that he was steering straight for a minefield, he apologised profusely, and told me that no one had told him of its existence! At Torbay, we completed the sea trials satisfactorily, and then parted amicably.

On the Sunday after arriving at Brixham, having completed some further fitting, we had a stand-easy. Four of our ratings wanted to go ashore from Brixham harbour, where our ship was moored, in order to attend church parade. They set off in the M.L.'s. dinghy, but there was a very nasty sea and swell, and they immediately capsized. Three ratings managed to swim to the side, or to lifebuoys in lines thrown to them, but Telegraphist Richardson could not swim, and he went under. Whipping off my jacket and shoes, I dived in after him. He had been under twice, and although he was lashing about deliriously, he was in a bad way. Five years before, as a boy of sixteen at Wellington, I had won the Proficiency Certificate and Instructor's Certificate Bronze Medallion. Now all the long training I had received for this came rushing back to me. Richardson was fighting frantically, and seizing my hands convulsively. At last I pulled them free, turned him on his back on my chest, and tried to float him. The conditions were rough and cold in the extreme, and a strong wind was blowing us out to sea. To fight against both current and wind was useless. I simply tried to keep the two of us afloat, in the hope that somebody would pick us up. Sure enough, some twenty minutes later, we were both hauled aboard a small fishing boat, which had been warned to look out for us.

I had dived in with my cap still on, and in consequence had hurt my neck. After a change of clothes, however, neither Richardson nor I were much the worse, though he was put to bed for twenty-four hours with shock. For myself, my main worry was my watch.

It had been given to me by my father three years before, and I valued it very highly. Unfortunately, however, it was not waterproof. I knew that my only chance of saving it would be to get it seen to immediately, but since it was a Sunday, no watchmaker was open. When I took it to one next day, it was too late; it had been ruined beyond repair.

I had little time to reflect upon our survival. I had only been back on M.L. 292 a very short time, when my cousin, Malcolm Forsyth-Grant, turned up. At the time he was a senior cadet at Dartmouth Naval College, and I had invited him and a chum of his to lunch. In fact it did me a lot of good to have them with me, taking my mind off the alarming events of the morning.

We were now fully commissioned, and ready for war in all respects. The next day, therefore, we set sail for Dartmouth, where I was to become Senior Officer of a miniature convoy, consisting of a freighter and a tug, with two ammunition barges. Under me I had a second seventy-two foot Harbour Defence M.L. commanded by a Sub Lieutenant Bennett. We sailed from Dartmouth one morning while it was still dark, bound for Falmouth. It was still dark when we arrived, amid big seas and a roaring gale. Once we had entered the Fal River, responsibility for the convoy became the onus of the port authority, so I went in above Falmouth to a mooring off Greenbank. Next morning, I saw that the two ammunition barges and the tug had all gone aground in the gale. I thanked God that by then they had left my charge.

The following day M.L. 292 was due to join the escort of a big convoy to Milford Haven, under the command of my old ship, Tynedale. Now Midshipman Dowrick, my second-in-command and only officer, had no experience of ship-handling whatsoever, except for an hour or so at Fort William. He had never in his life been in charge of a night watch. Under these circumstances, I deemed it incredibly risky to leave him in charge at night for more than minutes at a time. I rang the Chief of Staff at Plymouth, an admiral or commodore, and explained the difficulty. He was far from unsympathetic, but concluded that I would just have to make the best of it. There was nothing more that I could do. About four p.m., Tynedale entered Falmouth, and I joined my former colleagues in a roistering good night on the town. Next day at ten a.m. we sailed for Milford Haven with nine other M.L.s. in the escort.

By the time we reached the Lizard, the convoy was well formed up. It comprised about a dozen ships, three or four escort trawlers, ten M.L.s, and Tynedale, firmly in command. We rounded Land's End at dusk, and darkness saw us forging up the Cornish coast. I had been on the bridge ever since we had left Falmouth; there was a steepish sea, and the wind was increasing. I told Dowrick to keep close station on a coaster, while I went to the Wardroom for a cup of soup. Just as I was putting the cup to my lips, there was an almighty crash. I rushed to the bridge, to find that we had collided with the coaster. However, when I finally extricated M.L. 292 from her, the damage seemed slight, so I conned the ship back to its correct station, and never left the bridge again until we were alongside in Milford Haven.

Around midnight, however, the storm was raging in full fury, and the seas were about as bad as the M.L. could take. Doggedly I held my station, only to discover when dawn came that all the other M.L.s were gone. They had put into Padstow and other Cornish ports, through stress of weather. As dawn broke, therefore, I was delighted to receive the following signal: "From Tynedale to M.L. 292. Well done! Come hell or high water, I knew you would still be with us!" During the night, the seaman cook had been so sick that now he was lying apparently unconscious on the mess decks. I was worried for his life, and I had him hauled on deck and lashed to the mast. Now at last he was getting some fresh air, and he returned from semi-consciousness at any rate to the extent of being able to speak. He survived the trip, but I certified him unfit for sea service, and sadly he left us at Milford. He was a pleasant and loyal member of the crew.

On arrival at the Haven, Tynedale signalled me alongside, and her first lieutenant said that he had a personal message for me from the captain. Our crew could use all the facilities of the destroyer (a great and most unusual compliment!), and I was to dine in the Wardroom that night. I regret to say that, having had no rest for thirty-six hours, I fell asleep at the table. However, no one was upset. Next day, we sailed on alone to Fishguard, where I did have a good night's rest.

After our collision with the coaster, I had obtained permission not to sail at night until my second-in-command was more experienced. On leaving Fishguard, therefore, we spent a night in Holyhead, and thence sailed for the Isle of Man. On arriving at Douglas, I was just taking the opportunity of stretching my legs on the pier, when, to my astonishment, I ran into a close friend from Angus. He was in P.T. gear, and I naturally asked him what the hell he was doing. It turned out that he was a captain in an Officers' Training Unit which was based there, so we arranged to meet for a drink that evening. I had never expected to see him again for the duration of the war, let alone here in the Isle of Man, but that night we were able to have a pleasant reunion.

Soon after my arrival, a staff car arrived to take me to report to the port captain. On the way back, the driver asked me whether I had ever visited the Island before. He told me that I would be able to hire a car without deposit, and if I wanted a Manx licence, he would drive me to the police station, where I could obtain one for five shillings on production of my British licence. He also said that he would take me to a garage for hire cars. When I parked my hired car beside my ship, with all these arrangements complete, I could hardly believe my luck!

The only other M.L. which had survived from the Falmouth-to-Milford convoy was our "chummy", H.D. M.L. from Dartmouth. Now the skipper of this vessel and his second-in-command joined me and mine for a splendid tour of the island. Our circum-navigation of it was reminiscent of the T.T. race, but we did see where all the aliens and political prisoners were detained at Peel. It was now October 1941, and on the British mainland, of course, petrol was being strictly rationed, being available only on production of coupons. In the Isle of Man, on the other hand, the supply was unlimited. Again, food rationing on the mainland was by now biting severely, yet in the Isle of Man there was none. I actually bought two enormous legs of ham and two hundred-weight of sugar!

Next day I left for Stranraer, and thence for Oban, passing through the Sound of Islay and the dreaded Gulf of Corryvreckan, which has the worst tide rips in the United Kingdom. Even for a vessel of our size, it was an awesome experience to feel ourselves pitching and rolling in the whirlpools like a cork.

At Oban we tied up alongside the quay. I was breakfasting in the Wardroom when there was a massive thud, followed by awful rending noises. I rushed on deck, to find that a badly handled trawler had crashed along our side, wrecking all the guardrails, stanchions and so on, and ruining our shining new paintwork. I held my temper and took his number before sailing on to Fort William. From there we travelled on through the Caledonian Canal to Inverness.

Two incidents of that Canal passage cling to my memory. My mother, like all hard-pressed housewives, was very short of certain items, and had asked me to obtain them as and when an opportunity occurred. This I had done: salad cream (Fishguard), sugar and ham (Isle of Man), and other items which I cannot now remember. One which I had been quite unable to obtain anywhere, however, was Chivers' jellies. Now, however, in the course of passing through the Canal, we came to a loch where we had to stop for a short time while one of the basins was waiting to fill. While stretching my legs alongside the lock, I followed the other members of my crew into a tiny store to see what was on sale. It was full of Chivers' jellies, which the shopkeeper had found it impossible to sell! I believe I bought the lot!

The other incident occurred an hour later, again while we were stuck in a lock basin waiting for it to fill. A very irate lock-keeper declared that the crew had been chasing his hens. I rounded them up and interrogated them, but they all firmly denied the accusation. This I duly conveyed to the lock-keeper, not without a certain amount of indignation. That night we stopped at Fort Augustus, and to my horror, when dinner was served, the main dish was roast chicken!

After a fairly hectic ten days, we arrived at Inverness late on a Friday night. I therefore proposed to spend the week-end resting there. Now at Milton of Culloden lived an old friend of my family's named Colonel Usher. I believe that he had commanded the Gordons at Dunkirk, but by this time he had retired. He now asked me to shoot with him on the Sunday – in wartime it was the most popular day! I accepted with alacrity.

That same evening, however, my quiet Saturday in Inverness was shattered. First, a most officious lieutenant R.N.R., who appeared to be in charge at Inverness, told me that I could not shoot with the colonel, and that on Sunday at 10.00 hours I was to sail for Invergordon. I protested that my second-in-command had 'flu and could have done with a day off. In any case, we were not required in Peterhead, our final destination, before Tuesday. Thirdly, I pointed out, there was a very bad weather report for the Cromarty Firth. All my arguments were of no avail; the lieutenant would not listen to any remonstrations. Accordingly, I ordered a pilot from Clachnaharry for Fort George for Sunday at 10.00 hours. After all this, I was in a thoroughly bad temper when a Mr J.E. Kennerley called on me. He introduced himself as an Admiralty Civilian Officer Commanding Armament Supply at Inverness, and said that my sailors had been stealing his ammunition. Bearing in mind the chicken episode of twenty-four hours earlier, I gave him a drink and got rid of him as soon as I could!

At 10.00 hours the pilot arrived, and advised against sailing at all. I rang the lieutenant R.N.R., who was extremely rude and insisted that I was to sail – he would take no excuses. He accused me of merely wanting to shoot with the colonel.

I dropped the pilot off Fort George, and ploughed on into the Moray Firth. The seas soon became mountainous, and there was a full gale blowing from the west. I considered that I could not possibly steam through this without great danger, so I reversed course for the lee of the land, making for the Cromarty Firth and Invergordon, where I finally arrived at three p.m. on the Sunday afternoon. Dowrick collapsed on the settee from exhaustion and 'flu, and I told him to go to bed. Then, in a furious rage, I set out to find the flag officer in charge, a rear admiral. After all these years I do not remember much of what was said. But later I had the satisfaction of hearing that the R.N.R. lieutenant had been sacked that same week.

By Monday morning the gale had died down, and I set off for Peterhead, where the twenty-third M.L. Flotilla was assembling. I, an acting sub lieutenant aged twenty, was the junior commanding officer. I met the other C.O.s in the flotilla, and took to them without exception. Over the next week or so, we got down to training and working together.

The Naval Command at Peterhead was not entirely effective. Captain Hewitt R.N. (Retired), the N.O.I.C., was a charming fellow. One night I was duty ship, on instant call. I was having a cup of tea with the swing bridge operator, who had been a crew member of Lupina in 1940 and was a very old friend. Suddenly the harbour tannoy called out: "Commanding officer of M.L. 292, report to Naval H.Q. immediately." "Well," the fisheries lock-keeper remarked, "They can't send you to sea in this!" He was wrong. The duty officer said that I was to go to sea at once, and investigate a large collection of ships converging on Rattray Head from the north. It could be an invasion from Norway. I asked him about Naval H.Q. wireless frequencies. He replied that they had allowed the duty telephonist to go to the cinema. I was furious. "Recall him and have him man his set while we go to sea in this gale!", I spat. "Also turn on the harbour lights for me to clear harbour, and light Rattray Head at midnight for ten minutes, so that I can check positions!"

Within fifteen minutes I had cleared Peterhead Bay Harbour, and was steering into mountainous seas in a gale, with spray blinding the three of us, totally exposed as we were on the bridge. As we were searching blind for ships some miles off Rattray Head, we were suddenly almost blinded by a destroyer's searchlight. Quick recognition signals revealed that she was one of ours! The whole convoy was British. What a bloody mess! Angrily, I informed Peterhead that I was returning to harbour.

When I entered the Bay, the outer breakwater lights were still on, but the Bay itself was beset by a huge swell. The inner harbour lights were not on, so I had no option but to find a sheltered anchorage in the lee of the breakwater and let go the anchor. Our request for the lights to be switched on met with no reply from Peterhead radio. At last, after a rattle of signals in code to Aberdeen Naval Radio, the inner harbour lights came on. By that time, however, the swell was so great that I had insufficient power in the capstan to raise our anchor; we were stuck. Accordingly I told the first lieutenant to let all the brand new cable go, with a buoy to mark it, and, having done this, I steamed into the inner harbour and secured. At 10 a.m. that morning, in a thoroughly aggressive mood, I reported to Naval H.Q.. The calm, gentlemanly Captain Hewitt informed me that after my report that the ships were friendly, the duty telegraphist had been sent off duty again – before we had reached the harbour. He apologized for the upset, and said that a boat would uplift my anchor and cable and return it to me in the Inner Dock. The following day I heard that a trawler had caught the buoy wire in her screw, and that it had now had to be slipped to get the wire off her propeller. Thus my anchor and chain were lost for ever!

CHAPTER EIGHT

Coastal Forces (II)

The acting commander of our flotilla was Lieutenant Jimmy Lumsden R.N.V.R., while I was junior commanding officer. This, however, was unusual. Normally the commander of a flotilla of "B" M.L.s would have been not a lieutenant, but a lieutenant commander. The matter was of no particular concern to me, until one day an Admiralty signal arrived. It instructed me to exchange M.L.s with a Lieutenant Commander M. Shore Brundell; henceforward he was to be senior officer of 23rd Flotilla, while I was to join his ship at Brightlingsea, Essex.

On receiving this, I straightway lodged a protest with the C.O. of the Coastal Force based at Peterhead, a commander. Though I did not know much about this officer, there was one story circulating about him which I had heard. Being rather drunk in his office one day, he had made advances to a WREN. She had refused intimacy with him, whereupon he had given her a two-finger sign through the window, and in the process had broken the glass and severed an artery. That, presumably, was why, when I interviewed him, he had his arm in a sling.

At all events, while I was still in his office, he rang up Rear Admiral, Coastal Forces in London, to convey my protest. Though both of us were to have cause for disappointment, the admiral's reply was perhaps even more devastating to him than it was to me. As I overheard it, it ran somewhat as follows: "Before you start about Sub Lieutenant Forsyth-Grant, let me tell you that you are relieved of your command forthwith for a major breach of discipline. Forsyth-Grant is to act in accordance with the Admiralty signal. There is nothing more to say!"

When I arrived at Coastal Force Base, Brightlingsea, ominous news awaited me. Lieutenant Commander Shore Brundell had already set off to replace me at Peterhead. He had left the boat in charge of his second-in-command, who had promptly run it aground with severe damage. Thus there was no B Class Fairmile for me here. Worse, however, was to follow. I now found that I had been appointed to command a brand new motor anti-submarine boat, which was still building at Hythe, Southampton. I was simply furious. I had not the slightest wish to command anything except a B Class M.L. on convoy work, which I knew so well. High-Speed Attack craft simply did not interest me. The first lieutenant of the base was taken aback by my aggressive attitude. He warned me that Captain Farquharson (R.N. Retired), the captain, M.L., was a stern disciplinarian; one, therefore who, as a four-striped captain, would brook no nonsene from a sub lieutenant. He was away until six p.m., at which time an interview would be arranged with him.

As it turned out, Captain Farquharson proved to be an inspiring man. Aged about sixty, he had retired from the Navy fifteen years before and then, so I was told, had become secretary to the Bishop of Salisbury. Notwithstanding all that I had heard about him, I launched into an appalling diatribe, in which I complained of the atrocious messing about to which I had been subjected. I wanted no part in the High-Speed Attack brigade, I told him — nothing but a B Class M.L.. I was expecting his reply to take the form of a full broadside, but not a bit of it! The captain told me how badly the Navy had treated him, and said that he had every sympathy with me. He would arrange for me to go back to London and see Rear Admiral, Coastal Forces — the top of the tree, in other words — at noon next day, so that I could put my case to him direct.

At 12.00 hours the following day, therefore, I was ushered into the presence of the great man, whose name, Rear Admiral Piers Kekewich, sounded more Russian than British. Of his antecendents I know nothing, but Captain Augustus Agar V.C., D.S.O., R.N., a well-known author and the most distinguished Coastal Force officer of the 1918-20 era, wrote very highly of him.

Personally, I was very taken with him. Instead of giving me one almight blast, he listened to my story with sympathy and understanding. He said that I must take up my appointment at Hythe; it was quite out of the question for it to be cancelled. I should try High-Speed Attack Craft for three months, and then write to him personally if I did not like the job.

Although still bewildered and discontented, I was greatly mollified by what the admiral had said. There was in fact no need to report to H.M.S. Hornet, the major Coastal Force Base at Gosport, for several days. Accordingly, since the date was the 23rd December, I retired to the Great Eastern Hotel in London for Christmas. Here the head waiter was that same John Cobb who, as I have related earlier, had looked after me so superbly as a schoolboy at the King's Cross Grill Room. When that suffered a

Rear Admiral Piers Kekewich (right)

direct hit, he had narrowly escaped with his life. Now that he had
become head waiter of the Great Eastern, he saw to it that I had no
difficulty in obtaining a twin-bedded room there. I rang up my
brother, who was then a flying officer stationed at R.A.F. Debden,
and invited him to join me. Against all rules and regulations, he
managed to do so, and we celebrated Christmas in great style. John
Cobb was — God knows why! — delighted to see us, and we were
treated like royalty. Other guests complained at the unlimited
"goodies" that were put before us, since they were not available to
ordinary guests. John Cobb, however, blandly told them that we
had brought our own food, and that there was nothing he could do
about it! For three days we had a marvellous time, and explored a
London that I had never seen before. The extent of the devastation
left an indelible impression upon us.

After that it was back to work, and I reported to H.M.S. Hornet at
Gosport. I picked up my first lieutenant, Sub Lieutenant H.S.
Andrews, who was about ten years older than I , and off we set
across Southampton Water for the British Power Boat Company
at Hythe. Since the boat was not quite ready, we had some days to
wait there, and we made friends with several other officers
similarly placed. A Dutch Motor Gunboat, No. 46, had escaped
from Holland, and, under the command of William de Looze,

Royal Netherlands Navy, was also fitting out. Later our paths were often to cross in the course of our work in Coastal Forces, and William became highly decorated. I last saw him ten years ago, when he invited me to dine with him at Perth. At the time he was Dutch Consul General in Britain, and was in the process of inspecting his Scottish consulates.

My new command was a prototype experimental Motor Anti-Submarine Boat, the last of a batch of seventeen, but she alone was equipped with the new supercharged 1400 H.P. Packard engines, whereas the other sixteen had only the 500 H.P. Napier Lion engines. This alone made her, as compared with them, nothing short of revolutionary. Indeed, she was reputedly the second fastest boat in the Navy, and the fact that I had been given command of her should have made me feel more than honoured. Yet I was still hankering after my M.L.

After commissioning, we were based at Gosport (H.M.S. Hornet), where we joined some other M.A.S.B.s on Air Sea Rescue work. I was given a fairly free hand so that I could pay repeated visits to Power Boats at Hythe and try out different propellers etc. Down the Solent we used to achieve 50 knots. It made a super run for lunch! Generally speaking, Air Sea Rescue work was incredibly boring. It consisted of tying up to Seaview Pier, Isle of Wight, and waiting to rescue a plane. I was engaged in this sort of work for nearly eight months, and while Andrews and the crew seemed quite happy with their lot, I was bored and restless. Because of this, I started a correspondence course through a firm in London with the aim of improving my navigation. In view of the fact that I already had my own command, everyone thought that I was mad. At Seaview, the pier must have been about six hundred yards long, and at the end of it stood a large hotel. It boasted thirty rooms or more, but of these only three were occupied by Royal Marines for some purpose or other. In no time, therefore, I had arranged to take over one of the best remaining rooms, actually overlooking M.A.S.B. 39, where I could pursue my correspondence course in navigation in peace and quiet.

As I have said, normally speaking, Air Sea Rescue work was incredibly boring. During my eight months' experience of it, not one of the other three boats at Seaview was ever called out. However, we did one rescue which turned out pretty dramatic.

One Sunday morning I had left the hotel to have lunch in the boat, and was reading aloud to Andrews an account in the Sunday papers which described the exciting time the R.A.F. boys were having at Newhaven. It was there that their Marine Air Sea Rescue section was, and they appeared to be for ever rescuing bomber crews. As I read this, nearly fifty years later, it still seems hard to believe what happened next. The ship was linked via a pier connection to the telephone switchboard, and just as I was reading this account, the telephone rang. The message we received gave us the guts of a search operation which ran roughly as follows:

Around six a.m. that Sunday morning, somebody at Ventnor or Bembridge had spotted a rubber dinghy of the Bomber Escape type, with some men in it, trying to paddle for the shore. He had alerted the civilian Auxiliary Coastguards, who had pursued the rubber dinghy in a rowing boat. It was only hours later that the Navy had been alerted, and now, as we left the pier and raced off to search, it was about one p.m.

The High Command at Portsmouth promised me a Walrus Pusher plane to help in the search, but by this time there was dense fog, and the Walrus was unable to see the water below. Reluctantly, therefore, the crew gave up and flew home. I had little to go on — merely a vague report of a rubber dinghy somewhere between Bembridge and Cherbourg, and a definite report that a wooden dinghy with three local men had gone in search of it and were now missing.

As we ploughed on through dense fog, I was making a careful study of the chart and the available information on tides. We had no radar, and navigated by dead reckoning and echo sounding. We seemed to be already well on our way to Cherbourg, when suddenly we sighted the rowing boat less than a hundred yards away. In fact, we nearly ran it down! Once alongside, we helped the first two men on board, but the third refused to leave his boat. He said he would row it back to England. I was aghast, and tried to reason with him — said he should come aboard and let us sink the dinghy. The Admiralty would pay him compensation. Still he refused. Short of shooting him, there was nothing further to be done.

Now I turned to the two rescued men, and enquired what they could tell me. It turned out to be very little. It was now about five hours since they had lost sight of the rubber dinghy. To continue the search seemed pretty futile, yet we must not give up. Once again, I consulted the tidal information. I reckoned that the rubber dinghy must be within six miles, but how could we possibly find it in this fog? We steamed on at about twelve knots, every eye straining to peer through the fog.

Later, perhaps as much as an hour, we suddenly spotted the rubber dinghy with four figures in it. They were pretty far gone, but in no time we were alongside, and with ropes and ladders we quickly had them and their rubber dinghy on board. We carried no medic.

of any sort; I was the "doctor", and gave the orders. The four airmen were to be stripped, dried off and re-clothed as best we could, wrapped in blankets, taken to our bunks, and there given mugs of tea laced with rum. They were to drink it whether they liked it or not. That was my rough solution to the problem of hypothermia. Having given these instructions, I returned to my navigation. We must make for Portsmouth at top speed, but first we had to rescue the rowing boat and the missing civilian. An hour later, we nearly ran it down, but even now the oarsman would not abandon ship! I told him that if he came aboard, I would tow the dinghy back to Ventnor, and on this condition he at last agreed to do so.

Setting course for home in so dense a fog, and with no electronic aids, was a worry. So, for that matter, were the survivors. I nearly arrested the civilian, and blasted his dinghy, but I thought better of it. Anyway, once I made a landfall off the Isle of Wight, where the fog had cleared to a mile or so, I slipped the dinghy off Ventnor, and then proceeded at full speed for Gosport and Haslar Hospital Pontoon. An ambulance was waiting, but by this time the four airmen had made a wonderful recovery. In fact they were reasonably intoxicated, and firmly refused to be taken to the ambulance on stretchers. As they left, we gave them three cheers, and I promised to visit them in R.N. Haslar Hospital the following day. This, of course, I did.

Sad to relate, all the members of this gallant air crew were later killed in Bomber Command. Pilot Officer Ralph Allsebrook was their captain, and he received a D.F.C. for his exploit of safely crashlanding his Handley Page Hampden off the Isle of Wight, after bombing Mannheim. His station commander and his father, a county court judge, showered me with kind letters and gifts, and Ralph himself gave me a beautiful malacca cane walking stick with an inscription in gold recording this incident. Ralph, his father and I remained correspondents for two years, by which time he had risen to the rank of flight lieutenant and gained a D.S.O. But alas! He was killed while serving in 617 Squadron (the Dambusters). It is forty-six years since he gave me his photograph, and it has never left me since, still occupying a prominent place in my house to this day.

To return to my career in M.A.S.B.s, anyone entering Portsmouth Harbour from the sea will find the western extremity marked by Fort Blockhouse, or H.M.S. Dolphin, the Submarine H.Q.. Now, all Coastal Force craft at Hornet had to navigate close in to Dolphin as they passed up Haslar Creek to the base. Often submarines would be alongside the Dolphin jetties, and one day, as I was proceeding up to base, I must have been going too fast, for my

Flight Lt. Allsebrook

H.M. Motor Anti-Submarine Boat 39

wash rocked a submarine. Barely were our ropes secured, when a Naval messenger rushed aboard with a note commanding me to report forthwith to the Commander at Dolphin for using excessive speed and causing possible damage to submarines. Much chastened, I walked down to Dolphin, and was shown into the office of the great man. To my amazement, he turned out to be none other than Commander G.M. Sladen, D.S.O., D.S.C., who had recently torpedoed the crack German cruiser, Prinz Eugen. In pre-war days I had known him well. His wife was a distant relative of mine, and nearly twenty years before, when he was seven years old, he had had the same governess. He laughed off my speeding offence, asked me to dinner, and, over the next few months, allowed me to use the facilities of H.M.S. Dolphin, including the squash courts. This last I found a great boon.

Soon after this episode, I found myself involved with Captain Murray of H.M.S. Hornet, between whom and myself a mutual dislike existed. One day he sent for me to tell me that inquiries were being made concerning my rescue of Telegraphist Richardson in Brixham Harbour. It was possible, he said, that I might receive some form of recognition. At the same time, he warned me, it was possible that I might find myself facing disciplinary action for allowing the dinghy to be overloaded in bad weather. On his advice, therefore, I decided to forget the whole matter. Two months later, however, it cropped up again, and he gave me the same advice, to forego any chance of recognition in order not to incur disciplinary action. The upshot was that I received the Testimonial of the Royal Humane Society in vellum, and heard no more about disciplinary action. That, in fact, was the end of the matter.

During the spring of 1942, the bombing raids on Plymouth and Portsmouth were relatively light, but one particular night was an exception. Down came the high explosive bombs, followed by showers of incendiaries. The previous year, Hornet had been flattened by a massive boat explosion, and now we were told to get out into the Solent and disperse. At the time, my boat was half way through an engine replacement, and we had only half power. Thus we were far from operational.

Struggling down Haslar Creek, on one engine and with very bad steering, I entered the channel to the sea by Fort Blockhouse, where it was very narrow. At that moment we heard an appalling loud scream of bombs, and saw the entire stick falling right in the channel, about two hundred yards ahead. At about the same time I noticed that the "B" Class M.L. ahead of me had gone starboard as though to ram Fort Blockhouse, and that I was about to hit her broadside on. I immediately went astern hard on one engine, and pulled up with only a few feet to spare. The M.L. recovered, and, after some manoeuvres, continued out to Solent with myself in hot pursuit. When I finally came alongside this craft, and, once I thought we were clear of bombs, I gave the C.O. a piece of my mind. It turned out to be my own old ship, M.L. 292, still largely manned by the same crew as I had known. What had happened was that, when the bombs fell, the coxswain, had deserted his post. As a result, the ship had narrowly missed going aground. Shore Brundell's first lieutenant was Micky Hawkes. He gave me a stiff drink, and we laughed the incident off.

About July, 1942, I received order to take M.A.S.B. 39 to Fairlie on the Clyde coast for experiments with the Anti-Submarine School. As we could cruise at twenty-five knots, the passage was a different experience from that of M.L. 292 in the same direction. We made the passage independently, and on the way I made a beeline for Douglas, Isle of Man. Meeting Campbell Adamson again was the greatest fun, and we had dinner on board my boat with a most glamorous W.A.A.F. officer. I am afraid we overdid it, because the W.A.A.F. officer passed out, and had to be pulled up the dangerous dock wall on a Neil Robertson stretcher! Once released from this contraption onto terra firma, she walked, or rather staggered, between us to the "Waafery", where we rang the bell, pushed her inside the door the moment it opened, and fled for our lives.

On arriving at Fairlie, I was told by the O.C. Anti A/S school to take the boat for a top overhaul at Port Bannatyne in Bute. This I opposed; I did not consider that the small yard there could cope with 1500 H.P. Supercharged Packards, the like of which they had never seen before. However, I was overruled. While the overhaul was in progress, I was billeted in the Kyles of Bute Hydro, which was full of rich refugees from the Glasgow bombing. Two other Naval officers were billeted there, and one, Paul Berthon D.S.C., had been to Wellington, and had subsequently done outstandingly well in Coastal Forces. We very quickly became friends. At the Kyles of Bute, we found ourselves living in luxury, and there were plenty of Glaswegian refugees to escort, usually to Rothesay at night!

Earlier I mentioned that Rear Admiral Kekewich had told me to write if I was not happy in M.A.S.B. 39. As Rear Admiral, Coastal Forces, he was still very much a power to be reckoned with. I had already written to him once to ask for a transfer to M.L.s, and he had told me in a subsequent letter that I was lucky he had ignored my request; if it had been granted I would most probably have met my death at St. Nazaire, for here, in what has been described as "the greatest raid of all", the B Class M.L.s had been massacred, and there had been enormous loss of life. The admiral had extraordinary patience with me, particularly when I told him of the trials at Port Bannatyne, and the exasperating incompetence of the local engineering authorities. At the time, I predicted that this could prove to be the death of M.A.S.B. 39, and events were to prove me right. Could I please, I asked, have something more exciting, as, although I now enjoyed High-Speed Attack craft, M.A.S.B. 39 was not likely to see enemy action for ages.

Within a surprisingly short time, I found myself on my way to Dover, leaving Andrews in temporary command of M.A.S.B. 39. He had been an extremely pleasant and thoroughly adequate second-in-command, but he was much older than I, and happily married. Now he was more than happy to be left in the quiet of Port Bannatyne. As for me, my new orders were to take command of Motor Gunboat 9, whose comanding officer, Lieutenant Keith Kale R.N.V.R., had been killed in action.

CHAPTER NINE

Gaining Experience of Motor Gunboats at Dover and Ramsgate

Being new to motor gunboats, when I first arrived at Coastal Forces Base, Dover — H.M.S. Wasp, it was called — I felt very strange. However Graham Guthrie, whom I have mentioned before, was commanding some unit there at the time, and it was he who greeted me. Later, he was most helpful in introducing me to people. However, it turned out that the harbour at Dover was too small for gunboats or Air Sea Rescue Craft, which were based at Ramsgate; Dover was only the Coastal Forces H.Q.. Before long, therefore, I was instructed to leave for Ramsgate, and Graham took me to the station and put me on the train. Having just taken a direct hit from one of the heavy German Railway Guns, Dover Station was an absolute shambles. At the time this depressed me somewhat; had I known that within a very short time Graham himself would be killed by one of those same shells, I would have been still more depressed.

I arrived at Ramsgate not expecting to know a soul; yet whom should I promptly run into but Philip Wayre, the very man whom I had met at The Grand Hotel at Fort William, when he broke the window with a dart! The ice was broken, and the crowd whom I had now joined soon became the very best friends I made in Coastal Forces.

Motor Gunboat 9 had been severely damaged in action, and I was told to take her to the yard of Tough Bros. at Teddington and get her repaired. At Teddington I had the most splendid digs, conveniently situated right beside Toughs' yard in Ferry Road. However, after careful examination, the yard found the damage far more extensive than had been expected. The refit continued for three weeks, and meanwhile I was making a twice-weekly report to the office of Flag Officer, London, at the Port of London Authority Buildings. My immediate superior there was Lieutenant Commander Lord Reith of Stonehaven, the first Director General of the B.B.C., who was then serving as a Special Branch Commander

R.N.V.R. He was a stern unsmiling figure with bushy eyebrows, but a glutton for work and highly efficient.

For myself, there was little work for me to do while I was at Teddington, though both the crew and I were all hoping that the boat could be repaired. To while away the time, I sent an Anti-Aircraft rating to Birmingham to inspect a ten-bore shotgun that I had seen advertised in *The Field*. I gave him £22 — the advertised price — and instructed him to buy it if he considered it value for money; at the same time, he was to buy a hundred cartridges, for these were hard to obtain. That evening, as we were sitting at dinner in the house at Teddington, a policeman arrived and asked for the C.O. of Motor Gunboat 9. He told me that the police had arrested one of my ratings for shooting a wild duck on the Thames nearby! After much chatter and a few drinks, the rating was released with my gun. He had shown more than initiative!

In the course of my dealings with the yard at Teddington, I had become very friendly with Douglas Tough, the owner. One day, he asked if he might bring an old school chum to our normal noon drinks session in M.G.B. 9, and I replied that I would be delighted. When Douglas arrived with his chum there were about six other officers, also refitting, in my Wardroom. I recognised the "chum" at once; it was none other than A.V. Alexander, First Lord of the Admiralty! The party continued apace, and there were no repercussions.

However, the delay was making me restive, and a point came when Douglas Tough stated that in his judgement the boat was too badly damaged throughout to be repaired. Accordingly, I went up to see Lord Reith and told him so. Within days, the boat was paid off, and we all returned to Ramsgate. There was a sequel to all this. Motor Gunboat 9 was not scrapped there and then; she was moored beside the bridge at Teddington, where for many years she served as the H.Q. of the Sea Cadets.

On returning to Ramsgate, I was told that I was the C.O. designate of Motor Gunboat 6. The man I was to relieve was Lieutenant Winthrop Young, who had commanded a training boat at Ardrishaig, and whom I knew from those days. Where he went to after I relieved him, I do not know, but just after the war I read in the press that he had been appointed tutor to the crown prince of Greece.

For a month before taking over from Winthrop Young, I served as spare and auxiliary commanding officer on a number of different M.G.B.s. During one patrol I was spare C.O. on M.G.B. 13, whose C.O., McKetterick, was a good friend of mine. I spotted one of his ratings sporting a red star and the sickle and hammer on the chest of his oilskin suit, and took exception to this. Mac, however, only laughed. The rating's name, he told me, was Forrester, and he was an ex-public schoolboy from Haileybury, politically very left. That last piece of information was obvious. I told Mac that I would not have anyone like that in my crew, and at the time that was that. However, John Forrester was to have a considerable part to play in some later experiences of mine, which were to take place four thousand miles away.

It was not long before I had made a number of friends both afloat and ashore. Alan Lennox Boyd was an M.P., who also commanded a B Class M.L.. I had known both him and his senior officer, Ferdinando, at Portsmouth. Alex. Fear of M.L. 346, who also called in occasionally, had been at Peterhead with me. He had just won a D.S.C. for sinking a tanker single-handed in the course of the Dieppe raid. Lady Carson, the widow of Sir Edward, of Ulster and parliamentary fame, was soon asking me to tea and drinks at Cleave Court, Minster. At Pegwell Bay on the Stour, towards Sandwich, I had found some wildfowling. All in all, I was by now becoming fairly well socially settled in, as well as doing my first offensive patrols in the Dover Straits. It was a part of the world where people seemed to live and die fairly fast!

When I first took over Motor Gunboat 6, I discovered that the survival gear was non-existent. Indeed, I had heard other officers who had commanded Motor Gunboats discussing the same problem. If they had had to give the order "Abandon Ship!", petrol fires out of control, they would have had nothing to rely upon. I had heard vague suggestions of bomber survival gear being used, but no one high up had been able to get hold of anything in that line. Accordingly, I telephoned my brother-in-law, Group Captain F.J. Fogarty, who commanded R.A.F. Harwell, a prime bomber station in Berkshire. He told me to try Group Captain Waring, Deputy Director of Air Sea Rescue, or else Air Ministry, but to tell no one that he had given me Waring's name. When I tackled him, Waring was most helpful. Somehow he managed to let me have six large rubber dinghies, complete with air bottles. A month or so later, Lieutenant G.D.K. Richards D.S.C., my senior officer, was receiving an imperial rocket from the captain at Dover, who was inspecting our Base, for obtaining R.A.F. gear without Admiralty approval. Overhearing this, I told Captain Gunn that Dick Richards was blameless — I had brought it all on myself. Gunn was an excellent fellow. On this occasion he laughed and replied: "I might have known it!". Thereafter, no more was heard of the matter. Shortly afterwards, these dinghies became standard issue to Coastal Force M.T.B.s and M.G.B.s.

Air Chief Marshal Sir Francis J. Fogarty

In addition to the uniformed personnel of the Navy and the civilian personnel, contractors were also employed on special assignments, such as the servicing of power gun-turrets. One such contractor, I remember, was employed by Frazer Nash on armaments. He had a handlebar moustache, an upper-crust accent, and backed this up with an ability to produce a tall story. At a drinks party, he claimed acquaintanceship with the local landowners and aristocracy, including a certain Lord H. On one occasion he asked me and others to join a shooting party of Lord H.'s. It was to be on a Saturday, and unfortunately I already had an invitation for that day, namely to the wedding of Admiral Sir T.H. Binney at St. Martin's in the Fields, followed by a reception at Admiralty House. Even so, I could not bring myself to refuse the shooting invitation, and when the day came, off we went to the estate concerned near Ramsgate, to walk up partridges.

We had put up several coveys into a turnip field, and had lined up to walk this, when I saw a figure approaching on a reciprocal course. To my horror, I saw the party leaping a fence and running away! Alone, I marched on, bracing myself for a head-on clash with the approaching figure. It turned out to be Lord H's gamekeeper. We had all been poaching! I told him my story, and realising that it was genuine, he could not help laughing. Full of shame, I retreated with my tail between my legs to the Coastal Force Base. Then I remembered the wedding invitation. To restore my ego, I resolved to attend.

I arrived at St. Martin's in the Fields just before the bride, and then attended the reception. A thoroughly snooty toastmaster was announcing the guests to the happy couple, but the way he introduced me was a blow to my self-esteem. "Vice Admiral Sir William and Lady Whitworth", he intoned, as the victor of the Second Battle of Narvik and his wife went forward. Then, as I followed meekly behind: 'Sub Lieutenant Forsyth-Grant R.N.V.R.", he snarled. Anyway, I did meet some of my Angus friends there. One of them was Patricia Knox, a dedicated Red, who worked for the L.C.C.. I invited her to tea in an aerated bread café, which was the best I could afford! In the course of it, a violent argument developed between us, she being all for Stalin and I for Hitler. In the end, we were both asked to leave! As the train for Ramsgate drew out of Victoria, I noticed Canterbury, well alight from German bombs.

Just as I was becoming settled at Ramsgate and Dover, our flotilla, the 2nd, was replaced by the 9th M.G.B. Flotilla, equipped with the latest in gunboats, the 71 '6 Class. Meanwhile our Second Flotilla was ordered to Milford Haven to be embarked in merchant ships for North Africa, where we were to replace losses. Stuart Gould, the senior officer, had just been killed at Bizerta. Shortly after this order came through, therefore, the advance guard of our party, M.G.B. 13 and 6, sailed for Weymouth en route for Milford.

All the way to Weymouth, the sea was very rough, and when we arrived we were soaked to the skin. The C.O. of M.G.B. 13 was Lieutenant John Collins R.C.N.V.R.. He and I decided to spend the night in the Crown Hotel, and after early dinner, we each retired to the single rooms which we had booked. At about one a.m., there was a terrible crash in my room, and I put on the light. The figure of a totally naked man lay face down on the floor. At first I thought he was dead — that he must have been murdered. Before touching him, I rushed to get John Collins as a witness to what was happening. When John straightway diagnosed not murder but drunkenness, my spirits rose. We attempted to trace where the man had come from, and found a trail of all his undergarments spread out in a sort of "paper chase" and leading back to a bedroom with a light on. From this we deduced, correctly as it turned out, that he had been searching for the loo, had arrived at my room by accident, and had then passed out completely.

Far from amused, John and I turned him over. Yes — I had seen him before. He was a Dutch officer, "Happy" Vesey by name, who ten months before had been in M.G.B. 46 in Hythe (Subsequently he was to become Commodore, Royal Netherlands Navy.) We lugged him back to the bedroom with the lights on, and unceremoniously dumped him on the bed. Next day, when John and I went down to breakfast, he was being ordered out of the hotel. Apparently there had been more than one accident in his bed.

That same day, our orders to continue to Milford Haven were cancelled. The previous night H.M.S. Eskdale, a Hunt Class destroyer, had been torpedoed by E Boats off Start Point, and our orders were changed. We were to do a quick refit at Poole, before being based at Dartmouth as an anti-E Boat force.

We spent about a fortnight at Poole being refitted by the British Power Boat Company. In company with some others, I was billeted with a certain landlady in Longfleet Road, who demanded the whole of our ration cards for giving us bed and breakfast — other meals we must find ourselves. By this stage in the war, people were really starving in southern England — at least the civilians were. We used to lunch daily on spam. In the British Power Boat canteen we had it curried, cold, in shepherd's pies, rissoled, and given even worse treatments, while every night we used to have welsh rarebit in C and A Modes! It was the only time in my life when I felt genuinely near to starving.

On the brighter side, if you were interested in field sports, there was magnificent shooting to be had, and in fact there were about four of us who were. The Army had requisitioned Arne, near Wareham, as a tank range, and thrown out all the farmers, leaving their crops to rot. I soon obtained permission from the authorities to shoot pheasants, and on Brownsea Island I shot wild duck by courtesy of the Royal Marines, who even provided landing craft for getting us there, as well as a smokescreen, under cover of which we could, if necessary, retire — we were poaching!

However, all this soon came to an end once we were all gathered at Dartmouth to protect local convoys and to carry out offensive sweeps off the Brittany coast. Whereas all the Motor Gunboats were British, the Motor Torpedo Boats were British, Dutch and French. When not at sea, I used to live in a Navy-requisitioned base at Kingswear, and another officer occupying the same quarters was Philippe de Gaulle, a young sub lieutenant who was second-in-command of a French M.T.B. (Yes, this was the General's son, later to become head of the French Navy). At this time too, two Dutch C.O.s became close intimates of mine, Harry Jorissen and Cornelius Van Eeghen.

Midshipman Philippe de Gaulle aboard his M.T.B. at Dartmouth, 1942

*Dick Richards,
"Nelson of the Little Ships"*

Both off the British and the French coasts, we engaged in running battles with varying degrees of success. Philippe de Gaulle was wounded, but I don't remember anyone being killed. Hans Larive, the Senior Officer of the Dutch, was highly decorated and had an outstanding reputation. The same is true of Harry Jorissen, who had sunk a Jap Cruiser in the Far East. However, Coastal Force Attack Craft were not well thought of by Admiral Sir Charles Forbes, C-in-C, Plymouth. He belittled our efforts, and decided to throw in the "heavy stuff" to let others show us how it should be done. It was a disaster. He lost the cruiser Charybdis and the destroyers Grenville and Limbourne.

Notwithstanding all this, the long haulage from Dartmouth to Brittany was playing havoc with our boats in the rough seas, and also with our health. Officers and crews were supplied with drugs by the Navy, including, amongst others, bromide to make us sleep. People were suffering from hallucinations. On one occasion, we were raiding the convoy routes off Les Sept Isles when suddenly, without consultation, my Senior Officer made an emergency signal to C-in-C, Plymouth: "Enemy Report. Battleship, escorted by six destroyers, in position so-and-so, course so-and-so." I was flabbergasted. It was Les Sept Isles. He must have been in some degree hallucinating, and the next day he was relieved and sent on sick leave. I was ordered to take over his boat, M.G.B.8.

I regret that there was one coastal convoy that we failed to save. At the relevant time, I believe, we were patrolling elsewhere, and our participation came too late to be of value. One night, a coastal convoy consisting of several landing ships was decimated, and at first light we were sent to see whether there was anyone or anything that we could rescue. We found numerous bodies floating in Lyme Bay, and the wreckage spread everywhere on the surface included scores of crates of Army boots in huge floating packing cases. We salvaged everything of value that we could, but these packing cases were too heavy to lift, so we smashed them open with two axes which I had bought in Poole for Ecclesgreig! We ended up with hundreds of boots on board, and discovered that each crate contained either all left-foot or all right-foot boots, all of the same size. Thus there would be an entire crate of left-boots size eight, another of right-foot boots size nine, and so on. Loaded with salvage, we landed the lot at Dartmouth, and were told that we could each keep a pair of boots if we wanted them as salvage money!

Within a short time, M.G.B. 8 became the only operational M.G.B. fit for service. For a time, I was sent out to patrol on my own, and on one occasion prepared to attack a formation of three

E Boats alone. I was forbidden to do this, and told that I should shadow them and make enemy reports. Next day, the authorities decided — I think wisely — that one M.G.B. could not operate alone, and I was told to join M.G.B./M.T.B. Training Flotilla at Portland, and work with that.

CHAPTER TEN

Further Adventures and Some Misadventures with M.G.B.s.

For some weeks, M.G.B.8 operated in the training flotilla under Senior Officer Lieutenant Commander Truscott R.N.V.R., a most pleasant and efficient officer, with whom I got on very well. I decided to live in the barracks, H.M.S. Attack, which were up the hill from the dockyard. The commander here was Commander D.R. Miller R.N.V.R., who had been First Lieutenant Commander of H.M.S. Unicorn at Dundee. He was a hockey international, and when off duty I enjoyed playing a bit of hockey in the Borstal amphitheatre; it was the best pitch I had ever seen. We had great fun playing the Army. Here, our most dangerous opponents were the A.T.S. girls from the Anti-Aircraft Mixed Batteries. They gave no quarter and received none! My second-in-command at Portland was Sub Lieutenant Wright R.N.Z.N.V.R., a dentist in civilian life, and ten years my senior. He did his job well, but his interests were quite different from mine. Moreover, he was a New Zealander. When it came to time off and leave, I left him to his own devices. While we were at Portland, I let him have one leave which he spent in Dublin. The authorities were so angry about this that he might have been in Berlin!. However, so far as I was concerned, there were no repercussions.

All this time, what I wanted was enemy action, but I received no help from Commander Miller, who wanted me to stay in the training flotilla. When I put in a request for a transfer to a front-line flotilla, he turned it down. On one of my days off, therefore, I visited the appropriate appointments officer of the Second Sea Lord's Department in London and requested a transfer to Ramsgate. Much to my astonishment, the reply I received was: "Certainly! Very good of you to volunteer, Grant. You can report to Ramsgate tomorrow".

As I bought an evening paper at Waterloo for the return trip to Weymouth, I was still somewhat in a state of shock. The previous night, the 9th M.G.B. Flotilla had been very badly mauled, and casualties were extremely high. Dick Richards had been killed in action. That same evening, I met Miller in the officers' club; he was furious with me. "Serves you jolly well right!", he said.

The following day, I was back at Ramsgate, where despondency over the dead and wounded was deep and widespread. I was instructed to take over M.G.B.118, whose C.O., Philip Lee, had been seriously wounded. There had been heavy casualties in the boat, and it needed numerous replacements. I managed to organize all this, and was then told to take the boat to Weymouth for ten days intensive "work up" at H.M.S. Bee. This went well, and in no time we were back at Ramsgate.

The 9th Motor Gunboat Flotilla was now back in business, and Lieutenant R.B. Roper R.N. was appointed to succeed the deceased Dick Richards. For the next six months, from July to December, we harried the E Boats and convoys off the French coast — they seldom ventured to our side of the Straits. We were involved in numerous battles and landings, but to narrate all these in detail would, I feel, make this part of my story seem over-repetitive. The following examples, however, do rise up in my mind as having a special interest of their own.

In July, off Gravelines, under the command of Roper, two of us attacked and blew up E Boat No. 175. In September, two boats were detailed to land Commando saboteurs by night off Dunkirk, and mine was the second. At the briefing in Dover Castle, I asked whether the Germans had radar, as we had not been issued with effective sets. The reply was "no", but I did not believe it. There were strong grounds for supposing that by this stage in the war the Germans had either good radar, including Gun Control, or alternatively Night Vision Equipment which was years ahead of that in use in the Royal Navy.

We dropped our Commandos in canoes, and three hours later went in to pick them up. The Germans detected us, and a destroyer fired starshell, while six E Boats raced out of Dunkirk to attack us. Roper withdrew at speed, but in my boat all the engines cut out under the excessive boost they were registering under throttle. As we got going again, enemy fire was plastering the water all around us. At the critical moment, however, Roper laid a smokescreen across my bow, down which I turned for safety. The awe-inspiring sight of six E Boats racing through the smoke to hunt me down is something which I shall never forget. Luckily, we were at right angles to their course, and by this time were doing forty knots! Caught up right in the midst of this sea battle were the Commando saboteurs, but luckily the Germans failed to spot them. They were picked up at dawn by two Royal Navy Walrus planes.

By this stage, Hans Larive and his Dutchmen had already left Dartmouth for Dover. One night he led a flotilla in Harry Jorissen's M.T.B. to attack a valuable freighter. In support of this effort, Roper led three M.G.B.s and attacked from the other side. Jorissen sank the freighter with torpedoes, and we withdrew with some damage but no fatal casualties.

When, three nights later, exactly the same operation was attempted, I found myself inwardly questioning the wisdom of such a policy. Sure enough, the Germans were ready for us, and this time inflicted heavy casualties. Anticipating the enemy's moves, I crash-started and, without orders, shot out into the night, landing up alongside an E Boat who was blasting my colleagues on her other side. We raked her from stem to stern with all we had, and she burst into flames. My oerlikon gunner, A.B. Carrington, got a D.S.M. for this; all I received was a rocket from Vice Admiral, Dover, for acting on my own initiative without orders.

On one occasion, I found myself Senior Officer of a striking group consisting of two M.G.B.s, my own and a Polish one. It had been arranged that an Anglo-French force was to land, undetected if possible, at the mouth of the Somme at two a.m. Meanwhile, our task was to create a diversion ten miles up the coast by firing all our guns, as well as dropping depth charges and cans of blazing petrol. At 0030 hours I was in position. At that point, we found ourselves directly beneath a major sortie of enemy bombers from the French coast. Unwittingly, we had picked a spot right under a Luftwaffe airfield, and now the bombers were flying over our heads in wave after wave. While they could not see us on the sea, they themselves, silhouetted as they were against the sky, were sitting ducks to us. We were desperate to shoot one down, but could not give away our position without compromising the Somme raid. At 01.55 hours I decided to give in to the Poles, who were desperate to open fire, and beside themselves with excitement. No sooner had I given the order, than the waves of bombers ceased. Not a single plane more flew over!

Having created the necessary diversion, we were half way home, when, as we were crossing the Bullock Bank between Folkestone and Boulogne, M.G.B. 118 began to bump badly. My first thought was that we must be touching bottom. Then astern of me I saw a huge column of water. We were setting off acoustic mines, which those same bombers had laid the previous night! Frantically I signalled to the Poles to take station on my beam, and proceed at full speed. We were doing forty knots — too fast for the mine mechanism, and the mines were going up harmlessly astern. At least, by the time we arrived home, we had swept a channel through the new German minefield!

Although the sea-going crews of the gunboats at Ramsgate took the brunt of enemy action, the Base staff and civilians were also very much in the front line, as the following examples will show.

One afternoon I was playing tennis at Cleave Court. My three companions included Lady Carson's niece. Suddenly an aircraft fell out of the sky, crashing and exploding not far away. It turned out to be an appalling tragedy; the pilot had been engaged to the niece.

One night, a Polish gunboat and I had been on an offensive patrol of unusual ferocity. A German convoy had been attacked off the French coast by M.T.B.s, Fleet Air Arm from Manston, and the heavy guns at Dover. It had been a particularly savage night; the sky had been almost continuously lit up with flashes as the German guns around Calais retaliated by shelling East Kent.

About four a.m., having finished our patrol, Ludwig, the Polish C.O., and myself entered the Royal Temple Yacht Club (which was the Coastal Force Base) to have our breakfast. Then we went to our respective rooms, having to wade, as we did so, through large heaps of fresh rubble which had piled up both inside and outside the building. When I arrived at my room, it was to find that the whole of the ceiling was lying in small fragments on my bed. So I went to see how Ludwig had fared. It was as well that he had been on patrol with me that night. An eighteen-inch splinter of steel, weighing about four pounds, had sliced right through his mattress. It was part of the jacket of a heavy German shell. That same shell had passed right through the sides of a B Class M.L. in the inner dock, before bursting on the dock face. The C.O. of the M.L. had been decapitated. Another shell had obliterated the Bofors gun on the pierhead, together with its entire crew.

It was at the Royal Temple Yacht Club too, that I witnessed another dramatic instance of the destruction being inflicted almost nightly by enemy bombing and shelling. One night, as I was chatting to Harry Jorissen on the steps, we heard a German heavy shell whine overhead. Seconds later there was an immense explosion, with flames shooting up everywhere. That shell had scored a direct hit on the Ramsgate gasometer.

In spite of all this, it must be recorded as a fact that our base at Ramsgate was a particularly happy one, where we could find plenty to do. Personally, I spent much of my spare time in shooting. Alan Lennox Boyd often dropped in, full of energy as ever — and also of money! He had married a Guinness heiress, and when he was not rushing up to London in his role as M.P., or

H.M.S. Resolution under Air Attack

H.M.S. Musketeer sinking S.S. Samsuva

H.M.S. Arran

Night action in the English Channel 26/27 September 1943

driving his boat in the Second M.L. Flotilla, he spent much time shooting with me. I provided the know-how of where to shoot, while he provided the money for taxis to get there. We ate the game we shot at such luxury pubs as the Woolpack at Chilham. Another of my regular shooting companions — and a most amusing one at that! — was Philip Wayre. We were both often in trouble with our superiors over matters of discipline, for we used to get up to the most awful pranks. One rather prudish WREN reported us to the Base C.O. Her complaint was that I had had on my dresser a tube of contraceptive jelly! We had bought it as a joke, but she handed it in to him. When we were duly hauled before him, he was unable to find the evidence with which to berate us. Nonplussed, he opened his desk to make some notes, whereupon there was the tube of contraceptive jelly, which we had previously put there! "How disgusting!" we both exclaimed in unison. After this, as can be imagined, the rocket misfired, and the matter dissolved in laughter all round.

On one occasion I had a week's leave at the same time as Harry Jorissen, and was proposing to spend it in Scotland. On hearing that Harry had nothing particularly exciting in prospect for his leave, I asked him to spend it with me at Ecclesgreig. He accepted, and, during that leave, made such good friends with my parents, that he made Ecclesgreig his wartime home, and was often there while I was in North Russia or West Africa.

Christmas 1943 was approaching, and I had thought that there might be a lull. I was surprised, therefore, when, on the 23rd December, we were ordered to sea that same night to attack an enemy coastal convoy. As part of our preparations during the day, we were given demolition charges; this was so that, if any danger should arise of being captured in enemy waters, we could blow up our own boats. However, in view of the fact that the fitting and testing of circuits on them might require several hours of work, I told Ian Galbreath, my second-in-command, to leave them until after Christmas. In my case, therefore, without this particular form of equipment, we ventured forth in the direction of the enemy coast. My radar was working magnificently, and we tracked the enemy in from several miles, a fact which I duly reported to Roper in the leading boat, and which was logged in our book.

Once the enemy was within gunshot, I could see them plainly in the dark, and reported them. Seconds later, the night was turned completely into day by starshell. The large enemy escort was almost on top of us. I was second in line of the Gunboats, and my instinct was to go full speed ahead, attack the leading ship, and break off ahead. However, I have already described what trouble

Harry Jorissen and the Author in Czechoslovakia, 1958

such tactics had already got me into on a previous occasion. Roper was turning about, and the rule was that I should follow him, while my next astern, David Woolven in M.G.B. 117, should in his turn follow me. Because of Roper's position, I was forced to remain static to keep searoom, and was going ahead on one engine, astern on the other, trying to pivot on my axis, while at the same time engaging the enemy with all my guns.

We were a sitting duck for the German, as was M.G.B. 117 astern of me. In no time we were both riddled with shot, a tank in M.G.B. 118 was hit, and we were enveloped in a petrol fire. Almost at the same moment, I was all but blinded by a flash, as something hit the wheelhouse two feet below my head. By this time, all our engines had stopped. I shouted to Ian Galbreath to pass up the Secret Books for dumping before we abandoned ship. We were only about three quarters of a mile out from the French shore, and what hope could we have of surviving? Already I was trying to envisage what life would be like as a P.O.W. While waiting for Ian to fetch the Secret Books, we attempted to tackle the fire. We had a mixture of lethal methyl bromide and foam, and with this, to my amazement, we managed to quench it. Soon afterwards — surprise, surprise! — I felt the throb of an engine that had been re-started. I turned to try and assess the damage.

M.G.B. 118 testing guns off South Foreland before a patrol

Crew of M.G.B. 118

All this time Ian had not answered. I found him unconscious with a serious head wound. Joe Currie, the Glasgwegian radio operator, had bandaged his head most professionally, but already the bandage was soaked in blood, and his face was quite blue. I looked at my steel helmet, which he had donned as the action began; it had a huge hole in the ring formed by my two stripes. I knew then that Ian had been killed instantly by a cannon shell. Bill Archer, the pompom gunner in the fo'c'sle, and the most courageous of men, had been severely wounded by a shot in the knee; he was removed to the P.O.'s mess. The boat herself was riddled with delayed-action phosphorous bullets. Despite all this, we made Ramsgate approaches under cover of dense fog. In answer to radio messages, my chum Ronnie Barge left Ramsgate in his M.G.B. and fired starshell to guide me in through the fog.

At last we were alongside in harbour, and naval surgeons and ambulances were waiting for us. One petrol tank had been holed by shellfire, and there were several hundred gallons of pure octane sloshing about in the bilges. Once the wounded were off, we all abandoned ship, and the fire brigade took over. We had breakfast in the Base at 2 a.m. — bacon and eggs, that was the traditional treat for returning night patrols — while the casualties were discussed. Like ourselves, M.G.B. 117 had suffered very badly. Sub Lieutenant Woolven R.N.V.R., the C.O., was an old friend of mine. He was critically ill with gunshot wounds in the chest. About 3 a.m., after breakfast, I went to Ramsgate General Hospital to obtain a report. He was still critical, but holding his own. I am glad to say that he survived, and, after the war, qualified as a doctor and had a large medical practice in Hertfordshire. He also became a very good tennis player. To this day we still remain very much in touch.

As for M.G.B.118, she had become a write-off. She was so badly damaged that she never saw action again. After this I was sent on fourteen days' leave. However, I had not been at Ecclesgreig three days, when Ramsgate was on the telephone to me. Could I return at once to take command of another M.G.B. which was refitting, and which was urgently required for reinforcement? Realizing that in the foregoing action Coastal Forces had been severely mauled, I cut my leave, though it meant leaving my father decidedly downcast, and my mother in hysterics. My poor father had to have her tranquillized.

On arriving at Ramsgate, I was whisked off by staff car to Lady Bee's yard at Shoreham, where M.G.B.116, now called M.T.B.435, was refitting. Although the boat was in a hell of a mess, no one seemed in a hurry. I reported this fact to Ramsgate, and was told to get it seaworthy and bring it round to Ramsgate — they would finish the refit there. I read the riot act to Lady Bee's yard, and told them that we must sail in three days. After that I went to find digs for myself for a few days, and discovered a small hotel in Brighton. Its name I now forget. In the evening, I noticed a figure, half man half boy, who looked just like a sixteen year-old who had been a classmate of mine at Wellington eight years earlier. If it was indeed he, he did not seem to have changed. I felt sure that I knew him, but when I spoke to him he made no sound and showed no interest whatever. Later I spotted him with what was obviously a "minder". When the latter was alone, I asked him whether his charge was a man named Burrows. It turned out that I had been right. It was indeed the Burrows I had known. He had been a particularly clever youth, a year younger than I, but over-developed. At twelve his voice had already broken, and he needed to shave, so that he might easily have been taken for fifteen, while we who were thirteen still had our unbroken voices and smooth, unhairy chins. During my first term at Wellington, Burrows had been in the same form, and had actually sat next to me, but he was far cleverer than I and was soon forms ahead. After that, I never saw much of him. He was still only fifteen when I left Wellington. The "minder" told me that at sixteen he had been absolutely brilliant, achieving what most boys only did at eighteen. Then a major Speech Day had come, a particularly important occasion with royalty present. He had gone up to receive his prizes, but just as one prize was being presented, he had collapsed in a heap and had later been diagnosed as having severe brain damage. By this time, poor soul, he was little more than a mental cabbage.

Under the goad of daily exhortations from Ramsgate, I gave Lady Bee all the stick I could, but when the time came for me to sail for Base, the boat was still in a terrible mess. Nothing worked; there was no radar; the crew was hopelessly green, and the first lieutenant came from Air Sea Rescue M.A.S.B.S, and had never seen service in M.G.B.s. The sole tower of strength was Petty Officer Hill, a Royal Navy regular, who had been my marvellous coxswain in M.G.B.118.

I had been promised by Ramsgate that before I sailed on operations everything would be put in order. The radar in particular was something that I regarded as essential. In previous operations it had served me well, and I placed great faith in it. I also wanted to train my first lieutenant, in whom I had little confidence.

Before I had been at Ramsgate seventy-two hours, and with my radar still not working, a major flap became imminent. At that stage, to my horror, I was asked to go to sea; not only so, but I was to command the Force. I was a fool to accept.

I sailed from Ramsgate with the Polish Gunboat commanded by my friend Ludwig, and we took up a patrol line near Dungeness. About midnight, I saw a bomber explode, and in the glare I could see four parachutes descending. Obviously the crew was about to land in the sea. From my observation, and from information supplied by coastal sources, the likely point of descent was plotted, and we raced off to locate the bomber crew, but to no avail. I discovered that my first lieutenant had made a mess of the navigation, and told him in no uncertain terms that after this I would have to get a replacement.

We patrolled all night, and though we had some further excitement, it was not such as deserves explicit mention here. At about 08.00 hours we approached Dover in dense fog — so dense that it was recorded in the Daily Telegraph as the worst fog Kent had experienced throughout the war. I still have the cutting to this day. With Ian Galbreath as my first lieutenant, and with the help of radar, I would have gone into Dover Harbour without a qualm, though I found that even the Dover minesweepers were at anchor in the swept channel, afraid to sweep in such poor visibility. The senior officer, whom I hailed, asked me to breakfast with him, which I gladly accepted. As he knew his position perfectly, I now had no qualms about entering Dover. I told my Number One the position, got a course to steer, and both the Pole and M.G.B.435 were under way.

It is too long a story to relate here. My Number One plotted the position incorrectly, with the result that we steered the wrong course, and both Motor Gun Boats ran aground on Shakespeare Cliff. They were both badly damaged, eventually re-floated, and towed into Dover.

The captain of H.M.S. Wasp, Captain W.L.G. Adams R.N., was at first very sympathetic, and sent me by staff car to Ramsgate. I now had no boat. My Senior Officer had proposed that I should command a striking group from another boat as its Senior Officer. The Vice Admiral, Dover, vetoed this; I was to be court martialled.

I was very outspoken, and had upset several Senior Officers at Dover, but the court martial came as a most serious shock. Against the advice of friend and foe alike, I decided to fight it to the hilt. As my solicitor, I engaged a member of the firm of Aulfrey and Robinson, who was also the coroner of Ramsgate, and told him to engage a Q.C.. I was indignant. After the destruction of M.G.B.118, I had been poorly treated, and I had done my best.

Admiral Binney sent me a command to lunch with him in London, and he and his wife, a close friend of the family, told me to drop full legal representations; I should just let a good naval officer act for me, and trust to fair play and the court. I refused; I would make an issue of it.

I gathered that Vice Amiral, Dover, Sir Henry Daniel Pridham Wippel was incensed with me. I was placed under open arrest. While awaiting court martial, I played hockey for the Ramsgate Coastal Force Base at Broadstairs, and in the middle of the game an officer escort arrested me on the hockey pitch, and conveyed me, in my shorts, back to Ramsgate. To say that it was humiliating . . . !

Even in Dover Castle, which had seen so much in the course of five years of war, the court martial was a great matter. The Admiralty sent the Deputy Judge Advocate of the Fleet to advise. The court comprised four or five distinguished captains R.N.. Expert witnesses of high rank were summoned. Naturally, the Admiralty did not take all this kindly.

The trial itself was a sombre affair. It is improbable that the like of it has been enacted before or since during this century. It attracted far more interest and controversy than the usual run of cases — drunkenness, sodomy, embezzlement and so on. Flanked by my sword-bearing escort, I entered the court, and as I took my place beside the Ramsgate coroner and my learned counsel, there was a deathly hush. Laid across the table before me was a sword pointing from left to right. I would know my fate at the end by the position of that sword: whether it was laid with the hilt or the point directed towards me.

The trial lasted two whole days. I was charged under Article 13 of the Naval Discipline Act, in that I did hazard or strand one of H.M. ships. Thirteen charges of negligence were listed, but I was acquitted on eleven. On two only I was found guilty. As my record of service was read out, with the sword pointing at me, tears came to my eyes and I could scarcely control my emotion. My career seemed in ruins. All that I had striven for was lost. I was sentenced to be dismissed my ship and to be severely reprimanded. A day or so later, I left Ramsgate for Ecclesgreig on indefinite leave, to await re-appointment.

Here I shall digress for a moment so as to provide a postscript of events. While I was waiting trial, the Senior Officer M.T.B.s, Dover, who was a Lieut. Cmdr. R.N., and the highest Coastal Force Officer afloat at Dover, ran seven M.T.B.s onto the Goodwin

Vice Admiral Pridham Whippel

Dover Harbour (Courtesy of the Luftwaffe!)

Lieutenant M.O.F.Forsyth-Grant,
   Ecclesbreig,
      MONTROSE. Scotland.

----------------to--------------

Robinson & Allfree,
Solicitors,RAMSGATE.

1944 February	To professional charges in relation to attending you on your calling, when you consulted us with regard to certain charges brought against you by your Commanding Officer, which were likely to be the subject of a Court Martial - conferring thereon and at several subsequent interviews. Perusing Charge Sheet forming the basis of Court Martial proceedings; attendances upon you in connection therewith and receiving instructions to defend. Part journey to London on conference with Counsel. Instructions for Brief, including several long attendances upon you and perusal of various papers and documents. Drawing Brief and making copies of various documents to accompany; attending Counsel therewith. Perusing Summary of evidence of 21 witnesses for the Prosecution and other documents and further long attendances upon you in relation thereto. Copies of further documents for Counsel and writing him therewith. Attending hearing of Court Martial with Counsel - engaged two whole days. All other correspondence and work in connection with the matter.						31	10	-
	DISBURSEMENTS							
	Paid Counsel's fees.	35	12	-				
	Part fares and expenses to London.	-	17	6				
	Expenses attending at Dover (2 days)	-	18	6				
	6 Telephone calls to London to obtain Counsel and later to verify date of hearing and dispatch of Brief etc.	1	2	-				
		38	10	-		31	10	-
	Add Disbursements.					38	10	-
						70	-	-
	Less Amount received on account.					50	-	-
	With Compliments,					£ 20	-	-

17th March 1944.

Cost of a Court Martial

Sandbanks. This officer had a personal staff which included a qualified Lieutenant in Navigation, and yet neither he nor any of the others was court martialled. He was only logged. In retrospect I believe that the Vice Admiral was right. I was sacrificed for the greatest good, if only, to echo the dictum of Voltaire, "pour encourager les autres".

PART IV

In an Escort Destroyer on the Russian Convoys

CHAPTER ELEVEN

Musketeer

At the time of the court martial, I had been given to understand that, having spent over two years of fairly hectic fighting in the Channel and Dover Straits, I was now likely to be given command of a trawler, possibly on the west coast. After I had been at home for a week or so, I received a telegram instructing me to report to the Navy in Hull; it was the sort of summons which I had really been expecting.

Next day, when I reported to the duty officer at Naval Headquarters, I stated, as I gave my name, that I believed I was due for a trawler appointment. The officer studied various lists, scratched his head, said it certainly wasn't a trawler, and asked to see the telegram. Suddenly the impasse was resolved, but in a way which left me dumfounded. My ship was Musketeer, a fleet destroyer, and I had just missed her. She was now on her way to Scapa Flow, and thence with all speed to northern Russia for convoy escort duties. I was given all my travel documents, and instructed to go to Scapa Flow to wait for her return.

As I say, I was dumfounded. In a daze, I made my way to the Royal Station Hotel, booked a room for the night, and telephoned home. While I could not give much away on the telephone, I told my mother that there had been a change of plan, and asked her to parcel up and send on by rail all my warmest clothes, flying boots, fur jackets, long pants, and so forth. She should address these without delay to the Pentland Hotel in Thurso. That night I believe, though I cannot well remember, that I got very drunk. At all events, the following day, I retraced my steps as far as Perth, and there caught the night troop train, the Jellicoe, to Thurso. From there I made my way to Scapa Flow.

At this point, I must pay a tribute to, amongst others, the Pentland and Royal Hotels in Thurso. After years of war, they still greeted the personnel arriving at Thurso Station with the utmost warmth and affection, and the service they offered was magnificent. Yes, the hotel porter knew I was coming, and a suitcase had arrived from Montrose the previous night. In northern Scotland and Orkney there was no egg rationing, and I enjoyed a breakfast such as one would never have seen south of the border. Then I was on my way from Scrabster to Scapa on the ferry. On arriving, I went straight to the accommodation ship, Dunluce Castle, which served as a transit barracks for sea-going personnel awaiting the arrival of their ships in the Flow.

The cabin I was given was palatial, well furnished and comfortable, though already inhabited by a good few cockroaches and other pests. I had several days to wait before the return of Musketeer, so I amused myself by reading, visiting Kirkwall, and thoroughly relaxing. The Wardroom mess was quite large, probably forty officers or so, but I did not know any of them; nor was I particularly interested in making short acquaintances.

However, at dinner one evening I found myself sitting beside two media men, as I could tell from the war correspondents' badges which they were wearing, and we started talking. They asked me what I thought of the Dunluce Castle, and I replied that I was very comfortable; the food, I thought, was excellent — well above the standard to which we had been accustomed in Coastal Force bases in southern England. They told me that I should see how the other half lived, in other words visit the living quarters of the ordinary troops. I rejoined that I was really restricted to officers' quarters, and had no right of access to the mess decks. However, they did have right of entry there, and said that they would cover for me. All I had to do was to put on over my uniform an oilskin to which they affixed a press badge. Thus equipped, I set off with them for a tour of the ship. I was genuinely pretty shaken by what I saw. Most of the ratings seemed to be Canadian, and they were living in the bowels of the ship in Ben Hur conditions of semi-darkness and filth. It seemed all wrong, when the permanent staff, who were virtually non-combatant, were living in the lap of luxury. The press boys were disgusted, and wanted me to speak out, but I had no wish to get involved in a further clash with authority.

In a day or so Musketeer arrived, and I joined her. The captain was Commander R.L. Fisher, D.S.O., O.B.E., D.S.C., a most distinguished officer, who was the Senior Half Leader, Home Fleet. Destroyer flotillas ("squadrons" nowadays) were commanded by a captain, and usually consisted of seven ships. He, as Destroyer Leader, would have seven ships, the rest being under his second-in-command, known as the "Half Leader". Thus Fisher often had local overall command of four or more destroyers. The first lieutenant of Musketeer was Lieutenant Cornwall R.N., a very pleasant and able officer. I had a high regard for both him and Fisher. Musketeer and her consorts of the M Class were the most powerful gun destroyers of the 1939-45 war, having 4.7 guns of a new design housed in turrets, as opposed to other destroyers, which had only open mountings.

It did not take me long to settle down in Musketeer, and I understudied the gun control officer, who doubled as the ship's correspondence officer. His position in the ship was roughly equivalent to that of adjutant in the Army. Although I did not realize it, I was being groomed for his job.

Musketeer generally served as a close escort for convoys to Russia, on a route, therefore, which Winston Churchill once described as "the worst journey in the world". During one of my first convoys, I remember seeing a sloop named H.M.S. Kite torpedoed by a U Boat. She was not far off from us when it happened, and rescue operations were set in motion immediately, but in the Barents Sea there was little chance of surviving for more than a couple of minutes. Out of a crew of two hundred only six survived.

I remember vividly another incident on the occasion of my first sight of Bear Island. We were engaged in refuelling at sea, while I was taking a bearing on the compass platform. Suddenly there were two loud bangs, and to my horror I saw a nearby Russian ship break apart into three sections. She had been hit by two torpedoes. At the time, Musketeer was hooked onto the large tanker by steel wires and a flexible steel hose. Both ships were sitting ducks, and we had to separate quickly. Some of the crew hacked through the hose on Musketeer's fo'c'sle, the wire was slipped, and we raced off to hunt the submarines. Oil had been blown all over the ship, and it was as slippery as an ice rink.

As I watched the stricken Russian through my binoculars, I realized that I had seldom seen better discipline than her crew showed on that occasion. They got several lifeboats off the rapidly sinking ship, and as they did so, one after the other in perfect precision, the crew men shot down the ropes with the lifeboats. I believe and hope that the survivors would have been picked up by the rescue ship that was always attached to these convoys.

Murmansk in winter was a most dreary place, and the Russians were always pretty unfriendly. The place was full of political prisoners, labouring at the docks in conditions of the most appalling poverty. If it had not been for the dangers of the journey back to Scapa, everyone would have been delighted to leave the place.

Because we had not yet opened a Second Front in Europe, the

Soviet propaganda machine was anti-U.S. and anti-British. A Western propaganda film, "Desert Victory", had arrived at the Red Fleet cinema in Polyarnoe, the Arctic Portsmouth, but the Reds refused to show it, alleging "technical difficulties", until the Second Front was opened.

We units of the Home Fleet had to amuse ourselves as best we could, and the Naval High Command was worried lest there should be a confrontation between British and Russian forces. Feelings used sometimes to run high, and one episode in particular is a good illustration of this. All the dockyard cranes in Murmansk had been smashed by the Germans, with the result that cargo handling was a problem. Nearly every convoy carried a large number of railway locomotives as deck cargo, for the Luftwaffe had decimated the railway rolling stock. There were no cranes to off-lift these very heavy locomotives, so the British sent a "crane ship", the Empire Buttress, as a mobile wharfinger. The role of this ship was simply to wait alongside the Murmansk docks for the next convoy to arrive. Not unnaturally, as time went on, her merchant seamen became increasingly bored and drunken. One night, fed up with the miserable way they were living, they pelted Lenin's statue with snowballs. The police were not amused, and arrested those involved, giving them a very bad time. In consequence, the Empire Buttress went on strike. The Russians were dumbfounded. They demanded that all the ring-leaders should be shot. At that stage, however, the British decided to withdraw the ship and send it back with the next convoy, replacing it with another.

What fools they were! The effect of the proposed exchange of crane ships was that the next convoy was reduced to six knots, and that cost us dear. The obvious answer would have been to replace the crew by air or sea.

The Navy too had similar problems. The danger of sailors becoming idle and restless, and then upsetting the Russians during their free time, was very real. To prevent this, various sporting activities were organized, and on one occasion a boat race was laid on to occupy the time and strength of the disgruntled matelots, who had no other recreation in Murmansk.

Officers engaged in these fleet escorts had their own unofficial ways of maintaining their sense of humour. One day, a well-known writer for magazines produced a diabolical plan. Bogus invitations to senior fleet officers were printed, inviting them to an elk shoot as guests of the Commissar for Trade. They were to meet at the local Trade Commission H.Q., equipped with very special clothing for the hunt, and bringing with them the best sporting

Commander Fisher, D.S.O., O.B.E., D.S.C., R.N. (third from the left)

rifles and amunition they could muster. My captain consulted me, and, although privy to the deception, I kitted him out with a special "sporting type" Lee Enfield S.M.L.E., complete with dum-dum bullets.

All the senior officers duly foregathered at the appointed time and place, to be promptly arrested by the police. A minor diplomatic row erupted, and neither the Russians nor many of the senior officers appreciated the joke. At first there were threats of courts martial, but then a better sense of humour prevailed, and the matter was glossed over.

Our officers and troops could be high-spirited, and were by no means averse to "taking the micky" out of the sad-faced Russians on occasion. Perhaps our ways of doing so were not always to our credit. On one occasion at Polyarnoe, just to stretch our legs after a fortnight at sea, I led a party of fellow officers on a walk. The deep snow was frozen hard, and we walked without getting our feet wet. Then, by accident we came across a huge body of men — a thousand strong, perhaps — who were being drilled. Probably it was a Red Army battalion that we had stumbled upon. Because of the high-packed snow, we had no way of by-passing them, and were forced to pass within a few feet of the senior officer, whom I took to be a colonel. As we passed, looks of the blackest hostility were being thrown at us, so, hoping to placate them a little, we all saluted the colonel as we passed by him. As we did so, we uttered the only Russian words we knew, "Darasteje Tovarich", meaning "Good morning, comrade". The reaction of the Russians was for the entire battalion to present arms, and, more than a little shaken, we could only respond by ourselves standing to attention at the salute.

Nowadays, at a distance of nearly fifty years, it is hard to convey the tension that was experienced in Scapa Flow and Loch Ewe as ships made ready to sail on these Russian convoys. On one particular day, the first lieutenant of Musketeer gave us a "pep talk" to prepare us for the convoy that was sailing that night. He told us that he was worried about the morale of some members of the crew, and named one in particular who, he said, appeared to be terrified out of his wits. We were to make certain that he did not desert.

Sure enough, when we sailed that evening, the rating he had named was missing, and was posted as a deserter. Musketeer left Scapa Flow astern of Milne, with the other destroyers following. We were sailing out of the Orkney Islands, which was usually a safe and uneventful passage. Hence I was astonished when, soon after we left harbour, "action stations" sounded. It appeared that as we were steaming quietly along, a man had cried out from the sea, with the result that a general alarm of "man overboard" was sounded. Nevertheless, we never altered speed or course. A roll call was taken, first from Milne, from whom no one was found missing, and then from Musketeer. No one was missing from us either, except for the one man already posted as a deserter. Later, a rumour began to circulate which may provide the explanation of the mystery. It was said that the "deserter" had been thrown overboard by some of his mates. The terror he had shown earlier was due not to his apprehension about the passage to Russia, but to fear of what his mates might be planning to do to him. Why he met his fate I shall never know, but I am sure that that is what happened. He was never heard of again, and escape from Scapa Flow was as difficult as escape from Alcatraz. No one could get through Security at Scrabster, and the tides would certainly drown all small boat fugitives and swimmers. Some years later, I discovered that this fatality was recorded by the Chatham coroner as "Missing, presumed lost at sea"!

While at Scapa Flow, I had a chance meeting with a certain Alan Rothnie, which was to be of great interest to me later on in life. I had first met him in 1936 as a youth of sixteen, and he had been my first opponent in the Montrose Tennis Tournament. His

Ambassadors Jorissen and Rothnie with their wives, Royal Netherlands Embassy, Berne.

father was politically on the extreme left wing — left even of Socialist. Nevertheless, I had enjoyed the match with Alan, and we had struck up an acquaintance. We had met again and exchanged brief pleasanteries in 1939, when we had both attended the same course as midshipmen.

Now, five years after that brief encounter, I was preparing for sea in Musketeer when I spotted Alan crossing the deck to another ship. I immediately rushed forward and hailed him. He, in his turn, was astonished to see me in Musketeer, and I asked him if we both got to Russia, to have lunch with me in my ship. This he did. He was obviously very pro-Red, and told me that he had learnt Russian. He had been posted to the Naval Mission in Murmansk. I described to him the miserable time we always had in Murmansk, and asked him, if his friends could ever be persuaded to allow such a thing, to show me round a part of Russia other than her docks. It was obvious that Alan got on well with the local Reds, and, thanks to his influence, on subsequent visits I was always given V.I.P. treatment — so much so that my captain jokingly accused me of being an under-cover Communist, though he knew well how unlikely this was. More of this anon! At this point, suffice it to say that during my visits to Russia, Alan was a godsend to me, and I shall not easily forget him. Few other British officers had a Red Navy staff car at their disposal!

CHAPTER TWELVE

Gun Control Officer and Correspondence Officer of Musketeer

In May 1944, my captain told me to leave Musketeer for a few weeks in order to do a short course at the gunnery school at Devonport. The intention was that I should take over as Musketeer's gun control officer. During that brief period at Devonport, I met a number of chums who had taken part in the D Day landings and the aftermath to these. They had interesting tales to tell. On returning to Scapa Flow, I did in fact take over as gun control officer, and also as correspondence officer, so that at last I had a small status of my own. If I did not have command of a ship, at least I did have my own department.

From the perspective of over forty years later, it is hard to convey the stress under which we were all working, and as gunnery officer I was no exception. When I was not keeping watch on the bridge, I was often having to work out appallingly complex graphs and statistics, which involved spending hours of study, poring over mathematical tables — all this, quite often, in order to explain why we had not hit our target during battle practice off Scapa Flow before we had even started the convoy in which we were engaged! All too often, this involved eighteen hours and more of study, all alone in my cabin, with the ship pitching and rolling in the Arctic swell. To say that I lived in a sort of sick daze would be an understatement. By comparison, to suffer snow and spray on the freezing bridge was a pleasure! It must be remembered that in those days we had no covered-in heating control positions. We were all, seamen, signalmen, and officers, totally exposed to the elements of the Arctic. From those few months when I was gun control officer and correspondence officer, three events in particular stand out in my mind.

As correspondence officer, the captain placed great trust in me, and I handled many secret documents never seen by my colleagues. On one occasion, when we were engaged in boiler cleaning, and so temporarily immobilized in Scapa Flow, he went on a week's leave, telling me to open all correspondence, however marked. In the case of any secret matter, I was not to refer it even to his second-in-command. One day, an envelope arrived marked "Top secret. For Eyes of Commanding Officer Only". Acting on previous instructions, I opened it. The letter was from the Director of Naval Intelligence to the Commander-in-Chief, Home Fleet, to with copy to commanding officer H.M.S. Musketeer. It stated that, according to information received, "Lieutenant Forsyth-Grant, late of Coastal Forces, is an ardent Nazi sympathizer, and so possibly a major security risk. He should be placed under strict surveillance."

On the captain's return, I handed him this letter, which I had opened. He said that while he knew that some of my opinions were not popular, he had, nevertheless, the highest opinion of my loyalty and integrity. When I finally left his command, he was kind enough to state this in writing.

The second episode took place in September 1944, when I was engaged in one of the most powerful convoys I was ever to see, even though, at the time, the merchant ships were making the return journey from Murmansk, and so were empty. It included the battleship Rodney, co-victor of the Bismarck battle, aircraft carriers, and thirty-seven escorts. In fact it was just about the size that the entire Royal Navy had been in 1988! As we sailed for home, with several of our carrier-borne aircraft flying to and fro over the convoy to spot the U Boats and keep off the bombers, I believed this armada to be invincible. However, one beautiful afternoon in the course of the voyage — it was on the 28th September, to be exact — we received a rude awakening.

It was late afternoon, and I was off duty; but instead of sleeping on the wardroom settee, as I usually did during my off duty hours, I had remained in the gun director of Musketeer, and was simply dozing in my seat there. Suddenly I was awakened by a dull thud, accompanied by the noise of shrill voices and whistles, all blended together. Great columns of spray and some smoke were rising at the sterns of two merchant ships, the Samsuva and the Edward H. Crockett. U Boats had torpedoed them right in the middle of the convoy, using "Gnat" torpedoes, a type which homed in on sound and could be fired from a considerable distance. Within seconds, we were all at action stations. All I had to do was to remain exactly where I was! From the first, both the liberty ships which had been hit turned out to be incapable of steaming; they simply lay immobile on the still, calm water. The armada sailed on, but since the two ships were lying far too near the North Cape, two destroyers, the destroyer leader, Milne, and also Musketeer, were detached in order to sink them, and so prevent them from being salvaged by the Germans.

Musketeer despatched a boat, and somehow the crew of the Samsuva was rescued. However, although demolition charges, including a depth charge, were laid, they apparently failed to explode. All this caused a long delay. When at length the boat returned, the convoy had sailed on and was nearly out of sight. Accordingly, the captain ordered me to sink the ship by gunfire. This was the biggest ship on which I had ever fired, and our six 4.7 belched out 420 lbs of shell at every broadside. After I had fired several tons, Samsuva was well on fire, but it was incredibly hard to hit her on the waterline and so start her actually sinking.

Out of the corner of my eye, I could see, between our salvoes, that Milne was doing a far better job on the Edward H. Crockett. She was sunk in fifteen minutes, while Samsuva still lay on the surface a blazing wreck, with little sign, as it seemed, of actually going down. Berating me for incompetence, the captain said that we would have to leave in order to catch up with Milne and the convoy. I was beside myself with shame. I had waited for ages for this moment, and now when it came I had failed. How had Milne achieved so much in so little time? It was not much consolation to be told, some hours later, that Fleet Air Arm planes flying over the wreck had seen Samsuva sink at last.

On our return to Scapa, the captain, who had been decidedly unfriendly towards me for the remainder of the voyage, grumpily told me to report to Milne and find out what had gone wrong. He warned me that a successor would probably be appointed. With my tail between my legs, I reported to the flotilla gunnery officer and, before he could speak, poured out my apologies. He looked at me in astonishment and then laughed like a drain! He told me that Captain(D) had much approved of my shooting; it had been far better than Milne's. Milne had fired two torpedoes at point blank range; no wonder the target had collapsed! At all events, my captain was pleased and I was forgiven. In the end, I became honestly proud of my efforts in sinking the Samsuva, but that is more than I can say for two ghastly mistakes that occurred later.

We were one of the first destroyers to be fitted with shells carrying a new type of fuze that was entirely revolutionary. It was known as the "variable time" or "proximity" fuze. Its peculiarity was that it worked by a magnetic pole, which it activated as soon as it came into proximity with metal, thereby detonating the shell. As the magnetism increased the fuze began to activate itself, and as the field retired the shell exploded. The principle on which it worked was completely new, and the fuze itself was highly successful, particularly against aircraft. On one occasion, while returning from a Russian convoy, we were ordered to give a display on the Fleet flagship.

At the time, we were nearing Scapa Flow, and when I was told of the exercise, I was resting, dead tired, on my bunk. The plan was to shell the fo'c'sle of the Battleship Duke of York; but it involved the vital qualification *that we were to aim off twenty degrees so that the shells would fall and burst ahead of the bow.* My deputy, a regular R.N. warrant officer, with years of experience behind him, was on watch at the time, so I sent a message telling him to organize the first stage of the exercise. Our guns were controlled by the "director"; it was this , therefore, that needed to be de-clutched and repositioned in order to achieve that vital "aiming off" interval, causing the guns to fire twenty degrees to the right of where they were actually aimed. This "aim off" was, of course, crucially important.

Having given my instructions, I returned to doze, until a rating called me ten minutes before the exercise was due to commence. I took up my battle station and prepared to fire on the King George Class battleship, which was wearing the flag of Sir Henry Moore, Vice Admiral, Second-in-Command, Home Fleet. I was, I felt, experienced at my job, and had no reason to be nervous.

On the command "Open fire!", I gave the order, "Shoot!". Six 4.7s roared out their response. A second later black smoke and shrapnel could be seen bursting right over the quarterdeck of the battleship, or so it seemed! As the captain roared out a horrified warning, I realized the awful mistake we had made. That stupid gunner had off-set the director in the wrong direction! In response to the captain's anguished bellow, I just shouted: "Bad shot right!", clutched out the director, swivelled it forty degrees, and fired again. That salvo, and the six which followed it, detonated perfectly at a point beyond the bows of the flagship. I was still shaking with fear lest I should find that I had liquidated the admiral and his staff, when the intercom spluttered, and on came the voice of the captain. "Well done, Grant! The admiral has congratulated us on our performance!" Quickly I nipped down to the Wardroom and, to the horror of the steward barman, ordered a treble gin. He gave me the gin, but his face showed that I had committed a sacrilege at sea. For my part, I could not have cared less — I had survived!

The nightmare that I suffered over the V.T. fuze was not my only one. The next that befell me occurred when I was operating in a different capacity. It was the practice for the officer of the watch to exercise the gun crews in the sequence of movements which they had to carry out in order to get the guns loaded and aimed. A typical order would be: "Alarm! Enemy aircraft, green 10! Angle of sight, 20!" It was vital, however, that any such orders should be preceded by the words, "For exercise". The reason was that we had power-worked shell gear, which made it difficult, if not impossible, to empty the breach once a shell had been power-rammed. In these practice drills, therefore, turrets would carry out all the movements but would not actually load the guns.

One day, a dreadful crisis arose. An officer had failed to prefix his command with those vital words, "For exercise", and a V.T. salvo had been rammed. A very upset officer of the watch summoned me to explain the position. Two shells had actually been rammed, luckily in one turret only, since at "Defence stations" not all the turrets were manned. But what was to be done? The guns were loaded; according to the canons of strict orthodoxy they could be unloaded only by firing them. Yet to adopt this course would give rise to a major flap, and infallibly bring down the fury of the admiral.

My solution to the problem involved taking a very great risk. I ordered the gun crew to ram back the shell with a rod, as I stood beside the breach. In doing so, I had no idea what would happen. If the shell exploded, I would certainly be killed, so at least I would never be involved in a court of enquiry, let alone a court martial. The scheme worked; the shells did ram back successfully. When all was over, I repeated my visit to the Wardroom. This time the steward seemed less impressed. Perhaps he was becoming used to it!

All through my tenure of office as gun control officer of Musketeer, I yeaned for success; in the late autumn of 1944, I felt that it was within my grasp. At the time, as a change from the usual Russian convoys, we were engaged in an offensive sweep off the Norwegian coast, and, if I remember correctly, we were almost alone. A point came when an enormous ship was sighted and identified as a liner. "Stand by to open fire!" As I stood ready at my station, I could almost feel the monarch pinning a D.S.O., or at least a D.S.C., onto my tunic. I gave the order for all the guns to load, and waited with baited breath for the captain to utter those final magic words, "Open fire!". Only seconds now, and we would not miss. At that moment, I caught sight of a Red Cross on the side of the great ship; in the same second, the agonised voice of the captain screamed out: "Don't fire — it's a Red Cross ship!" It was the Swedish ship, Drottingholm, and she was loaded with British prisoners of war. As we were stood down, I almost wept. I believe that I was cursing all British prisoners of war, whether repatriated or sunk!

During 1944, we had many opportunities to judge of the discipline in Stalin's Red Navy. It was curious in the extreme, seeming to veer inexplicably from the grossly slovenly to the excellent. At any rate that Navy was never of the smallest help in getting the convoys through, despite the most outrageous claims to the contrary. The British had given the Russians the battleship Royal Sovereign, and also a number of ex-U.S. Navy destroyers — "flush deckers", as they were called. These latter, some fifty in number, had been handed over by the U.S. to Britain in exchange for the lease of naval bases in our Caribbean colonies. They were outdated and virtually useless. In the raid on St Nazaire, one of them was loaded with explosives and used to destroy the lock gates. That was about all they were fit for!

At the time of which I am speaking, the battleship and the destroyers were waiting in Scapa Flow to join the Russian Arctic Fleet. They sailed with us to Murmansk, but not as part of the escort. They were merely part of the convoy itself, which, in the course of the voyage, was subject to sporadic onslaughts by U Boats, these in turn being attacked by carrier-based planes and escorts. Hundreds of bombs and depth charges were dropped. One U Boat alone was plastered with no less than 180 depth charges. Later it was claimed as sunk — the only German casualty of that particular convoy. When we arrived at our destination, however, it was being announced on the Russian radio that, with some support from the British Navy, the Red Navy had escorted a large convoy into Murmansk. Many ships of the Red Fleet had been in action, it was asserted, including the battleship Archangelsk (late Royal Sovereign!). They had destroyed six U Boats. Yet those who were on that convoy can bear witness to the fact that no Russian ship taking part in it could have dropped a single depth charge without destroying the next ship astern.

One of my fellow officers in Musketeer was John Weedon. Like myself, he had been in Coastal Forces. At one stage, he had been sent to the U.S.A. to supervise the building of a flotilla of Motor Torpedo Boats which were to be handed over to the British. During the course of his sojourn in the U.S.A., however, the Americans changed their minds, and gave the M.T.B.s to the Russians instead. In the course of the change-over, John came to know the Russians quite well, for both the Senior Officer and the chief engineer of the flotilla spoke English. By chance, this M.T.B.

flotilla had landed up at Polyarnoe, and when John went to resume acquaintanceship, he asked me to accompany him. The conversation which we had with the Senior Officer was most interesting. He told us that the flotilla was playing havoc with coastal shipping around Petsamo. On the way back to our ship, nearly half a mile away, we ran into the chief engineer and had another chat with him. He told us that they had not yet been in action, but were very much looking forward to it. We were inclined to believe his version rather than that of the Senior Officer.

John Weedon had been well decorated for his service in Coastal Forces, and it is sad to have to record that shortly after the war he perished in a Sea Cadet whaler off Dover. So far as I know, neither his body nor those of the sea cadets he led have ever been found, and the incident remains a mystery to this day.

At the end of the day, the Red Navy did have some sort of drill analogous to "evening quarters" in the Royal Navy. I used to notice this while entering Polyarnoe at dusk, for a number of Russian destroyers were moored there. In the fading light one could just make out lines of ratings fallen in on the decks. Many of them would be smoking, and the "burns" would be clearly visible to us as we passed. It was not very impressive.

On the other hand, the grit of the Russian sailors was beyond question, and I could never denigrate them in that respect. One instance was the incident which I have already described, in which a Russian ship was blown up by two torpedoes striking her simultaneously. I also recollect a convoy to Russia in particularly appalling weather, even for those regions. It took seventeen days, and many of those we spent hove to. Even though part of the convoy consisted of patrol boats of the Harbour Defence type, they kept the most perfect station, and never failed in this, day after day, night after night, in the most atrocious seas. For days at a time, it must have been quite impossible for them to have a hot meal, much less to venture onto the open deck. Yet as they entered the Kole Inlet for their naval headquarters, every one of those boats arrived in perfect formation.

I am told that today's Red Navy is superbly equipped and highly efficient, and this I have no reason to doubt. However, the Italian Navy too had excellent ships and equipment, yet performed deplorably, simply because the personnel were useless. Anyone tempted to belittle the Soviet Navy today should ponder closely the difference between Italian and Russian Naval personnel. Surely then he will find himself unable to cast much doubt on Soviet ability.

On one occasion, I attended a lunch at Murmansk given by the

Kommissar for Trade, Anastas Mikoyan, later to become Stalin's right hand man. I studied him as closely as I could, and found him, like the Soviet sailors, a person of marked contrasts.

To augment the Russians' Northern Fleet, the Americans handed over to them the cruiser Milwaukee, and the U.S. Navy crew which had brought her over travelled back to the United Kingdom in British destroyers. At the time, the captain warned the ship's company that, compared to U.S. warships, our troops lived like pigs. We must try, he said, to make the Americans' passage as comfortable as possible. Luckily this worked out as well as could be expected. At the same time, I have to confess that in British ships the lower deck, with the possible exception of chiefs and petty officers, did live terribly rough and in appalling conditions. Nevertheless, as the captain stated, they were built for fighting and not for luxury. It was an understatement with a vengeance!

Conditions ashore were also decidely austere. At Scapa Flow in 1944 there was very little recreation available for either officers or men. My "big day" came round once a month, when I was able to have a game of hockey on a very muddy pitch. I much enjoyed the exercise, and the "luxurious" tea which was its aftermath — two hard-boiled eggs in a nissen hut. That was the Officers' N.A.A.F.I.! At all events, we managed to survive.

In October 1944, Musketeer became infested with black rats of the bubonic plague type, which had somehow got into the ship over ropes or gangways during our stay in northern Russia. After escorting our final convoy to Scotland, therefore, we were sent to Chatham to be fumigated, before being refitted for the Mediterranean. By this stage, the war was nearing its end, and the captain was kind enough to give me the choice of staying with the ship or trying for a shore job in Europe. I opted for the latter. I had always been deeply interested in history, and had read widely on the events in Europe which came as the aftermath to the Armistice of 1918. Now I wanted to see for myself what the powers that be would make of this new opportunity. With this in view, I particularly asked for a staff job in Antwerp, and was recommended for this when I left Musketeer.

On looking back on my time in her, I recognize that I was treated extremely well by all, and have the highest regard for those with whom I served. This applies particularly, but by no means exclusively, to the captain and the two first lieutenants under whom I served. The first of these latter was Lieutenant Cornwell R.N., and he was succeeded by Lieutenant Commander Davey R.N.V.R. Years after the war had ended, I was destined to meet all three of these officers again.

However, Europe did not fall as swiftly as had been expected. The Arnhem fiasco came and went, followed by the counter-attack in the Ardennes. Thus I had a longer time at home than I had expected. I was not entirely surprised, however, when, on my twenty-fifth birthday, the expected telegram arrived. I had a staff job all right — in Freetown, West Africa!

PART V

Shore-Based at Freetown

CHAPTER THIRTEEN

Fresh Experiences in West Africa

I was given sufficient time to get all the necessary range of "jabs" for yellow fever, typhoid etc., and also to obtain tropical naval kit, none of which I possessed. My mother insisted on packing my travelling bag, and included several items which I did not want, including Sotol mouth-wash tablets, and a huge bottle of lemonade in case I was thirsty! My father saw me off at Montrose, and at Glasgow I caught the Liverpool sleeper. Once aboard, I found myself in the same compartment as Paymaster Lieutenant Drummond Taylor R.N.V.R., who had joined the Dundee R.N.V.R. at the same time as I had. He too was being posted to Sierra Leone! Overnight, we caught up with our wartime experiences so far, stopping for breakfast at Liverpool's Adelphi Hotel. On opening my bag, I found that the lemonade bottle had burst, and so had the bottle of Sotol tablets, with the result that all my kit was enveloped in a beautiful strawberry flan!

After breakfast, we were due to embark in R.M.S. Andes, a 26,000 ton liner-turned-troopship belonging to the Royal Mail line. At this point I was anticipating some difficulties. I was equipped with three shotguns, two rifles, and a host of other paraphernalia — but no identity card. However, I need not have worried. The Senior Officer, Naval Contingent, was none other than Lieutenant Commander Jimmy Lumsden, who had commanded M.L. 291 at Peterhead at the same time as I commanded 292. Before long, I was settled, along with ten others, in what in peacetime would have been a family cabin for four. It had accommodation for two adults and two children! However, we did have a bathroom. Troopships were now teetotal, but that did not worry us. We had brought our own drink on board, and, in view of the fact that the ship's police were liable to do spot searches, most of it was stored in Jimmy's cabin. Jimmy, of course, was more senior, and therefore inviolate.

This experience of being a passenger at sea was completely

novel to me, and I enjoyed every minute of it. It consisted of nearly a fortnight's lounging about, with neither duties nor responsibilities, but with excellent food and water services. At one point we did run into a terrific storm, during which eighty percent of the troops were sick for twenty-four hours, and the dining-room was virtually empty. Luckily for me, however, I have never been much affected by sea-sickness. At the height of the storm, a valise, which one officer was carrying for the wife of a friend in South Africa, broke loose, and a terrible red stain appeared on the outside of the case. We opened it, and found that a bottle of red liquid had burst and soaked all the ladies' undies, smalls etc.. We did our best to launder them in the bathroom. Unfortunately, this coincided with a crash visit by the ship's police, who became convinced that we were concealing a female stowaway. Our protests that we were officers and gentlemen were brusquely ignored, and they subjected our quarters to the most thorough search.

I never like gambling (once bitten, twice shy!) even in fun, and when we were invited to roulette, I declined, only to be treated by all my chums in our cabin as a goodie-goodie and spoilsport. Most reluctantly, therefore, I agreed to join them. The croupier, or banker, was a flight lieutenant (admin.), and, in contrast to us ordinary passengers, was a regular member of trooping staff on the ship. Of course, that one session in which I was involved had to be the one in which he was caught. Somehow or other, it was alleged that he had magnetized the ball, and now he had been found out! I had the utmost difficulty in avoiding being cited as a witness at his court martial, for this was treated as a most serious offence, but thank God, I had nothing more to do with the matter.

I heard tell of magnificent sex life in the lifeboats after dark, but the men outnumbered the girls by ten to one, and somehow I never fancied my chances!

After about a fortnight, we anchored in Freetown, and Drummond Taylor and I went ashore to join H.M.S. Eland, the Royal Naval Barracks at Kissy, which was about three miles outside Freetown itself. At first sight, it looked quite awful: a dirty shanty of a barracks made up of nissen huts. I arrived at the officers' mess and went to pay my entry subscription to a chief petty officer steward, who was obviously in charge. "This place looks like the last place on earth!" I could not help remarking. The chief gave me a stony look. "This place is what you make it, Sir," he replied. How right he was, and how wise! Right from that moment, I followed his advice, and I never regretted it.

I spent my first day in H.M.S. Eland feeling like a fish out of water. Apart from the fact that life in the tropics was quite new to me, having a permanent job ashore was a completely novel experience, quite unlike the time I spent at Devonport the previous year, while on my gunnery course.

My official title was Senior Watchkeeping Officer, and my office was in the guardroom detention barracks complex at the main gate. My duties were to control the general inflow and outflow of the barracks, and to take charge of the twenty to thirty prisoners, all of them white ratings, who were locked up in the detention barracks. Under me I had three or four officers, a master at arms, and four or five regulating petty officers. The non-commissioned staff were for the most part regulars, with scant respect for any "Reserve" or "Hostilities only" officers; they ran the place their way. The lack of respect which they showed my predecessor was mirrored in the lack of respect which the prisoners showed them. In short, the state of discipline was appalling.

I soon let the staff know that I had been an officer for over five years of war, and for two and a half of these had served as commanding officer of one of H.M. ships. I knew my authority, therefore. For several days we clashed fiercely, but after that all conflict was over. For the rest of my time in this position, I got on extremely well with the staff, and had virtually no trouble with the prisoners.

On my very first night in the Wardroom bar I spotted a civilian whose face seemed familiar, and he in turn recognized me. It was J.E. Kennerley, the Superintending Armament Supply Officer, who, in 1941, had accused my troops of looting his depot at Inverness. In no time we became close friends, chiefly because of a common love of shooting and fishing, and it was destined to become a lasting friendship. After nearly fifty years it is still going strong!

During my first week of settling myself in to my new job, I came across a breed of "rating" which I had never met before. A large number of those working at H.M.S. Eland were really civilians and dockyard employees. However, lest they were captured by the enemy, they were given uniform and called "Special Repair Ratings (Dockyard)". In reality, they were simply dockyard mateys in uniform, and they accorded as much respect to rank as they would have done in Devonport or Portsmouth. In any case, they were nearly all "lefties", as were the officers, so-called, who wore officers' stripes but refused to accept officer discipline.

Early one morning, I was called to a disturbance in the S.R.R. (D)s' mess hall, where the men had refused to eat their breakfast. The barracks commander, Commander Dawson R.N., arrived just after me, and he sent for the captain. This was Sir John Alleyn,

Bart, a four-stripe retired officer. He was a nice old bird, who had left the Navy years before, and had been employed for the duration of the war in a much inflated position. In 1945 this was a new experience to him. Commander Dawson too had retired in peacetime as a lieutenant or something a little higher.

The disturbance now confronting these two officers was a serious matter. The troops were refusing to eat their porridge, and as Sir John addressed them, one agitator hurled a bowl of porridge at him, which burst on the wall just behind his head — and mine! I immediately requested permission to bring the riot squad in, but shaking his head, Sir John left the hall, leaving the commander and myself standing alone. The men refused to work unless the meal before them was replaced with a better one, and the commander agreed to their request. Thenceforward a lowering of standards was immediately apparent both in their dress and in the even scanter respect which they paid to authority.

Hardly had I surmounted this crisis, when, within a matter of days, the commander rang up in a terrible state to say that during the night the green baize of the Wardroom billiard table had been stolen, leaving the slate exposed. There would be no more billiards!

Now Kissy dockyard was the largest in West Africa, and several hundred black dockyard workers, all civilians, came through the gates every day to work there. They all had to show their passes at the gate, and by these means it was hoped to ensure that the same number left at five p.m.. I had already instituted random searches for stolen tools, but after this incident I arranged that about one in ten should be ordered to strip in my office. If necessary, I was prepared to emulate the Gestapo, about which so much has been written.

Sure enough, before long I discovered one of these boys wearing a magnificent pair of drawers made from billiard table baize, and within twenty-four hours I had recovered most of the baize from the table, though by this time, of course, it was all in dribs and drabs. My methods provoked much criticism from the more liberal-minded white dockyard ratings, and when one of them was being searched, he screamed that I would not be able to treat him like the downtrodden blacks. He was speedily proved wrong, and word soon spread. I had no further trouble from the S.R.R. (D) ratings, and only dirty looks from their bosses, whose rank in the officers' mess was higher than my own.

By early May, the collapse of the German forces in Europe seemed imminent, and great was the jubilation. The armistice itself soon followed, and was suitably celebrated. On V.E. night I

Victory Parade in Freetown, May, 1945

Duck shooting in Maswari Swamps, Sergeant Wallace in centre

was on duty in the barracks. Everyone seemed to be drunk, including warders and sentries, and some bright spark released some of the prisoners. Starting with some of my senior officers, I tried to restore some sort of order, but before I achieved this, five sailors had died in drunken accidents. Two were drowned or eaten by sharks while taking part in a swimming race from H.M.S. Philoctetes to the shore. Another two drowned when their 15 cwt. Bedford truck drove over a pier at full speed. I believe, too, that one died and several were injured in an explosion at a fireworks celebration. It was the busiest night I ever had in that particular job!

Three days later, there was to be a huge victory parade past the law courts, with the governor taking the salute. I was not scheduled to have any role in this, and the night before, I had my own private celebration in the Wardroom. At two a.m. I was rudely awoken. The officer leading the parade, I was told, had got malaria; I, as the only other officer qualified in gunnery and all the bullshit that went with it, had been selected as substitute for him. I was still far from sober when I was finally awakened at seven a.m. and told to get ready.

My task was to lead the parade for about one and a half miles along the straight, broad street, taking a cotton tree, an enormous hardwood standing beside the law courts, as my guiding beacon. On and on we marched — that bloody cotton tree never seemed to get any closer. My head was thumping and my knees felt weak, but at last I was abreast of the governor. I saluted, gave him an "eyes right", and the white Naval contingent followed suit. Three hundred yards further on I literally collapsed on the bonnet of a 15 cwt. truck. Fortunately, it had been scheduled to take me home, but I had to be helped in.

On and on went the celebrations — and the drinking. At the first guest night after V.E. Day, the loyal toast to His Majesty was drunk, followed by some others. Then the slightly inebriated commander who had succeeded Dawson proposed a toast "to the death of the tyrant, Hitler". Much to the laughter and jeers of my colleagues, who thought that I was unable to stand, I remained firmly seated. Then the commander named me to stand. At that point I rose to my feet and explained my attitude towards Adolph Hitler. A stunned silence followed, lasting several seconds. Then came the voice of the commander: "Lieutenant Forsyth-Grant will leave the mess". I clicked my heels, bowed, and left. The incident was never mentioned again.

Now that the German war had ended, a new role was added to my duties. Nazi war criminals, so designated, were reputed to be escaping to South America in Spanish merchant ships. British warships were constantly detaining these and sending them in to Freetown. On each one of them I had to place an armed guard while our so-called Intelligence Services (for whom I had the utmost contempt) went aboard to search and interrogate their crews. With ratings being sent off to the war in the Far East, I was often so short of staff that for this purpose I had to use ratings who had just been released from prison. The quality of officer employed on this duty was not very high either.

One day, I had an S.O.S. from one of these Spanish merchantmen which had been detained, to say that the armed guard that had been sent on board had mutinied and that the ship was in chaos. In response, I quickly had the mutineers under guard in my office, and sent a new detachment to replace them. To this deplorable state of affairs there was a fairly simple explanation. The sub lieutenant in charge was already under investigation for some unrelated offence. As soon as the armed guard had arrived on board, the Spaniards had plied every member of it with free brandy, with the result that some of them had had too much to drink. In the course of these proceedings, an able seaman of the Regular Navy had had an argument with Sub Lieutenant Wharton and had struck him.

I compiled an "on the spot" report of all this, and handed it to Commander Dawson. He told me to place the A.B. under close arrest, and said that he would be charged with mutiny — a very serious offence. Sub Lieutenant Wharton was not to be charged with any offence. Commander Dawson, and presumably his superiors, then convened a court martial, and, knowing that I had the most intimate knowledge of courts martial, he asked me to defend. I told him that I was unable to do so. If I defended the accused, I would have to implicate Wharton, who was a member of my staff. I could not remain impartial enough to defend him properly. By this time, Sir John Alleyn had gone home, and Commander Dawson was acting commander and acting captain. He now gave me a written order: I was to defend the accused. With this, unless I was to become a mutineer myself, I was obliged to comply.

For the accused himself I had every sympathy. He was an extremely tough Regular R.N. rating, about my own age, and of Glaswegian descent. He had already been in trouble many times, but in this instance, I believe, he was sinned against as much as sinning. I told him that he could, if he so wished, refuse my services, but promised, if he decided to accept them, to defend him to the best of my ability. He asked to do so.

The court martial was duly convened, and the trial began. I rather think that the president was Captain Bowes Lyon R.N., a close relative of the Queen. If he was not the president, he was certainly the power behind him. None of the members had ever sat on a court martial before; they were all quite ignorant of the procedure, as was the Acting Judge Advocate, a paymaster lieutenant commander R.N.V.R.. He in particular was quite oblivious of the rule book, Book of Reference No. 11, the Manual of Naval Court Martial Procedure. He had already asked if he could borrow my copy, and I had very frostily declined. However, they did get hold of a copy somehow. The accused was duly tried and convicted, but it was in the teeth of some irregularities. He received five years hard labour; it might have been even worse. I told him that he could appeal when he got back to Britain, and that he should discuss the matter with his lawyer or M.P. He thanked me most sincerely for all I had done. I was surprised that neither the court nor Captain Dawson who had recently been promoted, ever tried to retaliate for my outspoken criticism in court, but strangely enough there was no recrimination.

Two further incidents, both of them amusing, must be recorded from my time as head of security and prison governor (!). When I first arrived in West Africa, Commodore Menzies had been at Freetown with Dawson and Vice Admiral Peters, and I had told his secretary that I could not do the job to which he was assigning me without some form of personal transport. Menzies had decreed that I could have a motorbike — always provided that I could ride one well enough to pass the test. Subject to this condition, I was offered a brand new B.S.A. 350. Now my experience of motorbikes was limited to my escapades on Dartmoor during the time when I was serving on H.M.S. Tynedale. In my need, I turned to the nearest available expert, who was the Church of Scotland padre, and asked him to give me a crash course on the new machine. The padre had no mercy! However, by the end of four days, though scratched and scarred, I emerged a competent motorcyclist. I soon found that my rising self-esteem was due for a reverse. The civilian examiner attached to the dockyard decided that I could do the test in a car, and of course in this I passed easily.

The rainy season in West Africa was truly formidable. On one occasion during my stay there, forty-five inches fell in five days. Nevertheless it was during this season that Juba Kennerley and I made a journey to a place some forty miles from Kissy for the purpose of shooting bushfowl. Juba's friend Brian Liddell, who was a senior civil engineer with Admiralty, said that he would follow us. This was most unwise; Brian, who knew little of shooting or the country, was showing off to his girl friend, a white nurse from the 34th General Hospital, when the road gave way and the Austin pick-up landed in a ravine, by this time transformed into a raging torrent. He and his girl friend were lucky to escape drowning. He had no right to have taken a Naval vehicle to this area, and even less to have lost it. He could be liable for dire penalties.

Juba and I discovered him standing with his girl friend in torrential rain, both of them ruefully contemplating the nearly submerged pick-up. We rescued them and drove back to Kissy, where I mounted a rescue operation for the morrow. I told the barracks commander that I needed exotic tropical plants to "beautify" the prison, and was taking a convoy of lorries with me into the bush in order to obtain suitable varieties. Taking wires, winches, Summerfield tracking, and two huge M.A.C. lorries, I recovered the Austin pick-up from the bush ravine, as well as an assortment of exotic plants, and we returned in triumph to the barracks without anyone knowing how close to the wind we had sailed.

Soon afterwards, the post of Flag Officer, West Africa, previously held by Vice Admiral Peters, was down-graded, and a brilliant ex-submarine officer, G.C.P. Menzies by name, was appointed Commodore in Charge, Freetown. He re-structured the command, and I was promoted to Naval Transport Officer, West Africa, a position well above my rank.

CHAPTER FOURTEEN

My New Post as Naval Transport Officer

I found the position of Naval Transport Officer both exciting and challenging. Previously, the large numbers of units that made up this command had been under several different authorities, all operating independently. Thus the Naval Stores Officer had had control of vehicles ranging from motorcycles to enormous M.A.C. lorries, as well as of all the fuel that went with these. The Victualling Supply Officer had had tugs and lighters under his command, while the Boat Officer had had charge of a host of motor boats as well as the admiral's barge. Now all this was under one umbrella — mine! My command comprised several hundred personnel, Naval for the most part, but about 25 percent of them West African civilians. To administer all this, I had a white staff not exceeding ten, with Sub Lieutenant R.L. Westcott as my deputy, and Leading Writer Pope as my secretary. Our headquarters were on the waterfront of the extensive acreage of the Royal Naval Barracks, Kissy.

Morale, I found, was at a low ebb, and the state of the equipment reflected this. The sole aim of my predecessors had been, it seemed, to get out of Sierra Leone and back to the U.K.. Paint was easy to obtain, and the first thing I did was to initiate a general smartening up. The sight of so many newly painted boats and neatly maintained vehicles was enough in itself to lift morale. As for my own transport, from now on this was to be no problem to me; I had at my disposal vehicles ranging from large drophead coupés to 7 cwt. trucks and motorcycles — all with unlimited petrol.

It was not long before good order was. established, and the department was running smoothly. Hence I was able to take plenty of time off to explore further afield in Sierra Leone, and at same the time to meet a wider range of people. One day, I was playing hockey for the Navy against the Civil Servants (the white administration of Sierra Leone). During a lull in the game, I spotted a face that was familiar to me from eight years previously. It was Ian Husband, who had been with me in Wellesley House at Wellington in the thirties. In those days, he had been a prefect and I two years his junior, so that we had in no sense been friends. Moreover, he used forever to be searching my room for illegal contraband or guns. On this occasion, therefore, our initial greetings were a little frosty. Nevertheless, he soon became, and still remains to this day, one of my closest friends. In 1945, he was Deputy Commissioner of Labour. He rose high in the Colonial Service, becoming Commissioner of Labour in Kenya, and later a high official of U.N.E.S.C.O. in Geneva. Another hockey player was Tony Keeling, an Assistant Superintendent of Police, later to become Commissioner of Police in the colony, and to remain in that post when it became a republic. Both Ian and Tony became constant companions of mine on my many shooting trips up country.

Another remarkable character was Sergeant Wallace. He came from the Bournemouth neighbourhood, and his wife ran a nursing home. He had joined the Army as a gunner or bombardier, but had somehow arrived in West Africa, with the acting rank of sergeant, to run a huge vegetable complex at Hastings, twenty miles from Freetown. It provided food, chiefly in the form of salads, for the white Army in Sierra Leone. Sergeant Wallace was his own master, working without supervision of any kind. He had several West African servants of his own, and used to live a life of considerable luxury, entertaining other expatriates and being entertained by them in the style of a maharaja. I often visited his bungalow to shoot bushfowl in the acres of bush that flanked his very rural domain. Because of the colossal heat and humidity, it was only possible to shoot for an hour or so at dusk and dawn, and even then one returned to Wallace's house sticky with sweat and in need of a bath. This was provided by Lamoona, a beautiful black house girl, who not only supplied the water and washed one, but also, with Wallace's full knowledge and approval, provided sex for those who wanted it after their bath. It was an unusual and wholly delightful arrangement.

Yet another shooting companion to whom I had been introduced by Juba Kennerley was Brigadier the Viscount Down, O.C. Troops for Sierra Leone, and reputedly one of the richest men in Britain. I believe that he owned great tracts of London's Mayfair. He had his own private yacht, on which we sailed to most exotic places, including the islands in the Freetown area. On one occasion, we arrived with him and about four other whites on Tassoh Island, where we decided to camp inland in a deserted bungalow, rejoining the yacht the following day. Lord Down possessed three magnificent Woodward sidelock twelve bores, and we gave him his first experience of driven guinea and bushfowl. Afterwards, we were towelling down the sweat from our labours, and it happened that Wallace finished before the rest of us. I asked him, therefore, if he would make the soda for our whiskies in a wire-covered sparklet syphon that I had brought with me. Apparently he filled it above the danger red line, and the syphon exploded. The splinters of flying glass cut his face very severely, and, still worse, some of them lodged in one of his eyes. He was in considerable pain, and in danger of losing the sight of the injured eye. Under the circumstances, there was only one thing to do: operate quickly without anaesthetics. While some of us held him down, we extracted the glass from his eye and face, and thereby saved his sight. Within a day or two he had recovered.

Many of the officers and white ratings hated Freetown, and simply lived for the day when they were due to return to Britain. My own attitude was the exact opposite; I lived up to the advice of the petty officer who first greeted me in the Wardroom. "This place is what you make it," he had said, and while I was there I lived life to the full, always actively employed and never being bored. My colleagues were astonished at my manner of living.

Despite having the only warrant steward I ever met, one Tucker by name, food at the officers' mess was not particularly good. Because of the quality of his meals, Tucker's name was often miscalled. One day a fellow officer, who had held some appointment afloat, asked me to organize a bordello party after dinner for himself and four officer companions. It was arranged, therefore, that we should all dine at the Lion and Palm, the N.A.A.F.I. club for officers in Freetown, while I sent back my black Naval driver to collect a madam and six comely black girls. The madam informed me that the charge was five shillings per girl, and in addition an exorbitant fee of £1 for herself for organizing the whole thing. This I passed on to the sex-starved young men. Emerging somewhat alcoholically from the Lion and Palm, we all piled into a Bedford 15 cwt. truck with madam and the girls, and drove down to Lumley Beach. Here we staked out on the warm sand in the moonlight. Just as everyone was getting down to work, a plaintive voice sounded in my ears. It was the officer who had asked me to organize the party in the first place. "Mike," he called out, "I can't go through with this; I'm thinking of my wife!" "You'll have to pay your five shillings whether you have it or not!" I bellowed brusquely in reply, and that was the end of that.

I was well known at the Lion and Palm, and also to the masses of

Indian, Lebanese, and African traders who manned the bazaars and shops nearby. They always greeted me cheerfully, and knew me too well to give me any trouble. Officers visiting the colony, however, could have a different tale to tell, particularly those off troopships. One lunchtime I was entertaining Lieutenant Best Dallerson R.N.V.R., who was in charge of the Naval contingent in the visiting troopship Andes, and he asked me whether he could visit Chellarams, the big Indian bazaar across the street, while I paid the lunch bill at the Lion and Palm. When I went to collect him, however, he told me that he had been robbed of all his money and his wallet. Straightway I blasted the traders, telling them that unless the wallet was returned at once, I would boycott them for ever. It was returned forthwith — and intact.

It was not only in the plushier areas that I was well known. The back streets and slums too, though "no go" areas to white servicemen, were familiar ground to me. One day, on strolling round a corner in Kissy dockyard, I came upon a crowd of white sailors from a visiting sloop, kicking the daylights out of a black civilian who was lying on the ground groaning. I blasted them for their cowardly mass attack upon him, and they fled. Meanwhile the black picked himself up.

I never did discover what the cause of the trouble was, but the black, who turned out to be a fairly well-to-do clerk, thanked me profusely and asked me to visit his club in Freetown. I thought that this would be interesting, so after dark I put on a khaki jacket to cover my epaulettes and whites, parked my motorcycle in the "in bounds" zone, and marched into the slum area to knock on the door of the house to which the clerk had directed me. It was, of course, a black brothel, but the patrons were mostly white civilians.

I received a warm reception from the clerk, who was the owner, and was given a glass of black market "Grouse" whisky. After chatting to the girls, I finished my drink, declined sex, and took my leave. I had started to return through the slums to my bike, when suddenly about six people hurled me to the ground, sat on me, and robbed me of my wallet. Just then, as I lay motionless in the half light, a furious fight developed over my prostrate body. Next, friendly arms pulled me to my feet, and my wallet was handed back to me. The grateful owner of the bordello had known that I risked being mugged as I was returning, and had sent an escort to see me safely out of the slums. It was an episode which I shall never forget.

One day, Ian Husband suggested that we took a long week-end in order to visit the police training college at Port Lokko, eighty miles from Freetown. At the time, our friend Tony Keeling was already staying there. Accordingly, at five a.m. the next morning, I met Ian in Freetown with my 7cwt. Austin pick-up. On the way to the college, we had to cross a wide river by means of a hand-operated ferry. We were due to reach it about dawn, so we decided that, while waiting for the ferry, we would breakfast on the river bank. I was to provide the bacon and the eggs. That breakfast was a disaster! My tin of navy bacon was rotten and stinking, three of the eggs were addled, and the fourth had a dead chick inside. Anything more calculated to put one off one's breakfast could not be imagined.

Nevertheless, it did not dampen our spirits, and we duly arrived at the police college in time for a huge curry lunch. The commander of the college was a Superintendent of Police, Oliver Lucas, who hailed from Devon. We had some interesting hunting and exploring, though it was rather marred by a misadventure which befell Tony Keeling. He had the misfortune to sit on a drum of petrol which sprang a leak and squirted petrol up his rectum. For the space of about half an hour he was literally "hot arsed"!

What Ian and I were really anxious to find was a remote area called Kasanko, which was famous for duck flighting. However, West Africans are, generally speaking, poor hunters and trackers, and we never did find the place. To this day I still dream about it sometimes!

One evening, Oliver Lucas, Tony Keeling, Ian Husband and I were dining in the commandant's garden. Two pointers, which were the property of Deputy Commissioner Apthorpe, the second highest ranking policeman in Sierra Leone, had been left in Oliver's care while their owner was on leave. Suddenly, as we were sitting in the garden, a West African policeman rushed up to tell us that both dogs had developed rabies and were attacking people. Oliver decided that they must be shot at once, and he asked me to do the job. Reluctantly, I did as he requested. I presume the dogs did in fact have rabies, but I must emphasize that my whole part in the affair was to do as I had been asked. Afterwards, I wished that I had not been so co-operative, for Apthorpe never forgave me, and thereafter bore a grudge against me.

In those days, shoots in Sierra Leone were far more dangerous and exciting than the highly organized affairs familiar to us in Britain today. As an illustration of what I mean, I may relate one episode which took place while we were guests at a duck-flighting shoot organized by Commissioner Swayne, a very senior district commissioner at Maswari, some fifty miles from Freetown.

Incidentally, he had a very beautiful Nordic wife. It was flight time in the afternoon, and the commissioner had deputed me to take up a position on one side of a sheet of water, about one hundred yards long by thirty feet across, onto which the duck might flight. My host arranged to pick me up before dark, and then left me, completely on my own, in my position.

I had already shot one or two duck, and left them still floating on the water, when, at one end of the lake, a whistling teal flashed in, flying exceptionally fast and low. As it came abreast of me, I took it, and it fell stone dead into the water. Then, to my horror, out of a tree directly opposite me, I saw a man fall. It was Wallace. I had felled sergeant and duck with the same barrel! Never to this day have I discovered what he was doing in that tree; he could not possibly have shot fast, flying duck from it. At all events, when I rushed over to him, I found that though he had been hit by thirteen pellets, his worst injury was a bruised ball! One pellet had hit a metal fly-button on his denims and cannoned against a testicle. At least it had prevented him from being penetrated in that region! Luckily, the rest of the party must have heard the commotion, and came over to investigate. It was agreed that I should take Wallace back to Swayne's bungalow and send for an ambulance. Meanwhile, the rest of the party would continue the shoot.

I gave Wallace two shots of morphia omnipon, which I had kept from my M.G.B. days. Then I started arming him along the track to my vehicle. Needless to say, my gun was still loaded. We had got half way back to the Austin pick-up, when I disturbed a huge flock of guineafowl, a most valuable quarry. Cold-bloodedly, I abandoned Wallace, and then proceeded to drop a right and left of guineafowl. I believe it was my very first right and left at this quarry. Picking up the guineafowl first and Wallace second, I continued our painful journey back to the car and the bungalow.

The ambulance duly arrived, and Wallace was carted off to the 34th General Hospital to have the shot removed. Meanwhile, a black court messenger — they were the equivalent of police in rural areas — got off a rather garbled message which arrived at the 34th General in the following form: "Expect arrival of Sgt. Wallace, riddled with thirteen machine-gun bullets"! In those days, they bred them tough in Sierra Leone. Within a few days Wallace was back at work, none the worse for this awful experience.

Sadly, the lives both of my host, Commissioner Swayne, and of Sergeant Wallace ended in tragedy. Not long after our shoot Swayne committed suicide. A group of R.A.S.C. personnel had caught and beaten up a party of men who had robbed them, and in the course of this, one of the robbers had been killed. Swayne had attempted to "cover up" for the R.A.S.C. men but had been discovered.

Wallace too was to meet an untimely end. After being demobbed in 1946, he had some affair with a girl friend and left his wife. He then killed either one or both of the two women near Bournemouth, before shooting himself.

CHAPTER FIFTEEN

Further Experiences in Sierra Leone after VJ Day

The smooth running which had been achieved in my department was in part due to the excellence of my secretary, Leading Writer Pope. It came as something of a bombshell, therefore, to hear, at fairly short notice, that he would shortly be returning to Britain to be demobilized. At the time, I had volumes of paper work to get through, and to be without a secretary at this point would put me in a near-impossible position. What was I to do?

Commodore Menzies knew of my difficulty, and sent for me to suggest a solution. He had with him in his office, he said, a man who would be just right for me, an A.B. who had been to public school, was very well educated, and could do office work. To my horror, I discovered that this proposed replacement for Pope was none other than A.B. John Forrester, that same rating whom I had encountered at Ramsgate in 1942, when he had been a neo-Communist member of Motor Gunboat 13. At the time, he had been wearing the hammer and sickle emblem on his oilskins, and I had taken strong issue with his C.O. about it. Now here he was again! I told Commodore Menzies that I considered Forrester unsuitable, and he was instructed to wait outside in the ante-room. I then unfolded the whole story to the commodore. However, it turned out to be a case of Hobson's choice. There really was no one else capable of doing the job. Forrester promised to serve me well and truly, and that had to be the end of the matter. I had my new secretary.

One day in August, on walking into the Wardroom bar, I ran into my old chum Drummond Taylor, now a lieutenant commander (S). In pre-war days, it will be remembered, he had been with me in Dundee, when he was a sub lieutenant. On this occasion, Drummond was bubbling over with excitement. He declared that he would soon be standing me a drink in Dundee. I stared at him in blank amazement. Had he gone off his rocker with the heat?

"Haven't you heard," he went on, "about the new super bomb that has been dropped on Japan? Now they have dropped a second, and the Japs are asking for an armistice!" At this I nearly dropped myself. It was absolutely the first I had heard of the imminent end to the war with Japan. The secret of the atomic bomb had been well kept. Of course Drummond was absolutely right; within days, World War II was over.

The previous June, my father had written to me to suggest that it might be advisable to sell my 1933 Vauxhall, now twelve years old. Cars, he told me, were making very good prices in Britain, and with the end of the Japanese war apparently far distant, I would not be likely to be back in the United Kingdom before 1947. At the time I had agreed, but now, unexpectedly, the Japanese war was over; I would soon be finding myself back in Britain, but without a car. The end of the war in the Far East did in fact vastly accelerate the progress of demobilization, and now there was a constant stream of people leaving Freetown for good.

This was my situation when I found myself at dinner one evening sitting next to a somewhat inebriated lieutenant, who had a sad story to tell. He had just sold his 1939 Vauxhall saloon to a Syrian, had got drunk on the strength of it, and then, while still celebrating, had driven the car into a ravine, and been obliged to return the purchase price to the Syrian after all.

What I did next makes me believe that I had had one over the eight myself. Having no cheque book with me, I got hold of a sheet of lavatory paper and a twopenny stamp, and, with these unlikely materials, there and then made out to the lieutenant a cheque for £85 sterling on the North Bank of Scotland at Montrose, payable in the U.K.. In return, he assigned to me full salvage rights and ownership of his car. He actually gave me its registration number, F (for Freetown) 1549. I had often seen it in barracks, but the transaction was completed between us without me ever having seen the state it was in after landing up at the bottom of a ravine.

The following day, I went out to inspect my purchase, and, if possible, to extricate it. With the help of some N.T.O. plant, which even included a bulldozer, I duly recovered it, and put it into M.T. workshops to be tidied up. As it turned out, the damage was not all that bad anyway. When I told my colleagues that I was proposing to get it back to Britain, they all laughed at me, declaring that I would never manage it and anyhow that it would cost a fortune. Nevertheless I persisted. I obtained the necessary export licence without any trouble at all; now all that remained for me to do was to find a ship.

At that time, the battleship King George was being used to transport troops back from the Far East, and she called at Freetown to re-fuel and take on water and provisions. I was instructed to visit the captain and lay on whatever he might require in the way of boats and motor transport. He asked me to have a drink with him in his cabin, and, while we were thus engaged, remarked what a God-forsaken place Freetown was, and what an awful time we must be having there. He wished, he said, that he could do something for me. I replied that it might be possible for him to do just that. Could he take my car back to the U.K.? At first his response was to laugh heartily at such a suggestion. It was now nearly noon on Saturday, he pointed out, and he would be sailing at seven p.m. He very much doubted whether I could manage it, but if, before sailing time, I could get my car aboard his ship, anchored though she was in the roads, he would take it for me.

As soon as I had returned from the battleship, it was down to work in earnest. I got the dockyard to flash up a huge fifty-ton shear-legs, laid down a wire cargo net with a tarpaulin on top, put the car onto this contraption, and with slings and shear-legs, hoisted it onto the stern of one of my tugs. Then off we set for King George V. No sooner had we started, than the black tugmaster ran the tug aground on a sandbank. Furious but unbeaten, I recovered the slings of the shear-legs, fitted an enormous wire to the towing bars of the tug, and told the shear-legs to pull us off. This was soon achieved. By 4.30 p.m. we were alongside the battleship.

All this time, I had been working with the blacks like a black myself. I must have looked like one too. I was covered in coal dust, probably hatless, and devoid of epaulettes. The officer of the watch, standing immaculate on the quarter deck, mistook us for a bumboat and told us to go away. I replied in a brand of Oxford English as impeccable as his own that the captain had given us permission to put the car aboard. "Wait a moment," he replied, and then, after a swift exchange of words on the telephone, we were under the crane, the car was off-loaded, and we were scudding back to our rat-hole in Kissy Dockyard. My car was delivered at Portsmouth in perfect order. It kept me going for two years, until I was able to buy a new one.

To return to my career in Freetown, I was still continuing the way of life I had worked out for myself. It did not include attending many parties of the "high society" type. Nevertheless, I was invited to a very grand wedding between a colonel of the R.A.M.C. and a war widow. Three days before she arrived in the colony, her husband had died of yellow fever. That had been three years before, and now here she was about to marry the colonel. The wedding was a very "upstage" affair — the biggest wedding the colony had seen since the war. To help it on, I had smuggled in cases of champagne from Konakry in French Guinea.

The Governor had a particularly high-sounding name; "Sir Hilary Blood", I believe it was. At the reception, I was standing just behind him and the Controller of Customs. The time came for the main toast to be drunk, and at that point the Governor exclaimed that he had not seen champagne like this for years. To this the Controller of Customs replied: "I would like to know where they got it from!" If they ever discovered the answer to this question, they never let on!

Another upper-crust function that I attended was a curry dinner, at which about twelve people were present. It was held at the house of the assistant chief of police, Assistant Commissioner Turnbull. It was a pretty formal affair, and I was probably the most junior of any service officers present — if, indeed, not the only officer present from the armed services. Some high-ranking civil servant had recently brought out his bride, and this was her first experience of the tropics. I was sitting about six feet away from her when she began to fill her plate with hot peppers and gingers, far too many of them and far too hot even for my gin-rotted guts. I froze in horror, quite unable, by reason of my lowly status, to scream out the warning that was on my lips. Helplessly, I looked on as she spooned up a mouthful of all the hottest varieties on the plate. Two seconds later she detonated, and was rushed upstairs by two elderly memsahibs who had seen many a tenderfoot virgin collapse in similar fashion.

In August of the same year, in the course of a game of squash with Tony Keeling, he asked me to come to dinner afterwards with Commissioner Ward and two colleagues of his at the police mess. One of the two colleagues was a man named Ted Grange, an ex-prison warder from Armley Jail in Leeds, whose only claim to fame was that he had been on scaffold duty when Dr. Buck Ruxton was hanged. Ruxton had been one of the most notorious murderers of the thirties. It had been intended that Grange should join the prison service at Pademba Road, but the police were short-staffed, and somehow he had transferred to them, starting off as an assistant superintendent, the lowest rank at which a white policeman could join. He was a somewhat graceless fellow, and politically left wing, so that we often clashed. On this occasion, even before dinner we were all pretty inebriated. It must be remembered that this was Commissioner Ward's dinner, and that he was the chief of police in the colony. Suddenly, however, forgetting all protocol, Grange rose from the dinner table saying: "I can't sit at the same table as that Fascist, Forsyth-Grant". He then stormed out of the room. No one took the slightest notice, or was in the least put out, least of all Commissioner Ward.

Ten minutes after he had left, however, a black policeman rushed into the room exclaiming: "Masser Grange, he had bad accident in car. He not well". Rather bored, we went to the scene of the trouble. Once outside, Grange had driven a police car straight into a wall, wrecked the front of it, and then passed out at the wheel, probably from concussion. In any case we were not particularly interested. The Commissioner simply told the black police to take Masser Grange to his bed and leave him there. Then we returned to continue our interrupted dinner.

Meanwhile, a one-hour hurricane, a phenomenon not uncommon in those parts, had struck Freetown with immense ferocity. It had brought sheets of rain, thunder and lightning, and hurricane-force winds. I had come on my motorbike, but had no intention of driving back in such weather, so I waited, drinking of course, until calm was restored. Then, after saying farewell and thankyou, I returned to my cabin-bungalow in Kissy Barracks.

I had certainly imbibed more than was good for me, for as I lay on my bed in the dark, I seemed to see things spinning before my eyes. the night was now still, but all at once I heard a major commotion on the waterfront six hundred yards away. Bleary-eyed, I started my motorbike and rode to the pierhead. There I was met by my personal coxswain, Chief Petty Officer James P. Danielson, West African Navy. This man, who was two years younger than myself and the son of a tribal chief, was the finest specimen of manhood I ever met in West Africa, loyal, utterly efficient, smart, and highly disciplined. He now told me that six white sailors from visiting sloops were missing. Boats returning liberty men to their ships had overturned in the hurricane. Several of the white sailors had been rescued, but six were still missing. Within a matter of seconds I was sober, and ordered the search which had already been started to be continued. In the end, we retrieved all but three of the missing men, and those three had to be posted as missing, presumed drowned.

By the time all this was finished, it was two a.m., and I was very weary and stone-cold sober. I made my way to the commander's night quarters. Commander Black R.N. had retired as long ago as the thirties at a far lower rank than his present acting one. It was he who had ordered my exit from the Wardroom some months before. Now he greeted me in fairly alcoholic fashion. He congratulated me on the rescue work, but changed his tone

Chief Petty Officer Danielson, R. West African Navy

completely when the officer arrived who had been on duty in the Barracks at the time of the disaster. This was Sub Lieutenant (Special Branch) Brastead, and to him the commander was thoroughly abusive. To the uninitiated, I should explain that Navy Special Branch had nothing to do with the police. It comprised many officers who, though enlisted in the R.N.V.R. in wartime, had, for various reasons (usually medical), been pronounced unfit for sea or for combat duties. They could still perform useful administration work ashore, thereby releasing others to fight. They were analogous to those who were miscalled "the wingless wonders" in the R.A.F.

As we left together, Brastead was almost in tears. The poor boy was only about twenty, and had probably been at some university for the early part of the war. Unlike hardened old sweats like myself, he had never seen people die. Now I had no high opinion of Black, and had often been extremely rude to him myself. As Brastead poured out his misgivings to me, I was anxious to save him some self-respect. While he was speaking, I interjected a few remarks to the effect that no one could possibly have forecast the hurricane that had caused the disaster. Once outside the Commander's Quarters, however, I spoke more openly. I insisted that Brastead himself had done his best, exactly as I would have done, and that he should just forget the abuse to which he had been subjected. Finally, for the second time that night, I returned to bed, where I slept like a log and awoke in the morning completely refreshed.

At the time of which I am speaking, the splendid Commodore Menzies had been replaced by another most able active service officer, Captain de Winton R.N.. He, I believe, had acquitted himself quite outstandingly in Atlantic destroyers. It was with the greatest pleasure that I worked under these experienced, battle-trained leaders. What a contrast to certain of the officers resuscitated from the peacetime Navy (the "dugouts", as they were somewhat contemptuously known), who had seen no active service under modern conditions! At the same time, it would be most unjust to forget the heroic work done by some of these Naval officers of the pre-war vintage, including several admirals who became commodores of convoys.
commodores of convoys.

In the aftermath of the disaster I have just described, Captain de Winton sent for me to tell me that one of the bodies of the drowned sailors had been washed ashore at a remote spot called Lungi, some thirty miles away on the mouth of the Sierra Leone river. He wanted me to lead an expeditionary force to find the body. A doctor was to carry out a post mortem and assign the cause of death, and a padre was to conduct a funeral service. This was a much tougher proposition than it might appear. I had to organize a B Class M.L. to tow a launch, with another surf boat in tow, and, through sandbanks and huge Atlantic rollers, land a party of about twelve, including a surgeon lieutenant commander and a padre, on a piece of unknown coast.

After some initial "hairy moments", which looked pretty serious at the time, we arrived safely at Lungi, and found and identified the body. The doctor carried out his post mortem, while I and some sailors dug through some very tough shale stone called laterite to make the grave. I rather believe that I expedited the digging operations by firing a charge of amatol, so as to ensure that the grave was of sufficient depth. At all events, in the end, the mission was completed. Sadly, albeit with a certain sense of a job well done, we sailed back to Kissy without further "casualties or damage".

By now, Wallace had recovered from the gunshot wounds that I had accidentally inflicted on him, and we were still the best of friends, visiting one another regularly. On arriving back from the burial party, therefore, I had a quick bath and change, and was just in time to meet Wallace for a drink, dinner, and the weekly cinema.

While we were in the bar, Brastead came over to commiserate with me and ask me to describe the events of the day. He showed himself still emotionally very upset, and I told him not to be stupid; that I had seen too many deaths before to be upset by them, and that this was simply one more. I also invited him to join us hard-bitten old bastards for dinner and the cinema. However, he declined. Instead, he went off alone and hanged himself. That, I felt, was a tragedy indeed, and a terrible one.

Drummond Taylor's wife was dying of cancer, and on these grounds he had claimed Class B Release for demobilization. I, however, had no such claims upon me, and when I told Captain de Winton that I was in no hurry to go home, he was delighted. I think he suspected me of being slightly mad, and no wonder! By other people's standards I certainly was, but I was enjoying every minute of my life in the colony.

I never really saved money, except for the purpose of buying worthwhile presents for my parents, yet I undoubtedly prospered. I lived better then than I had ever lived before, or was ever to live again for many years. In my own way, I lived the life of a colonial sub-ruler of the old empire days, with a personal staff of about twenty blacks, all paid for by the Navy. I even had my own gun-bearer and tracker, whom I inherited from Juba Kennerley, and I also inherited his English name; it was Pig's bladder! "Pig's bladder — where the hell are you, Pig's bladder?", I used to roar in stentorian tones, and the other whites used to collapse with mirth.

My Naval and civil pay combined was at least £20 a week. As for my food, clothing and accommodation, that was all paid for by the Navy. At golf, caddies and other attendants could be had for ninepence (old money) per person per round. Thus, when I played, as I sometimes did, at Lumley Beach, I could afford to do it in style. I used to have no less than five black attendants accompanying me: caddie, umbrella man, drink-bearer, rifle-man (carrying my .22 for shooting doves out of palm trees when I was bored), and a frontsman, who was well accustomed to my ways, and stood at the limit of my golf shot to recover my ball in case I landed in the rough.

Of course, minor hiccups used to occur from time to time. The blacks were gaining more power. They were already making moves to assert their authority and rid themselves of us colonizers. I had my own form of local intelligence which served me well, and, for reasons which I will not now disclose, I was even better served by my friends in the Black African Independence Movement. I also had valuable informants among the rich

Syrians, Lebanese, and Indians, who feared the emergence of a black republic. I enjoyed it all; the scheming, the bribing, the fraternizing, the drinking of beer and black coffee, the ability to go where few other Europeans ever trod. After all, it was while I was there that Graham Green wrote his best seller, *The Heart of the Matter*. Though he states that his characters are fictional, I believe I could have named them all. All in all, I learnt to handle the Navy, the police, and the black republicans.

During this period, the black magistrates used to use their authority to indulge their hostility towards the whites, particularly servicemen. On one occasion, two white petty officers, who had run down and killed a black pedestrian while driving a navy truck, were indicted for manslaughter. Questions were already being asked in the Westminster parliament about their arrest, and the captain's office instructed me to do what I could for the accused men.

At this time, I had a number of other problems on hand, so I told my second-in-command, Sub Lieutenant Westcott, to see what he could do at the coroner's inquest. I assured him that I would back him to the hilt. He returned. That same afternoon, a black gentleman, unknown to me, knocked at my door and entered, saying that he wanted an exide accumulator for his car. I explained politely that the Navy did not deal in such small types of goods. "Oh," he said, "I must explain. I am the coroner of Freetown, and the verdict was accidental death." "Wait," I replied, "we have a new battery waiting for you to collect." We both bowed politely, well satisfied with our conduct of the day's business.

By December 1945, great efforts were being made to get rid of war stores and even ships. Even the huge liner, Edinburgh Castle, which had served as a depot ship in Freetown, was taken out to deep water and sunk by gunfire. B Class Fairmiles and H.D. M.L.s were being sold for about £200 apiece, and those that were not sold were burnt. Yet the Gardner engines of those H.D. M.L.s alone were worth over £3,000 each in Britain at that time, and some of those returning to the U.K. bought them and sailed home in them.

Juba Kennerley had tons of unwanted explosives to dump in the sea, but we purloined a considerable quantity of amatol for explosive fishing, a practice which was strictly illegal. By these means, we were able to glean many a good basket of both sea and freshwater fish for the table. Again, hundreds of valuable watches were placed on anvils and smashed with a sledgehammer. It was in accordance with a deal which the government had made with the manufacturers during the war, so that markets would not be excessively flooded with surplus government stores.

One day, I visited the armament stores to find brand new ammunition trucks being destroyed, together with their 16 x 4 rubber tyres. Now back in Britain tyres of this size were desperately needed for wheelbarrows. I begged a torpedo box from Kennerley, and into it I stuffed wheels and axles, until the entire vast package weighed over two tons. Now the Navy operated a scheme whereby the personal luggage of officers serving abroad could be transported home and delivered to their doors free of charge. I took my two-ton box to H.M.S. Unicorn, an aircraft carrier, and a crane hoisted it aboard. An officer asked me what it contained, and I replied that it was my tennis gear, golf clubs etc. Despite the unusual weight, the Navy's undertaking was in this case fulfilled to the letter. The box, with its contents, was duly delivered to Montrose, with the result that before long all the broken-down iron-wheeled barrows on my father's farms were sporting the latest that Dunlop could provide!

At length it became increasingly borne in upon me that now that the war was finally over, there was no excuse for continuing to maintain a major naval presence in Freetown. When even the B. M.L.s and H.D. M.L.s were being sold off, it was time for me too to sell up and go home.

CHAPTER SIXTEEN

Hunting for Elephant in the Wilds

It was now the turn of Juba Kennerley to join the general exodus, and I saw him off by air on Christmas eve. My own demobilization was long overdue, but, as I have already explained, though I could see the writing on the wall, I was in no hurry to leave. Soon after Kennerley's departure, however, I was told that I would be Senior Officer of a group of three large trawlers which were due to be sailed back to the U.K. in late February or thereabouts. I was to be given command of H.M.S. Arran.

Before leaving Africa, I had intended to take a last leave in Portuguese East Africa. Friends of my father in Rhodesia were organizing a big game safari there and I had been invited to join. However, by this stage my health was completely undermined by amoebic dysentery, malaria, and other tropical diseases, which I had picked up in the course of my shooting forays. I therefore decided that before I left, I would spend a final two weeks' leave on an elephant shooting expedition with Ian Husband. It was to be in the wildest of the wilds of Sierra Leone.

Outside a circus or zoo, neither Ian nor I had ever seen an elephant. Nevertheless, because there had been no hunting during the war, elephants had multiplied enormously in the hinterland of Sierra Leone, and the local inhabitants were asking the government to have them culled. In no time, therefore, and without any cost, we were granted licences to shoot elephant. It was not permitted to shoot them with any shot under .450 calibre, so our next stop was to buy jointly a very ancient elephant gun, together with 50 rounds of ammunition. It was a single-shot Martini Action 577 rifle, and it cost us £5. Now we were legally equipped. Ian obtained leave a few days before me, and went up country ahead of me to a base camp, where I was to join him.

I set off in great style from R.N. Barracks. I had a lorry, and a personal retinue of fourteen Africans. These comprised a group of servants ranging from gun-bearer, cooks, and laundry boys, down to ordinary porters. Needless to say, most of them were on the

N.T.O. payroll. By way of armament, in addition to the Martini, I had a brand new Mauser rifle, which I had inherited as my part of the plunder from a U Boat. I was also taking with me my own .22 Browning and .375 Mannlicher, my shotguns, and a British service rifle, complete with mine-sinking, armour-piercing ammunition. This last, I felt, would be suitable for an elephant! For provisions I had raided the Naval Victualling Stores, and obtained corned beef, baked beans, herrings in tomato sauce, tinned bacon, and a large chest of whisky, gin, rum and brandy.

The first part of the journey took us through Port Lokko, but soon afterwards the road came to an end at the large Kaba River. I told the lorry to return to Freetown, hired canoes, and we crossed the Kaba. Thereafter everything had to be carried on the heads of the Africans. At dawn and dusk each day, I led my cavalcade, marching about six hours a day and camping in native villages at night. A major problem was the language, for the coast Africans do not speak the local tribal tongue. However, with the aid of maps and compasses, I found my way to the largest area village, where the paramount chief held court. The name of this village was Sendugu. From Sendugu I marched on to Kabala, on the Kolente or Great Scarcies River, which was roughly on the boundary between French Guinea and Sierra Leone. I was told that Ian was two days' march ahead of me and already hunting, so at this point I made my base camp and waited for his return.

The country was weird and wild. Many of the natives had never seen a white man before. In contrast to the game of the coastal regions, in this area the game birds had seldom been shot at, and were remarkably tame. In order to feed my retainers, I needed fresh meat or poultry, so I shot six large guineafowl with a single twelve-bore cartridge! It was quite unbelievable. I also bought eggs and poultry, either for cash, or for some of the textiles which I had bought in Freetown especially to barter with these people. Deer abounded, and so did hippo. The latter resembled three-ton boars. I knew that any one of them would provide food for my host for days, so I decided to shoot one. Picking out a huge bull swimming in the Kolente, I fired my Mauser at him. The beast sank without a splash, but I was sure that I had got it. Using sign language, one of the locals asked permission to dive in, but before agreeing to this, I threw in a Mills grenade to make sure that there were no crocodiles about. Only then did I let him go ahead.

He dived in and came straight up, and we saw at once that he had suffered an appalling injury. He had hit a rock, and the whole of his nose had been cut out of his forehead. We pulled him ashore, semi-conscious and in great agony. I doubt if any European could have survived such an accident, but — and I say this seriously, with no disrespect — Africans do have very thick skulls. I brought out my ever-present morphia omnipon and injected him, and we all tried to make him comfortable in the shade. I had no intention of moving him until the sun had begun to go down, so I returned to base and sent an urgent message for Ian to return. Not only was he part of the government, but he had with him the court messenger, or local native policeman, from the district commissioner.

I felt that the reaction of the local people to this incident might be a violent one, and shortly afterwards it seemed that my forebodings were about to be fulfilled. I was dozing in my camp bed in the late afternoon, when a crowd invaded my camp all shouting and gesticulating. I grabbed hold of my revolver under the pillow, but soon realized that the cause of their excitement was not what I had feared. The injured man had not died, but the hippo which I had shot had floated to the surface, and they were hauling it to the river bank by means of ropes made from vines. I arrived at the scene just as the huge bull was being beached. There, amid scenes of wild jubilation and great rounds of applause, I was photographed with my gun-bearer on top of the carcase. The poor beast was soon butchered, and huge legs of pork, cutlets, heart, and brains were being haggled over with great relish by the entire village. Personally, I did not fancy either the flesh itself or the beanfeast that was being held over it, and I was left, a solitary figure, in my base camp. I had rented a hut for the injured man, and native nurses were attending to all his needs.

After a day or so, Ian arrived with the court messenger, and all seemed well. We continued hunting, and ended up with three elephants, two hippo, and quantities of small game, with which to feed our retainers. My leave was much shorter than Ian's, and regretfully I was forced to leave him and return to the Naval barracks, but before that, a huge celebration was held, in which gifts were exchanged with the chief. It was the tradition to give two bottles of gin per elephant, as well as various presents of cloth and European clothing. Meanwhile the village beauties, aged between thirteen and sixteen and reputed to be virgins, were paraded for the great white hunters to take their pick for the night.

The next day our miniature army footslogged its way back past Sendugu, where I rested for at least three hours at midday in the shade of a native hut, and so on to the Kaba River. One day, in the course of this return journey, I awoke with a start as a loud commotion broke out. A crowd was carrying a young black on a litter. He had been badly injured by the horn of a semi-domesticated bush cow, which had suddenly attacked and gored him. He was brought to me, as the great white doctor, to undergo whatever treatment I prescribed. I did carry a very extensive first aid kit, and of course I started with the invaluable morphia omnipon. Then I got to work with bandages and sticking plaster. We had decided to take the injured man with us, so when we resumed our march at three p.m., we had two casualties accompanying us. Whether they were on litters or able to walk, I cannot now remember.

On arriving at the banks of the Kaba, we searched for canoes to ferry us over. From the river we made our way to the roadhead, and there, at last, we were able to hire a lorry from a banana plantation to bus us back to Port Lokko. I arrived at the mission station, where there was a resident white doctor, but unfortunately he was up country. I therefore handed over the casualties to a black orderly. Later the doctor wrote me a pleasing letter in which he congratulated me on my first aid, and said that the two injured men were restored to good health.

How we managed to obtain transport from Port Lokko back to Naval barracks I cannot recall, but what I do remember is that when we did finally arrive, the sentries at the barracks at first failed to recognize me, and refused to let me in. In the circumstances it was, perhaps, understandable. I was absolutely filthy, I had not shaved for days, and in place of uniform, I was wearing torn and stained mufti. However, after a good bath and a shave, I was back in the Wardroom for dinner, as if I had just had a day out on Lumley golf course.

CHAPTER SEVENTEEN

The Voyage Home

Within days of my return from my shooting expedition, I handed over my responsibilities as N.T.O. into the very capable hands of Dick Westcott. Some time later, he too was to make a fresh start, in his case in Rhodesia, where he quickly rose to the top as Commissioner of Native Affairs, remaining in this post until the Marxists took over.

Meanwhile, I took command of H.M.S. Arran, the officers and crew of which were new. They were all whites and, like myself, were going back to the U.K. for demobilization. Some of them, being shore-based personnel, had barely been to sea in their lives, and the same was true of the crews of the other two ships under my command as Senior Officer of the group, H.M.S. Oxna and H.M.S. Copinsay. Technically, these were Isle Class trawlers, but having been built for fighting rather than fishing, they could almost have been classed as corvettes. With Captain de Winton's consent, I spent a few days getting the crews better trained, and once this was completed, we sailed for the U.K.

A few days after we had put to sea, a wireless message was received instructing me to put into Dakar or Bathurst. The father of one of our officers, Lieutenant B.G. Allsworth, had died, and he was to be flown home. That night, as I was resting in my cabin, the navigator shouted down my voice-pipe that we were running aground, and that he could see huge breakers ahead. I rushed to the bridge, and rapidly altered course by over ninety degrees, signalling to the other ships to follow me. To this day, I cannot understand why we were on the wrong course. The navigator responsible was alleged to be well qualified, yet he had made an enormous and rudimentary error. Instead of lashing into him, I told him to have a couple of hours sleep below, while I took over the rest of his watch. (This was unusual. When there are over three watch-keeping officers, it is not the normal practice for the captain to take a watch himself; unless or until he explicitly says he is taking over, he confines himself to appearing from time to time to supervise the officer of the watch.) On this occasion, I was quite happy to take over. The crisis was past and we were back on course. In fact, I was rather enjoying the rise and fall of the ship, when suddenly I felt myself turning faint. I remember crashing to the deck and a frightened look-out shouting: "Christ — the skipper's passed out!" In a sense that was true. I could neither see nor speak and I was paralysed. Yet all the time I was able to hear.

Gently I was carried below, and I realized that I was now back on my bunk. A splendid and most efficient rating, who must have been my personal steward, tried to force some tea into my mouth, but after a time he gave up the attempt as useless. I simply lay there paralysed.

About seven hours later, I found that I could move my fingers a little, and then at last my sight returned. The steward came back, and this time, with great difficulty, I managed to drink the tea. Then once more he left me for an hour or so. Before noon that day I was out of my bunk, though still feeling, and obviously looking, extremely poorly. However, as the day went on, I improved, and by evening we had made the port of Bathurst, where we tied up for the night.

Bathurst had no Navy personnel, but I was examined by the Chief Medical Officer, who said that it was imperative for me to abandon the voyage and come ashore for treatment. He then left, saying that he would see me again in the morning. The following day I decided to hand over command to my Number One. There appeared to be no hospital in Bathurst, which meant that I would also have to find accommodation of some sort. I put on civilian clothes, complete with my Old Wellingtonian tie (How much that has done for me both before and since!), and then made my way to the Senior Civil Servants' Club. Before long, a member came up to say that he had been at Wellington, and to ask me when I was there. It turned out that he was the Colonial Secretary, next in rank to the Governor. Once I had explained my plight to him, he most kindly invited me to stay at his house. With the utmost regret, therefore, I left H.M.S. Arran, and she sailed for home.

At this point, I must pause in my story to explain something of the background of health problems which had led to my collapse. By early 1946, my health had been truly appalling; that, of course, had been my reason for cancelling my trip to Portuguese East Africa. At the time I had undergone several weeks' treatment at the hands of a black doctor who had qualified in Cambridge, and whose skill in the field of tropical medicine was far superior to that of the Naval surgeons stationed at Kissy. I had been suffering from constant fevers, diarrhoea and constipation. In fact, when I passed out aboard Arran, my bowels had not opened at all for ten days — this in spite of my taking large quantities of aperients. After examining me and hearing my tale, the Bathurst doctor told me that he was going to give me the largest dose of castor oil he had ever administered. He did so and . . . nothing happened! He was flabbergasted. Then at last, slowly and without any rush, my bowels did open again, and I felt a little more comfortable.

Soon afterwards, I received a telegram from F.O.G.M.A. (Flag Officer, Gibraltar and Mediterranean Approaches), instructing me to fly home to the U.K. as soon as I could obtain a seat on a plane. However, as it turned out, it was nearly two weeks before I could do this. When I finally did manage to book one, it was on a British South American Airways plane starting at Buenos Aires, landing at Natal in Brazil, and with Bathurst the next stop after that. It was then due to fly overnight to Lisbon, and so on to London the following day. At the end of my two weeks' sojourn, therefore, I found myself waiting for my plane at Gambia Airport. I waited . . . and waited. Finally, three hours after the plane had been due to land, it was announced that it had crashed at Natal, killing everybody on board.

Sombrely, I returned to the house of my kind host, to stay with him until I could book myself onto another plane. Then F.O.G.M.A. sent me another telegram, this time instructing me to fly to Gibraltar for further orders. There was, I found, no direct flight from Gambia to Gibraltar, so I flew to Rabat in Morocco, and spent the night in an R.A.F. transit mess there. Next day, a large party of all ranks and all three services were told to board a troop-dropping Dakota for Gibraltar. It had no seats, only roof-straps similar to those used on the underground. No one counted numbers or checked weights. We were simply stuffed inside until it could hold no more, at which point we took off. With a great bump, we hit the ground again, and a large number of the passengers were thrown against one another. Another mighty bump followed, and then finally we became truly airborne. The plane seemed grossly overloaded, and on arriving at Gibraltar we nearly overshot the runway. However, we had arrived safely and in one piece.

The following day I reported to the office of F.O.G.M.A., where I was told that a mutiny had taken place at Las Palmas aboard one, if not all, of the trawlers which had initially been under my command when I left Sierra Leone. I was to go there, resume command, and bring them to Gibraltar. A destroyer would ferry me to Las Palmas in a few days time. Meanwhile, until all this could be arranged, I was to stay at the Bristol Hotel, at the same time undergoing examination by the medical people for my tropical diseases. When I reported for this, the medical staff at Gibraltar, who were pretty efficient, were aghast at my condition. They said that I must return to a temperate climate forthwith. Abandoning its original plan, F.O.G.M.A. concurred, and I was detailed within the next few days to join the destroyer Tuscan as a passenger for Portsmouth.

Nearly all my kit was still in H.M.S. Arran, and I had no warm clothes to wear in the chill spring of the U.K. Moreover, the Naval paymaster with whom I had to deal refused to give me any subs; he had been "conned" too often by those undergoing rapid demobilization. In the end, I had recourse to Gieves, the famous Naval and Military tailors. They were marvellous. Having checked that I had a long-standing account with them, they gave me all the clothes I wanted, a suitcase to put them in, and £50 spending money.

The journey home was uneventful. It was not the first time that I had had dealings with the Commander of Tuscan, Lt. Cdr. Lewis. During the D Day landings his destroyer had been in collision with H.M.C.S. Athabaskan, and he had had to face court martial proceedings. At the time he had asked me to defend him, but I had been unable to comply. I never asked him any of the details of how his trial had gone, but at any rate, here he was still in command of her.

Once I arrived in Portsmouth, I found that my car had been safely and most kindly delivered by the battleship, H.M.S. King George V. At not a penny cost, there it was, waiting for me to collect it. The following day I reached home, and had the enormous pleasure of being reunited with all my family, for now that the war was over, the other members too had returned from their various battle stations. Not surprisingly, the Admiralty "lost" me for several weeks, but the boss of my old company said that it was time that I made up my mind whether I wanted to stay in the Navy or rejoin them. I therefore took the next train to London, and the following day I was demobilized. After nearly seven years in the Navy, I was a civilian once more.

PART VI

Return to the Peacetime R.N.V.R.

H.M.S. Montrose at the Coronation Fleet Review

CHAPTER EIGHTEEN

Back to the R.N.V.R. in Dundee

Following upon my demobilization, came an uneasy period when I was slowly readjusting to civilian life. One day, however, I received a telephone call from Captain D.R. Miller R.N.V.R. in Dundee to tell me that he was re-forming the reserves there under Tay Division R.N.V.R.. He hoped, he said, that all pre-war officers who were still in the neighbourhood would rejoin. Within a year I had done so. In fact, of the midshipmen who had been in Unicorn's gunroom in 1939, four now came back, in addition to about five of the higher ranks. With these as the nucleus of our force, therefore, we settled down to resume peacetime training.

In late 1948, each of the R.N.V.R. Divisions was given a motor minesweeper of the single-screw, wooden hull type that had given invaluable service in wartime. Our ship, refitted with the latest equipment, was to be called H.M.S Montrose in honour of Commodore the Duke of Montrose, who had founded the R.N.V.R.. The commanding officer was to be the staff officer supplied by the Admiralty. He would be a serving officer in the R.N. of lieutenant commander's rank. It was not long before we were training in our ship on day and week-end trips, as well as taking part in numerous other activities.

In 1943, the Commander of H.M.S. Attack, the Coastal Forces Training Flotilla, in which I had served, had been Douglas Miller. He had now risen to the rank of captain. He was a most forceful character, who not only knew how to get his own way, but had powerful friends in the Department of Admiral Commanding Reserves. He now pressed for an R.N.V.R. officer to command H.M.S. Montrose for the day trips and week-ends. The lengths that Miller went to to get this idea off the ground — as well as to secure a duty-free licence for us! — were magnificent. It would involve a change which was highly revolutionary, and was certainly never contemplated in peacetime conditions prior to 1939. Nevertheless, Captain Miller persuaded the Admiralty to try the experiment, and it was suggested that I should be appointed to command

H.M.S. Montrose for a seventeen-day trip to the Western Isles. Only two of us in Tay Division had held command of H.M. ships during the war, and for this initial cruise I was lucky enough to be selected.

When we finally sailed, we were still missing a whole range of essential items, including charts of the treacherous Minch and Pentland Firth, through which we would have to sail. However, if we had waited for all the requirements for which we had indented in due form, and which were necessary from the strictly legal point of view, we would never have got off in 1949 at all. We made Inverness, and stopped for the day at Corpach, at the south-west terminus of the canal.

One of the people I had met in Eastern Scotland in the course of shooting had been a certain Joe Hobbs. He had bought Inverlochy Castle, and had started the Great Glen Cattle Ranch, a tremendous cattle enterprise, and at that time unprecedented throughout the U.K. It had been inaugurated with much publicity and acclaim on the part of the Socialist Secretary for Scotland, Hector MacNeil. Joe was a very rich man; he had made a vast fortune in Canada and the U.S.A. during the Prohibition era, and, in more ways than one, had considerable experience of the sea. We had become close friends, and now he sent a Rolls Royce to the ship to collect me and several others for tea at Inverlochy, which struck me at the time as being plushier and better maintained than Balmoral itself.

Joe told us that he had instituted a lawsuit against the British Aluminium Company at Fort William, to stop the pollution of the atmosphere by hydro-fluoric acid; it was causing the teeth of his cattle to fall out. It was a case of David versus Goliath, but in the end, I believe, Joe won. Whatever the outcome, of its kind it was the biggest lawsuit of the decade in Scotland. That evening, after we had taken our leave of Joe, we decided to visit Fort William, and at the Grand Hotel there I ran into Sandy Kinnear, who had been a midshipman with me in 1940. He was now forestry manager for British Aluminium at Fort William. He launched into a tirade against Joe Hobbs, saying what a terrible chap he was. We did not dare to tell him that we had just been visiting his bete noire! Sandy was subsequently to rise to the post of chief land agent of the whole of that vast conglomerate at Fort William.

The day following this visit, we took a pilot on board to take us through the dangerous sandbanks at Fort William. While we were in the Wardroom, I offered him a cigarette. A candle was spluttering on the table at the time, and he produced a spill to light his cigarette from it. To my astonishment, I realized that it was a pound note of the British Bank of West Africa. Thereupon, he told us the following story.

During the war, a freighter carrying tin boxes of freshly printed West African currency had been sunk off the west coast of Scotland, and some of the tins had washed ashore. The locals had purloined them, and had illegally attempted to cash them. The police had arrived, with customs and other officers, and several of the locals had been prosecuted. No more money had been exchanged, and the old notes had simply been used as lighter spills. This story has a curious end to it. Thirty years later, a London salvage company consisting of about four divers and three labourers, bought the wreck and salvaged the metal, together with the money. To use it as currency was, of course, illegal, but nevertheless that is what they were accused of doing in both Zurich and Amsterdam. They were, I believe, caught. All this I read in the press many years after the meeting with our pilot at Corpach.

On passage from Fort William to Oban, I received a signal instructing me to leave the ship at Oban and, in company with three other officers, proceed by rail to Liverpool to row in the Northern R.N.V.R. Officers' Championships. I left the ship in the hands of the "surviving" Senior Officer, and we duly arrived at breakfast time at Liverpool's Adelphi Hotel.

Having nothing better to do until early afternoon, when the boat races began, we decided to explore the heavily-bombed Liverpool docks and see how the re-building programme was progressing. Suddenly I began to feel ill. I asked my companions to continue the tour without me, while I went back to rest in the foyer of the Adelphi. By the time I had parked myself in a comfortable seat, I was feeling so awful that I thought I was about to die. Sweat came pouring down my face, I was convulsed with shooting pains, and hot one minute, cold the next. I realized that this was a return of the maladies from which I had suffered in West Africa. Seeing what an appalling state I was in, the head porter asked whether he should get a doctor. I managed to reply that I preferred to wait for my colleagues. When they arrived soon afterwards, they too were horrified by my appearance. They called a taxi and took me to the School of Tropical Medicines. The doctor, who was highly experienced, said that he did not believe I was about to die, but that in no circumstances was I to row in the Officers' Boat Race.

We were now in a terrible quandary. No spare officer could possibly be found to take my place, and my colleagues, both those who had come from Dundee direct, and those who had accompanied me from the minesweeper at Oban, had been to enormous pains, and expended much time and energy, in order to get to Liverpool for the race. Desperately ill though I felt, I was not going to let my chums down. In defiance of the doctor's warnings, I did row in the race. Of the race itself I remember almost nothing; all I know is that against half a dozen other contenders we actually won it! A huge celebration drinks party and dinner followed, attended by about two hundred people. I barely managed to keep my feet or my seat at table without either passing out or being sick. It was one of the worst ordeals which I have ever faced. Even as I endured it, I was aware of another looming ahead, and I was not looking forward to that either. After dinner we were to catch the 11.30 train to Wigan, change onto the Stirling train, then change at Stirling for Oban, and so arrive back at the ship the following day.

Somehow I survived that awful journey, and by the time I had rejoined H.M.S. Montrose at Oban, I was feeling quite recovered; all the fever and the aches and pains had disappeared. This was the first experience of a plague from which I was to suffer for twenty years after leaving West Africa, but it was one of the worst attacks I would ever have to endure. In most of the others I lost consciousness for a time!

From Oban we sailed to Stornoway. It was here, nine years before, while serving in H.M.S. Shower, that I had had my first sexual experience with a girl, for at that time the local populace had accorded the visiting troops an ecstatic reception. Now, in 1949, things were different. Stornoway was full of "illegits.", who had been fathered by the forces during their stay; hence Stornoway no longer wanted the likes of ourselves. After being treated for the space of twenty-four hours as unwanted guests, we departed.

Though we did have some charts, they did not include any covering the area between Stornoway and Duncansby Head, so that it was without a chart that we had to navigate those extremely dangerous waters of the Minch and Pentland Firth. This was downright criminal; had anything gone wrong, a civil enquiry or court martial would have been convened, and it would undoubtedly have been condemned as such.

However, expediency is the mother of invention, and we made our own chart. Lieutenant Rennie Stewart had been a R.E.M.E. captain in Burma during the war, and was an expert on improv'sation. He now produced a chart by combining information from two unlikely sources: Dunlop's *Road Map of Great Britain*, and a book called *The West Coast Pilot*, which provides a detailed description of the coastline and certain soundings round that part of Scotland's barren outline. Thus we sailed from a hostile shore.

Over half our crew were only eighteen years old, volunteers who had never served in the war. When, therefore, we ran into a truly savage storm in the Minch, they were terribly seasick. The same was true of some of the officers, who had seen service on battleships and cruisers, and were unaccustomed to small minesweepers. Hence we were hard put to it to find enough personnel fit for duty. The rain gave way to fog, and at one point we nearly ran aground on the Island of Handa, which loomed up — need I say, unexpectedly? — far too close for safety. Still the storm raged, and I decided that I would not sail on through the night. We made our way safely into Loch Inchard and there dropped anchor.

Loch Inchard was beautiful and calm, and I sped ashore in our motor boat. My purpose was to telephone my naval superiors ashore from the Garbert Arms Hotel at Kinlochbervie. Some of us, both officers and crew, were due to attend the R.N.V.R. Rowing Championships in London in seventy-two hours time. By this time I had had my fill of train journeys and rowing, and had declined to compete, but two of my officers were keen, and, to the delight of all concerned, I undertook to land them at Aberdeen within the next thirty-six hours, so that they could entrain for London.

The following day, the quartermaster called me at four a.m., and I sniffed the air on deck. Above the steep sides of the loch the clouds were racing, yet press on I must. Up anchor, and we were away. To describe the Minch as rough would be a complete understatement. Once round the well-named Cape Wrath, however, we were in calmer seas. Off Thurso, in fact, the sea was dead calm. When I threw a penny over the side, I was able to trace its course down several feet before it disappeared. I scanned the Old Man of Hoy in the Orkneys as we passed, and images flashed back into my mind of mighty gun exercises of years gone by, and of the immense power of battleships and cruisers as we manoeuvred with the Home Fleet. By this time, I reflected, it was a mere skeleton as compared with those hectic war years.

On to Duncansby Head and the Moray Firth. About one a.m., I told the officer of the watch that he seemed to be steaming the wrong course. If he continued, instead of clearing Kinnaird Head, he would ram Macduff. Politely he replied that the helmsman was steering the correct course. I was puzzled. Then I discovered that someone had left a loud hailer "mike" on top of a compass, which was registering an error of forty-five degrees. We altered the course, and said farewell to Macduff.

It was about six a.m. when we entered Aberdeen, and there was a heavy swell. Aberdeen is not a nice harbour in an easterly, but I duly landed the officers and troops who were to catch the train for the rowing championships. Then back to sea again and off to Dundee, where we secured in the Earl Gray Dock that afternoon.

That was the first time a warship had been commanded by an R.N.V.R. officer in peacetime, not counting the continuation of the state of emergency after the war had ended. The trip had proved a success. Before long, it was to become routine practice for R.N.V.R. officers to command R.N.V.R. minesweepers. We had shown the way.

CHAPTER NINETEEN

Cruises Farther Afield and a Sojourn in Portsmouth

Our 1949 cruises had been acclaimed as a success, and in 1950 I had the honour of being offered a far more ambitious cruise. We would sail down the North Sea to Dover, and thence to Boulogne and Ostend, thereby including both France and Belgium in our itinerary. As we were rather stuck for any form of shore transport, I decided that this time I would take my motorbike with me.

To see Dover again, and actually to berth in the Submarine Basin, from which I had seen so many fighting patrols set out seven years earlier, was an interesting experience indeed. From there we sailed, according to plan, to Boulogne, where I rented a room in a poor class of hotel, with the sole purpose of having a bath when we needed it. We found, however, that this was strictly forbidden! Only the registered guests might use the bath. I was a philatelist, though only on a decidedly amateurish scale, so when I saw, in a shop window, stamps of the German occupation with Hitler's head upon them, I immediately bought them. As I was paying, the old lady who served me spat out the following caustic remark: "The Germans very bad, but the English worse!" Because of the heavy bombing which such people had had to endure before the Germans were driven out, we were far from popular.

Damage to boats was much in evidence, and, because of the huge marine minefields still remaining, for many years to come, shipping would have to stick to carefully swept channels known as "Nemedri routes". On our second day at Boulogne, a French frigate did actually blow up with great loss of life; at the time it was believed to have hit a mine. Years later, however, I came across an account in a book which I was reading to the effect that in fact the ship was blown up by a time bomb. The individual who had organized its planting, it was said, was none other than the famous Soviet spymaster, Colonel Rudolph Abel. This was the man who was finally unmasked and imprisoned in the U.S.A., only to be exchanged soon afterwards for Gary Powers, the pilot of the notorious U.S. spy plane shot down over the Soviet Union.

A friendly football match was arranged: the crew of H.M.S. Montrose versus the Boulogne football team, who had just beaten Arsenal A. The match turned out somewhat of a fiasco, for we lost thirty nil!

At Boulogne, I had great difficulty in getting my motorbike ashore. In the end we bamboozled the dockers into off-loading it for us with a twenty-ton crane. Thereafter I had the greatest fun exploring all the ports, such as Etaples, Berck and Le Touquet, which I had raided during the war. On one occasion during our stay, we used my motorbike to ferry four of us at the same time to Calais. However, after a brief visit, we were quite pleased to leave; the native population, from the Maquis captain commanding the port down to the ordinary dockers, struck us as devious and unfriendly.

Our next port of call was Ostend, but here we discovered, to our horror, that the British First Sea Lord, Admiral of the Fleet Lord Fraser of Northcape, had just arrived in H.M.S. Redpole, a sloop, to inspect the Belgian Navy. Dutifully, I called to pay my respects, and was introduced to him by the Secretary, Captain (S) Aulfrey R.N.. Aulfrey's younger brother had been at school with me, and this paved the way for a very pleasant interview.

To make way for Lord Fraser's staff, H.M.S. Redpole had been cleared of most of its technical officers, with the result that before long we in Montrose received a signal from her asking whether we had a doctor, as a rating had very serious toothache. We sent over a Surgeon Lieutenant (Dentist). Soon after, another signal was transmitted, asking us to send back the Surgeon Lieutenant (D); he might be able to help with a rating who had broken his ankle. This time we sent over a Surgeon Commander. The next day Redpole had trouble with its electrical layout, and yet another signal arrived for the humble minesweeper: "Do you carry an Electrical Officer?" We sent over a Lieutenant Commander Electrical. Lord Fraser treated all this as a huge joke. He sent a signal of thanks, in which he added jocularly: "I am thinking of transferring my flag to you!" Of course it was not the practice for minesweepers of the class of Montrose to carry technical officers, whether medical, dental or electrical, but on annual training cruises a number of officers, including "brass hats", used to queue up for such chances as this of seeing Europe.

During our stay, a luncheon banquet was given by the port in honour of the First Sea Lord, and I was included in the invitations. It was quite the largest meal I have ever seen. After eating a huge steak, and believing I had won, I found myself being presented with a whole partridge!" I was reduced to picking a few morsels of it. My neighbour at the table happened to be the harbourmaster, and he noticed my apparent lack of appetite. Much to my mortification, he remarked: "I see you do not like our food." For once, I was quite lost for a suitable reply!

After our visit to Ostend, I took H.M.S. Montrose to Chatham and berthed her alongside a large depot ship commanded by Lieutenant Commander A.C.G Mars, D.S.O., D.S.C., R.N., a famous submarine captain. I listened to some of Mars' exploits during the war, and also heard his description of how he had been given leave to contest Windsor as a Liberal candidate for Parliament. It was only after failing in this that he had rejoined the Navy. He was a remarkable character, yet much as I liked him, I could not avoid the impression that he was still suffering somewhat from the strain of the war years. One year later he was court martialled in a blaze of publicity for refusing to take up a new appointment. The outcome of the trial was that he was incarcerated in a mental hospital, Netley at Southampton. Later, however, he was rehabilitated, and survived to write the submarine history of World War II, with a preface by the famous Admiral Roxburgh. Eventually, therefore, he must have been forgiven.

The following day, I handed over command of H.M.S. Montrose to Lieut. Cdr. R. Young R.N., who had just been appointed Staff Officer to Tay Division, and it was he who sailed her back to Dundee. Meanwhile I went up to London with two of my officer colleagues to row in the Officers' Whaler Championships on the Thames from Westminster Pier. I regret to say that we were unplaced, but it was a pleasant experience to be feted by the London Division, R.N.V.R.

The year after this trip, I decided to opt for a shore course in minesweeping in H.M.S. Vernon at Portsmouth. The captain of Vernon had just lost his son in the tragic loss of the submarine Affray. Ships based at Vernon were still sending down divers and photographing the wreck to see whether it could be salvaged. As I was introduced to the captain, and presented my credentials, I felt most deeply for him, particularly as I already knew him slightly from an earlier encounter.

In 1951, Portsmouth was still in a fearful mess. Nothing seemed to have been done to replace the Hard since those awful raids ten years before. On most evenings, therefore, I stayed in the Wardroom mess. In fact this was the pattern for most of us Reservists. The Regulars would vanish to their homes nearby, leaving the Wardroom to about ten of us. One evening I was drinking with a Reserve officer when, to my great interest, I noticed that he was wearing the George Cross. It was Lieutenant Commander "Buster" Crabb, the frogman, who was later to be killed by electric shocks emitted by the Russian cruiser, Sverdlov. At the time he was investigating her under water in Portsmouth. It was Crabb who was in charge of installing the underwater television cameras which were being used in the inspection of H.M.S. Affray. The damage was being assessed with a view to salvaging the wreck later.

Before I left Montrose, I had sent my motorbike to Portsmouth by train in the hope of riding round the countryside and familiarizing myself with it. However, true to form, British Railways took over two weeks to deliver it, with the result that it arrived only three days before my course ended.

Bob Hood, another lieutenant from Dundee, was following the same course as myself. One evening I suggested that he should ride pillion on my motorbike, so that we could both meet a naval celebrity I knew who lived in Alton. This was Captain A.W.S. Agar V.C., D.S.O., R.N., who, in 1918-20, had served with the utmost distinction against the Bolsheviks in the Baltic. That had been in Coastal Motor Boats (M.T.B.s), but in the Second World War he had commanded a cruiser squadron in the Indian Ocean. In 1942 both his ships, Dorsetshire and Cornwall, had been overwhelmed and sunk by the sheer might of the Japanese Naval Air Arm. Gus was a splendid and most interesting character, always full of information, and he was just beginning to set down his experiences in writing. Since then, several of his published works have met with considerable acclaim, and it is a matter of the utmost regret that his career as a writer was cut short by his early demise. I am glad to say that to this day I still keep up a correspondence with his widow.

After this final amusing night at Alton, our course was virtually over. I was so exasperated by the incompetence of British Rail in failing to deliver my motorbike in reasonable time, that I decided to sell it in Portsmouth, and who better to buy it than ex-Chief Petty Officer Writer Fisher, who now had a motorcycle shop in Portsmouth? This was that same Petty Officer Fisher whom I had known so well six years previously, when he ran the Secretariat for Commodore Menzies at Freetown.

By the time I had completed my course at Portsmouth, I was considerably better trained for the more serious minesweeping exercises which were to be undertaken in the following year. Speaking in general, it would be true to say that by 1952, throughout the United Kingdom, the Royal Naval Volunteer Reserve was highly organized, well led, and well trained.

In May 1952, I was again ordered to command H.M.S. Montrose. We were to join other minesweepers from Edinburgh, Newcastle and Hull at Bridlington, where we would sail in company to Portland and attach ourselves to the Home Fleet. We performed some exercises at Portland, and the commanding officers of our squadron, called the 101 Minesweeping, were invited to lunch with the Commander-in-Chief in H.M.S. Vanguard, Britain's largest and last battleship.

Speaking personally, I felt that this was the highlight of my Naval career. To be piped over the side of the Fleet Flagship, an honou due to the commander of one of H.M. ships, was something I had never dreamed of in my days as a lowly midshipman in H.M.S. Iron Duke. We were met at the gangway by Lieutenant W. Staveley R.N., Flag Lieutenant to Admiral Sir George Creasy. I doubt whether Staveley knew his horoscope when he met me. He was himself to become First Sea Lord in the 1980s. Sir George was interested to hear that H.M.S. Montrose had her own kilted piper, who played us in and out of harbour. (This was Lieutenant Commander W. Rennie Stewart R.N.V.R.).

The next day, we were due to sail at 8 a.m. for intensive minesweeping exercises in Lyme Bay, and the Admiral said that he would be watching from the quarterdeck of the Flagship to see and hear our piper in his full naval-cum-Scottish regalia. Accordingly, about 8 a.m., the 101 Minesweeping Squadron got under way. As we sailed close to the stern of H.M.S. Vanguard, Rennie Stewart was piping "Scotland the Brave" with all his might, the sound of the pipes only being silenced for a few seconds as we saluted Vanguard, and as she replied to our courtesy. It was a pretty inspiring sight.

For the next week we practised minesweeping in Lyme Bay most rigorously. We harboured in Dartmouth, where we took out some of the cadets from the Naval College. For the training period the Senior Officer of 101 Squadron was Commander B. Pengelly R.N.. I am sorry to say that I disliked him intensely, and that the feeling was mutual — I am not sure exactly why.

Once the training was over, we sailed independently for various ports, with a view to fun and recreation after the very intense two weeks we had spent. We went to Flushing (Vlissingen) in Holland, and it was my duty to present my credentials to the Senior Dutch Naval Officer in the cruiser Heemeskirk. I remembered this vessel well from our tough convoy battles of 1941. The Dutch naval officers were most welcoming, and showed themselves even more so when I told them that I had served with their compatriots in M.T.B.s/M.G.B.s 1942/33. Two of these former colleagues of mine,

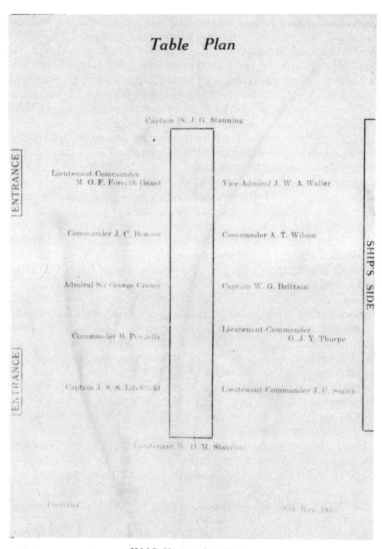

H.M.S. Vanguard, Table Plan

I discovered, were now working at the Dutch Admiralty in the Hague.

In no time telephones were ringing, and the following day I took three other officers to the Hague to meet Lieutenant Commanders Schroeder and de Looze. We were shown over the Hague, and then taken to the Hotel Bali at Schevingen, which was famous for its cuisine, and where I partook of the greatest reistafel I have ever seen. A reistafel, to the uninitiated, is a special curry dish, a great speciality of Dutch Indonesia. The basis of it is a large bowl of rice. On this one piles all kinds of delicacies, generally of Indonesian provenance, from the surrounding side dishes. On this occasion, I remember, we had no less than thirty-two different dishes from which to choose. What made that lunch even more memorable was that in the hotel we recognised President Mossadeg of Iran. He had toppled the Shah of Iran for the first time, and in addition our own Royal Navy had been in confrontation with the Iranians at Abadan. He was now attending the Royal Courts of Justice in the Hague in an attempt to have Britain penalized.

To return to the luncheon party. It had been so superb, and we had partaken of so much food and drink, that for the next two hours I was happy to snooze in a seaside deckchair. The Dutch officers could not have been kinder or more hospitable. They took us back to the Hague, and then on to the train for Flushing. Later William de Looze was to come to Britain as Consul General of the Netherlands, and was still going strong when I dined with him near Perth in 1985.

We had all of us immensely enjoyed our stay in Flushing, and at the end of our three days there, sailed back to Dundee without further incident.

CHAPTER TWENTY

Further Adventures in the R.N.V.R. during the Fifties

1953 was Coronation year, and the Navy's way of paying special honour to the newly crowned sovereign was to hold a Grand Fleet Review in June. In this extravaganza, H.M.S. Montrose would have her part to play, and yet again I was offered, and accepted, command of her. By late May all preparations had been made, but then a major misfortune befell me. My father, who had been seeming none too well, suffered a coronary. It had been arranged that the village celebrations should take place in a grass park just below our home, and at first it was thought that in view of my father's illness the festivities would be postponed or cancelled. However, even though he knew that he was dying, he would not countenance any such thing, and insisted that the arrangements should go ahead. So the Coronation was duly celebrated at Ecclesgreig, and a few days later I sailed from Dundee in H.M.S. Montrose. I was sure that that was the last time I would ever see my father alive. In the course of seeing us off at Dundee, Captain W.F. Keay kindly enquired after my Dad, but I could only tell him that I had bidden him a final farewell.

However sad the parting had been for me, there was no reason to dampen the spirits of the officers and crew, which were highly exuberant. All the R.N.V.R. minesweepers were concentrated opposite Southampton at Hythe, the very place where, in 1942, I had spent so much time fitting out M.A./S.B. 39. Now, in 1953, however, there was no sign of M.G.B.s.

My uniforms, which had not been replaced since the war, were by this time looking somewhat shabby, and I was told in no uncertain terms that I could not possibly attend the new Queen's cocktail party in "that tatty outfit". This was only three days before the event itself, so I went to the magnificent Gieves at Southampton, and they promised to provide me with a brand new suit, complete with appropriate medal ribbons, all ready for the Big Day. To show my appreciation, I invited the manager and one of the assistants to bring my suit on board on the day of the Review, and throughout the proceedings to be my private guests aboard H.M.S. Montrose. I am delighted to say that they accepted.

The immense throng of ships, representing so many different nations, and all anchored off Spithead, was a superb spectacle in itself. The event itself passed off without any untoward incident, although I believe that one sailor's wife was delivered of a child by the surgeon commander. That took place in an aircraft carrier, but not, I think, in Indomitable, which at the time was commanded by my old Skipper of Musketeer days, Captain R.L. Fisher.

H.M.S. Britannia was not yet in service, so it was in H.M.S. Surprise that the Monarch held court for all the Commanding Officers of the Fleet. I noticed a number of faces which I had not seen since the war, and it was particularly interesting to see so many members of the Royal Family present together at one function. It was certainly the largest assemblage of them that I had ever seen, or was ever to see again.

Once the great event was over, we were allowed to sail to a port of our choice in Europe, and by a unanimous decision we chose Flushing. By this time the troops were heartily sick of being at anchor for endless hours of rehearsals, and once we arrived, they let their hair down with a vengeance, doing considerable damage in the process. While all this was going on, I was having a quiet dinner alone with my old friend the Port Admiral, whom I had met the year before. Next morning I visited him to offer my apologies for the chaos the troops had created the previous night. He, however, was most understanding, and I am thankful to say that the whole matter was glossed over and hushed up.

Two years later, in 1955, the authorities laid on the largest minesweeping exercise ever undertaken by the R.N.V.R., now re-named the R.N.R. It was scheduled to take place in August at Invergordon, and both submarines and aircraft were to be in attendance. Vice Admiral Sir John Cuthbert, Admiral Commanding Reserves, was to be in charge. By any standards, it was a major, and extremely serious operation, and many valuable lessons were learned from it.

I had booked a room at the Royal Hotel at Invergordon, and when I was not required to spend the night on board, I slept and bathed there. One evening, knowing that next morning at six a.m. we were due for a major exercise, I dined at the hotel with the Gunnery Officer on the Admiral's staff, who was also staying the night there. Now the Royal Hotel was a state pub; in common with all the hotels in the Invergordon and Carlisle areas, it had been created during World War I so that the government of the day could control the drinking! It is fortunate that they have all now passed into private ownership, for they used to offer the worst possible service. Our experience on this occasion illustrates well the point I am making.

Before retiring to bed, Lieut. Cmdr. Donner and I saw the receptionist, who promised to leave the key in the main door that night, so that we could leave the hotel quietly at 5.30 a.m. the next morning. By 5.15 a.m., Donner and I, both dressed in full uniform, went downstairs to let ourselves out. The key was not there! Not only so, but the lower half of all the ground floor windows was, as we quickly found out, barred. The only way in which we could make our egress was to open the top half of a sash window, sit on it, and then reach out and grope blindly for the window ledge before finally leaping to the ground.

With great difficulty, we managed to lower the upper sash of the window to a little over half way down, but that was as far as it would go. Like all the fittings in that ill-equipped hotel, it would not function as it was intended. At all events, I managed to climb up and sit on the window frame, from which I intended to jump the last two feet onto the ledge. I was now sitting with my behind on the frame and my hands over the edge of it. Suddenly, beneath the weight of my body, the window sash was forced down to its proper position. It had happened too quickly for me to remove my hands, and now they were trapped between the upper and lower sashes. Luckily I was not hurt, but I was held as completely helpless as if I had been crucified there. At this juncture, hundreds of sailors began clattering down the street to join their ships in time for sailing. The spectacle of a Lieutenant Commander helplessly and hopelessly crucified in the main window of the Royal Hotel must have made them think of pink elephants. Whatever their first impressions may have been, however, the Jack Tars came to my rescue. Resourceful as ever, a large band of them hoisted me skywards, thereby taking my weight off the frame sufficiently for it to be moved up and so release my hands. Then they lowered me to the ground unhurt, though somewhat shocked. Donner managed to make his egress too, and without becoming involved in a similar hideous predicament. Luckily, we both managed to get aboard our ships in good time for sailing, for the Admiral himself was going to lead out his fleet.

That day the Moray Firth was a scene of great activity, with a submarine laying dummy mines, lines of minesweepers dotting the sea, hordes of fighters and helicopters roaring overhead, and the Admiral directing operations from a frigate. At about noon, I received a message that the Admiral's chief-of-staff, Captain

Beattie V.C., R.N., was to land on our quarterdeck in a helicopter so as to inspect our activities. At the very moment when he was landing, I had sweeps out astern, and was in the middle of some decidedly tricky manoeuvres, which could easily have gone wrong. At such a moment, the last thing I wanted was someone breathing down my neck as I worked out my next move.

At this time, we had as our engineer officer Commander (Engineer) Jimmy Young R.N.R., who was doing his training with us. Now, at this moment of need, he turned out to be just my man. He took Captain Beattie to the Wardroom and gave him a couple of his special "Jimmy Young blockbusters". By the time I had extricated Montrose from what could have turned out a bad tactical manoeuvre, Beattie was in cracking form. From then until the evening, we were engaged in intense minesweeping exercises, but they all passed off smoothly. When we had completed them we shaped course once more for Invergordon.

Jimmy Young was an old friend. In 1942 he had been my flotilla engineer at Hornet, and we had both done some training with Captain Beattie, who in 1948 was commanding the destroyer Whirlwind. However, it was at St Nazaire, in the course of the greatest commando raid of the war, that Captain Beattie had won his Victoria Cross. At that time he was in command of the destroyer Campbelltown, and in her he had rammed the lock gates. Campbelltown had been blown up, and Beattie himself had been taken prisoner.

On this occasion, all of us, both severally and in concert, did our utmost to entertain him well, and I always remember a remark which he made when he was due to return to the frigate by helicopter. He said that while he might have won the Victoria Cross at St Nazaire, he had no intention of winning a second that evening. Would we please return him to the frigate in our motor boat? No sooner said than done, and after a pretty heavy day, we were glad to have a good night's rest in port at Invergordon.

The summer of 1955 was wonderfully hot and sunny, but unfortunately it did not suit everybody. In the forests and woodlands of the Moray Firth region, innumerable fires were started, often by sparks from steam trains or by picnickers. Even while we were minesweeping, the Moray and Sutherland coasts would often be wreathed in thick smoke from the burning forests, as many of the fires raged out of control. Just before we left Invergordon, we received an S.O.S. asking for any spare hands we could lend in order to assist the local firefighters, but regretfully, we were forced to refuse. By this time, we were due to cross the North Sea and pay a courtesy visit to Hamburg.

Lt. Cdr. S.H. Beattie, V.C.

During our passage across, which was otherwise uneventful, we received a wireless message instructing us to pick up "MID" at Brunsbuttelkoog on our way up the Elbe River. At that time Germany was still under the control of the occupying forces, and Hamburg was in the British sector. We speculated as to who this important MID might be. Obviously, we concluded, he was something to do with the Military Intelligence Department. Off Brunsbuttelkoog we stopped, and a motor boat sped towards us with the important personage.

No ship of lesser status than a cruiser is entitled to bugle calls, but we were Reservists, and had not only a Highland piper, but our own bugler too. We prepared to receive the mysterious but important personage with full Military and Naval honours. Hence it came as something of an anti-climax to discover who MID really was: just a very ordinary National Service Midshipman! He needed a passage up the Elbe to the Naval H.Q. at Hamburg.

Up river, I took on a German pilot who proved particularly agreeable. He asked me whether I would require help from a tug to berth the ship. At the time, I judged this to be unnecessary, but that was before I had experienced the velocity and strength of the Elbe currents! As I tried to berth alongside, in very restricted space, I found myself wishing that I had taken the pilot's advice, and for one awful moment I thought I was about to be carried stern first into a bridge. Luckily, at the critical second, the engines came full ahead, but it was only by inches that we missed smashing that bridge! As we secured safely alongside the jetty, I thanked the pilot and we parted on the best of terms.

Barely were we alongside, when the Naval Staff Officer (Intelligence), Lieut. Duff Still R.N., came aboard with all kinds of papers and instructions as to how to treat the Germans, etc. He was a splendid and most helpful fellow, and it was largely due to him that our next few days were such a pleasant interlude. Amongst the papers he produced was one bearing the names of scores of naughty clubs, brothels, and so forth, that were out of bounds. Of course all our troops — really civilians — wanted was simply the addresses!

Duff Still warned us that the Area Military Commander, Brigadier Long, had an aversion to the Navy, and had recently been very rude to the captains of two destroyers and an aircraft carrier which were visiting the port. He told me that he was instructed to take me to Brigadier Long to present my credentials, and was horrified when he discovered that I would be improperly dressed for the occasion. I had left my sword in the Royal Hotel at Invergordon, and as I was ushered into the presence, I noticed the Brigadier cast a critical eye over my dress and (lack of!) side-arms.

The introductions over, the atmosphere was still decidedly frosty, and the brigadier had already almost signified that the audience was at an end. At that point I played my last desperate card. It turned out to be the trump! "Were you at Wellington, Sir?" I asked. For a second he frowned. Then, with a slight change of manner, replied: "Of course I was! Were you?" On my replying in the affirmative, his attitude changed completely. He roared with laughter and called for sherry. After that, in spite of his fierce reputation, we got on famously, but when he went so far as to say that he would return my call aboard H.M.S. Montrose in person, I was astounded. It was highly unusual; an officer of his rank normally arranged for a colonel or major to return a call upon an officer as junior as myself.

So the Brigadier, flying all flags from his staff car, duly visited us in St Pauli, to the accompaniment of the maximum amount of bullshit that I could organize — and at that I was no mean hand. Bugles blew, a special detachment on the gangway came to the present with fixed bayonets, and the brigadier came aboard with his Chief of Staff to be right royally entertained in our Wardroom. Duff Still was flabbergasted, and the local Germans even more so.

They though that we must be having a political commissar on board.

After a few drinks, I told the brigadier how disappointed we were that all the good places appeared to be out of bounds. He roared with laughter and said that we were really nothing more than a bunch of civilians in uniform. In our case, he went on, he would make an exception. If and when any of our men was arrested, I should ring up his chief of military police, and they would be released. In fact, before we left Hamburg, I was very glad to invoke this arrangement. Without it, my crew would have been four short!

I could not believe that any city could have the night life we saw in Hamburg at that time. Even thirty years later, after visiting countless other countries, I still consider that Hamburg has a "mystique" of its own. Some years after all this, I was not at all surprised to learn that the Beatles had made it the "launching pad" for their career.

I have mentioned that we had a bugler, an extremely rare embellishment even in destroyers — let alone minesweepers! Our performer was Alex. Henderson, a Reservist A.B. from the town of Montrose, whose father had been a close friend of mine in 1940, when we were at Loch Ewe, he as a petty officer, I as a midshipman. Though he had at least one, and often two, other jobs, Alex. used to add to them the third one of looking after me, the captain. When, therefore, on our first day in Hamburg, he called me with my early morning tea, I asked him what the food was like in the minesweeper. "Absolutely filthy," he replied. I was particularly shocked at this. After all, many of the officers and troops were making this training cruise their annual holiday. However, I had a scheme up my sleeve which I thought might solve the problem.

Surgeon Lieutenant Tim Crowley R.N.R. was our ship's doctor. In civilian life he was an anaesthetics specialist in Foresterhill Hospital, Aberdeen, but during his annual training, as now on the present trip, he fortunately had little to do. I told him, therefore, that I was placing him in charge as inspecting officer of mess deck meals, and in this role he was magnificent. It turned out that the person who was doing the damage, in his personal interest, was the coxswain, or chief petty officer, of the mess deck. In no time Tim Crowley and I had sorted him out, and thereafter, I was told, the food was excellent. That was one occasion when I was more grateful than I can say for my early experience in Shower, when I was so close to the troops, and was treated much the same as they were. It was because of that experience that I knew my mess decks as well as my Wardroom!

During our stay in Hamburg, the Navy were particularly kind to us and offered us all kinds of options in the way of entertainment. One day, eighty percent of both officers and troops turned down the prospect of a visit to Kiel, and chose instead to visit the famous Elbeschloss Brewery. However, Tim Crowley and I, together with three adventurous ratings, opted for the alternative: a staff car to Kiel, an inspection of everything of interest there, and a journey home by train. That was an education in itself. All in all, I believe, everyone of us had a marvellous time in Hamburg. Speaking personally, in all the years of my Naval war service I never enjoyed anything so much as the days I spent there. I have often been back since, and on those occasions too, have never failed to enjoy it to the full.

At last the time came for us to leave, and, with the help of my old friend the pilot, we sailed down the Elbe, dropping him off at Cuxhaven — into a pilot boat, not into the sea! Half way home, we ran into a full North Sea gale. The ship was a twin-screw "Ton" minesweeper of 1950 vintage, and we had almost new Deltic engines, but at the time they were having teething troubles. At this particular juncture, in fact, we were on only one engine. The crew was well trained and highly competent, but even so, in view of our engine trouble, I signalled Chatham to say that I would like another minesweeper to stand by me while I crossed the North Sea in this full gale. Absolutely nobody came to help us, and when at last I made North Shields in near hurricane winds, we were quite alone. It had been a gruelling experience for us all.

That was the end of an exciting episode, but two years later I met Commander Knight R.N., Senior Officer of the Ton Class minesweepers at Harwich, who was refitting his vessel in Montrose shipyard. Over a drink, I mentioned this experience of ours of two years before. "Oh yes," he replied, "I remember it well, but recollect that nearly all our crews were green National Service. We could not face a hurricane like that, and we would not have been of any use. On the contrary, with crews such as that, we would have been in grave danger ourselves!"

By this time my service in the R.N.R. and all that went with it was drawing to a close. Although in the years which followed I did on occasion command ships for short periods, the demands upon my capabilities as a civilian were becoming too great, and my career in the Navy was coming to an end. In the late fifties I left the R.N.R.. I had served either full- or part-time for twenty years, and I felt that now was the time to hand on the torch to others, more able than I, and having more time to give than I would thenceforward be able to manage.

As I look back on my career, I realize that I enjoyed it all. Bad times there may have been — the cruel Russian convoys, for example. Yet I have forgotten all that; what I remember, rather, is the good times I had and the countless comrades I met, many of them still in touch with me to this day. It has all been so worth while!

PART VII

Business and an Excursion into Politics

Early Struggles to Establish Myself in Business

I must now return to 1947, and my first wavering steps on the road back to civilian life. After nearly seven years' full-time service in the Navy, they were not easy. To begin with, I had to take a massive drop in pay. While in command of H.M.S. Arran, I had been receiving £20 a week; now, as a trainee manager, my weekly pay was £5. Added to this was an equally massive drop in status. Virtually up to the time of my demobilization, I had been issuing orders to three hundred men; now I was receiving orders from all and sundry. By January 1947, I was ready to chuck in my hand and go back to sea, and very nearly did so. However, the senior managing director, who himself had spent five years as a prisoner of war, persuaded me to give it a longer try. It was wise counsel indeed.

Slowly but surely, I readjusted to civilian life, and before long I had developed a sideline to my principal job by running a timber contracting business. Though only on a small scale, it proved highly profitable. During the war years, timber had been virtually unobtainable. Now fishing boat builders and textile machine makers in Dundee were crying out for it. With the help of a small staff of four, I bought, felled, and transported heavy timber for the boatyards and factories.

My largest customer was James V. Hepburn Ltd., a boatyard in Montrose which had gone into voluntary liquidation. Despite its condition, it was paying me cash against delivery of supplies of oak and larch, and I was able to use its sawmill to convert large beech trees into slabs for hacklemakers in Dundee. Eventually the liquidator was forced to put the company up for sale, and I interested some wealthy financiers in raising the purchase price, so that I could continue to supply the yard with timber. One day, the liquidator, a chartered accountant, 'phoned me to say that he had bought the company, and that the post of chairman was mine if I wanted it. With the agreement of the financiers whom I had consulted, I accepted this agreement.

There were now six directors in all: the chartered accountant himself, who had been the liquidator, a well known ship repairer in Aberdeen, a second chartered accountant, newly qualified, the former manager of the shipyard, who had survived the liquidation, a Montrose solicitor, and finally myself. From the start, it seemed clear that none of the directors had sufficient cash to raise the working capital required, which was a minimum of £30,000. Before long the ex-liquidator was proposing a new arrangement. He said that we should all sign a Joint and Several Guarantee to the North of Scotland Bank, and in that way raise the necessary sum. To this four of the directors agreed, and the only two to decline were the Montrose solicitor and myself. The bank's general manager assured me that to sign such an agreement was no more than a formality, but I pointed out that I did not have the money to guarantee £30,000. He replied that he had known my father and grandfather, and that the name was good. Still I declined.

We built boats all right — no question about that! I personally obtained one notable order from the Fairmile Company, who had contracted out all the Bs and Ds of the war years, and were now in business as civilian suppliers at Cobham in Surrey. The order was for a fish carrier for Lake Victoria, and the vessel was duly completed and delivered. In fact, on paper, Montrose Shipyard was prospering, yet the overdraft grew and grew. Every Thursday, in my capacity as chairman, I used to cycle from Johnstons' offices on the waterfront across the river bridge to the shipyard, in order to sign the wages and other cheques. One day, however, there was a message from the bank asking me to telephone. The manager told me that unless I added my name to those of the other guarantors, neither the wages cheque nor any of the others could be met. I remonstrated, but in vain, and he indicated that without my name they were insufficient.

I signed. It was a body blow to me, for I knew that I had possibly signed away far more than I possessed. Within two years I had developed a duodenal ulcer from the sheer worry of it. Noticing my condition, my father asked me why I never smiled. I kept my secret. The overdraft had now reached £40,000, but a large fishing boat had been built, and as soon as it was launched the new owner paid exactly that sum: £40,000. On the day that it went down the slipway, the other directors threw a large launching party at a local hotel, after which they held a celebration meeting. Stonily I informed them that from that moment I resigned as chairman and director, and would remove my name from the guarantee that same day. I would sell my shares; I would walk out.

Walk out I did, telling my lawyer and chartered accountant to sell my shares. The best offer they could find, however, was half a crown for each £1 share. Some little time later, they jointly rang me to say that the offer had now been increased to seven and sixpence a share, which I accepted. It was my first encounter with big business.

Although I was much troubled with the affairs of this company, which I had started as a sideline, my main occupation, which was in Joseph Johnston and Son Ltd., was on a more ascendant path. The wonderful old chairman of Joseph Johnston & Sons Ltd. was W. Douglas Johnston, a former provost of Montrose. When I was learning the business, I had found him a wonderful teacher, and he had been like a father to me. When he died, he left me £1,000 in his will — an enormous sum in those days. Although the company had done badly in 1945-46, and not much better in 1947, in 1949 it suddenly began to prosper. By that time I had become a junior managing director, but it would be quite wrong of me to suggest that this had much to do with its new-found prosperity!

The true reason for this was that salmon poaching, which had reached appalling dimensions during the war years, was now at last being effectively stopped. All through the war the poaching of salmon in rivers, often with explosives, had continued more or less unchecked. Hence it was only from 1949 onwards that salmon began to return in appreciable numbers to the Scottish shores. A great spell of prosperity ensued for salmon merchants in general, and for Johnstons in particular. It was to last for a further twenty years.

My first real challenge came in 1952, when my two senior colleagues wanted to lease coastal salmon fishings from the Crown Estates in north Kincardineshire. For these, they proposed to offer the highest salmon fishing rents for coastal nets in Britain. I opposed so high an offer; I was sure it was excessive. In doing so, I unfortunately incurred some displeasure for my views. At all events, the upshot was that our tender for the lease was accepted by the Crown Estates, making us the largest of all ratepayers in the county. Once our offer had been accepted, and we were free to operate our new fishing stations, I abandoned all opposition, and was put in charge of a campaign which now developed to get our operations under way. It was then that the fun really started.

The previous tenants refused to give Johnstons the havens and stores on the coast from which the nets would have to be worked. Furthermore, they were determined to remove all the landmarks which they had in use, so that Johnstons would not know where to moor their nets. Faced with all this, my first action was to contact an old friend, Ltd. Cmdr. Bill Bruen R.N. of the Fleet Air Arm, who had flown spotter aircraft in the Graf Spee battle. I asked him to photograph all the relevant sea salmon nets in the water between Stonehaven and Aberdeen from his base, H.M.S. Condor, near Arbroath. This he completed in excellent time, with the result that now I did not need any of the old landmarks; we could perfectly well put in our own! The poor departing tenants got wind of this "ruse de guerre", which was, of course, quite illegal. For a time there was a threat of questions being asked in Parliament, but of this nothing further transpired.

Our next task was to build miniature harbours, with roads leading to them, along the rocky Kincardine coast. We also had to buy up plots of land on which to build stores and install cranes, known as blondins, in order to lift the gear as well as the catches we were hoping to make.

I set to, and worked at the problem throughout the winter of 1953. In all aspects of the work I was supported by David Dundas, a boat skipper from Montrose, who had been promoted to local superintendent for these fishings. We worked in complete harmony. I personally dynamited the rocks and bought all the building materials, much of it on the black market. The reason for this was that construction materials were in short supply, and after the war we needed licences, many of which would have been refused. Luckily, there were no such things as building controls or planning consents, and if there were, I completely ignored them. Before the latter controls became so highly organized, and the penalties so heavy, I had put up over £500,000 worth of buildings without a single licence. I would only stop when the authorities became thoroughly nasty!

At all events, the buildings and installations were all finished in time. That did not mean, however, that our troubles were at an end. The previous tenants had succeeded in persuading their employees to blacklist Johnstons, and we could not find fishermen to man the boats. In those days Scotland used to have a number of "feeing markets", and the Altens Market at Aberdeen was the largest of its kind in Britain. Here, once a year, in Hadden and Market Street, hundreds of men congregated: salmon fishers, managers, rope manufacturers, box makers, cork merchants, net makers, and all the paraphernalia of commercial salmon fishing. Here salmon fishers used to "bargain" for their labour for the ensuing year, while the merchants were plying their wares, anything from twine mending-needles to sea cobles worth many thousands.

This 1953 market was not the first Altens Market that I had

Private Air Force

attended. In earlier years, Johnstons had sent me there to gain experience. This particular one, however, was certainly the first that my two senior colleagues had visited, and the only reason for their coming now was to support me in my efforts to engage salmon fishers. That is why they came armed with a suitcaseful of written agreements!

The three of us took a table in the Market Arms in Hadden Street, one of the most "famous" of its era, and we began buying drinks for all the salmon fishers. As the drinks flowed, and the men became more and more inebriated, it was apparent to all that we were standing more drinks than our rivals. The opposition cracked. Salmon fishermen in large numbers thronged to put their names to our employment agreements.

One such salmon fisherman, in particular, I shall always remember. His name was Tom Blues, and he was pig-headedly recalcitrant. Nothing would induce him to sign. He accepted drink after drink, but remained resolute in his refusal. As the day wore on, we had engaged almost all the men we needed, but not Tom Blues. Eventually I discovered him in a gutter, and all but out for the count. I massaged his hand persuasively, but by this time all he wanted to do was to sleep. "Just sign here, Tom," I said, "while we get you another drink." He signed, and then finally passed out for the day. We had won!

The following year, there were some teething troubles, but we fished the coast successfully, and my two colleagues decided that after business was over at the Altens Market, they would give the successful fishers a splendid meal at the Imperial, one of Aberdeen's larger and more prestigious hotels. Personally, I warned against it; I had my premonitions of disaster.

We had the usual massive orgy of drink in the Market Arms, and when time was called, the fishermen were shepherded into the Imperial Hotel for lunch. I say they were shepherded; perhaps that is putting it too mildly. Some of them had to be frog-marched, or even carried! Tom Blues was there all right. He just managed to get himself seated at table as the plates of soup were being placed on it. Calmly, he took out his false teeth and threw them into the water jug! That was the last luncheon Johnstons ever gave after the Altens Market.

It was really the salmon in Montrose and Lunan Bay and the surrounding areas that contributed so much to the prosperity of Johnstons in that era from 1954-75. There the men knew their jobs and everything used to run smoothly. If anything did go wrong, it was nearly always in the area between Stonehaven and Aberdeen.

One of our earliest problems was caused by the outbreak of typhoid in and around Aberdeen in 1964. It caused a tremendous scare, and the dangers were blown up to panic proportions by the media. People were going down like ninepins, and when I was told that it had spread to our crews, and that one man based just under Girdleness Lighthouse had caught it, I rushed up to investigate. After all, we were food suppliers. If our men were infected, they could be spreading typhoid.

When I arrived, about four a.m., I lost no time in finding out what had happened. The previous day, it seemed, one man had arrived for work with a glazed expression on his face, and had been unable to stop staggering about. The skipper had telephoned for an ambulance, the man had been shoved into it, and it had driven off. From that moment, all trace of the suspected typhoid victim had disappeared. It was imperative for me to find him. By six a.m., I was calling at police H.Q., where they were keeping lists of all the doomed. Still no trace of our man! They told me to call back at 10 a.m., when the Ministry of Health would produce the latest information on admissions to hospital. In the end, I found out that the man did not have typhoid at all; he had simply got drunk. He had arrived outside the isolation hospital before he had sobered up sufficiently to realize what had happened. Then he had made a run for it, and gone missing for three days.

I rang the office, and told them that the panic was over. Then I decided to treat myself to a luxury lunch at the Station, Aberdeen's most prestigious hotel. I found myself the only guest in the bar, and was relaxing there, when Freddie Milne, the head waiter, brought me the menu. When I asked what was special, he said that since I was the only guest for lunch that day, all the kitchen and waiting staff were at my exclusive service. Such was the fear and panic of the beleaguered city of Aberdeen at that date.

Despite such isolated problems, the fortunes of Johnstons the salmon fishers were going from strength to strength. However, the chairman, who had been so good to me in 1947, was feeling the ill effects of five years in a P.O.W. camp in Germany, and was often absent. That left most of the running of the business to the second managing director, and to me as third, or junior managing director. Although my senior colleague had a splendid brain, and had excellent and very definite ideas as to how the business should be run, he was a retiring person, and I think he enjoyed having a "frontsman" who was never afraid of publicity, favourable or otherwise.

A time came when the old R.A.F. aerodrome at Montrose came up for sale by public auction, and he asked me to go and buy it on behalf of the company. He made the proviso that I should not go higher than £10,000 for it — this, although it was several hundred acres in extent! This was before oil had been discovered in the North Sea, and the land was of low agricultural potential. Hence it was not expected to make the reserve which the Ministry of Defence had placed upon it. If it failed to reach that reserve, the sale would be cancelled and it would be exposed again at a later date and at a lower price. As I was waiting for the auction to begin, I was sitting next to an employee of the M.O.D., and he whispered to me: "There will be no bids." I told him that I agreed. We listened as the auctioneer tried first £15,000, then £12,000, then £10,000. Not a sound in response! "Well," he said, "I can't offer it for sale for less. First call at £10,000! Second call at £10,000! Third and last call at £10,000!" At that point my arm shot up. He never waited. "Yours!" he shouted, and that was that! Some years later, in the oil boom, that airfield was probably worth half a million!

On another occasion I was holidaying in Berlin when a major building company of Montrose — it was one of the largest in Scotland — went bankrupt, and the liquidator put up the vast premises for auction in the Town Hall. Even though the reserve price was only £10,000, there was not a single, solitary bid. The following week, my colleague remarked what a pity it was that I had been in Berlin at the time, because he would have liked me to attend the auction and buy the premises as a speculation. If necessary, I could even have gone to £5,000 above its reserve. "Would you be happy," I asked, "if I bought those premises today for the £10,000 of the reserve price?" "Oh yes," he replied, "I wish you could, but now it is too late." I worked out my strategy, and that afternoon at three p.m. I rang the liquidator, a Mr Munro of Romanes and Munro, Edinburgh, Chartered Accountants and Liquidators.

Says I: "Mr Munro, I hear you failed to sell R. Pert and Sons Ltd. at the Town Hall last week. I was in Berlin and missed the sale. I will offer you £9,000 for the premises right now." "How very interesting," replies the chartered accountant, "I will write to my committee of inspection." I feel that his front is cracking. "No use," I answer, "Ring them! My offer only exists until 4.30 p.m.!" "Nonsense," protests Munro, "You could never have the money in my office by 5 p.m.!" "Try me!", says I.

He agreed, and by 4.30 p.m. I had bought the premises. By 5 p.m. our Edinburgh company lawyer, Oliver Williams, had paid a fifty percent deposit on the price, and irredeemably bought the huge office, together with warehouse and stores. Within two years we had sold it to the Water Board at a very handsome profit. The whole episode brought forcibly back to me a maxim which I often used in the course of my wartime service in Coastal Forces: "He who hesitates is lost!"

It must have been quite obvious to our employees that the profits we were making were very high, and I sensed that some kind of public relations exercise was needed. Relations between employers and employed had always been excellent, but in the circumstances, something extra was called for to keep them so. We decided to give our employees a special day out. The only other occasion remotely like the one we were now planning had been the Coronation ceremony in 1953, when a magnificent meal, full public screen coverage of the ceremony, together with free drinks, had been laid on. That had been a once-and-for-all affair, and nothing of the kind we were now contemplating had ever been attempted.

My two colleagues agreed that we would lay on a bus trip for the older people, and a company dance for the younger generation. It did not take me long to organize the two functions, and from then on, as a way of expressing our appreciation of all those years of prosperity, we used to hold an annual bus trip for three hundred individuals, and a dance at the Town Hall for roughly the same number. This last was particularly appropriate in view of the fact that the chief contributor to the building of the Town Hall had been a member of the Johnston firm — one, therefore, who had made his money out of salmon fishing.

Some of those three hundred-strong bus trips turned out to be highly amusing affairs. There was, for instance, the occasion when, the tourist season having ended, we arrived, of all places, at Tomintoul, the highest village in the United Kingdom. I will leave it to the reader to imagine what happened when about one hundred and twenty men, together with their long-suffering spouses, were let loose in this village after waiting all day for a drink. It was like the rape of the Sabines!

For the first few years of my marriage, whenever I was the organizer of these trips, my long-suffering wife used to accompany me on them. On one occasion we were in Crieff, a small Highland town. For the sake of being the "fuehrer", and also from motives of family respectability, I, for once, kept off the booze. After a singularly temperate lunch, we were the first to arrive back at the six waiting buses. We then discovered that David Mackie, a pensioner of seventy, together with his wife, had never even left the bus for a meal. He asked me whether I could spare him a copy of the Courier, to which I replied that I only had the Express. "Never mind," said David, "that'll do. It's only to wipe up the sick!" It was a fairly rough interlude!

In the year following, I decided to up-grade the event. Instead of holding a marathon drinking spree, we visited the Edinburgh Military Tattoo. With considerable difficulty, I managed to marshall about three hundred employees, wives and children into the area for the ten p.m. peformance, and with my wife and two boys sitting most respectably beside me, we watched the whole superb spectacle without any cause for anxiety. It was when I was marshalling the three hundred back to the buses that my troubles began — I wished that I had a few sheepdogs with me! Nevertheless, at last I had the throng amassed, and off we set down the M90 motorway and over the Forth Road Bridge. Just beyond the bridge a crisis erupted.

On such occasions as this, Buster Strachan. a salmon boat skipper of long standing, and an excellent "gaffer", was prone to alcoholic fiestas. Now he came rushing up and stood before me and my wife holding his privates. "Michael," he said, "I can't wait any longer!" (My wife, meanwhile, was pretending to be shocked.)

I told him that we could not stop on the motorway, but that he could relieve himself as soon as we left it. This was greeted on all sides by a hearty roar of applause, which at the time I mistook as support for Buster rather than what it really was — self-interest!

Just off the motorway in Fife, I told the leading bus to stop, and the entire flotilla of six stopped in perfect formation astern. Immediately there was an appalling rush for the door of our bus —it might have been the disaster of the Titanic, except that this was quite different. As captain of my ship, I watched all the crew and passengers take to the lifeboats, and then asked my wife whether she was ready to abandon ship too. This she coldly declined. I noticed my two sons literally jumping with ecstasy, stimulated in their case by coca cola. Being the last to abandon ship, the only places available to us in the queue were in the full glare of the bus headlights. There I stood, brave as General Gordon before his murder at Khartoum, my two young sons beside me, and there I duly helped, together with some fifty other eager spirits, to wash down the bus. Once relieved of our agony, we resumed our seats, and drove off back to Montrose.

My wife was furious. "You always were an exhibitionist," she declared, "but I did hope you would not educate your two sons to go the same way. I will never come on a Johnston bus trip again." Nor did she.

Sadly, around the 1980 mark, the fortunes of commercial wild salmon fishing began to decline. There were no more trips and dances at the Town Hall. Like an old soldier, I did not die — just began to fade away.

Although it was a few years more before I retired completely, my active part in commercial salmon fishing was drawing to a close. There was some criticism from younger successors. I was no longer, they said, pulling my weight. I was not the dynamic force that I had been years before. Nevertheless, despite anything that I or anyone else could have done, the writing was on the wall. It was the end of an era, and much as the enthusiastic new generation tried to rejuvenate the age-old trade of commercial salmon fishing, which had been so profitable, the end was coming faster than they anticipated. By 1988, the industry as we had known it had virtually collapsed.

CHAPTER TWENTY-TWO

Two Salmon Wars

Ever since I had entered employment with a commercial salmon netting company, the battles with poachers had been endless and endemic. In a previous chapter I have alluded to the menace posed by sea salmon poachers. By the end of World War II, however, sea salmon poaching was almost non-existent, and was to remain so for the next sixteen years. The only exception was the waters of Berwick. Generally speaking, however, it would be true to say that during this period it was the river poachers who were causing all the trouble.

One poacher who was a terrible thorn in our side was Willie, who used to string a hang net across the South Esk estuary by night at Ferryden. In this he was well supported by his family, who supplied intelligence and set up their own version of an early warning system. We had tried using a ten-knot salmon coble to intercept him, and also racing to the roadhead by car. All had proved futile. The early warning system which he and his family had set up was all too effective, so that by the time we arrived on the scene he had invariably disappeared.

The chairman of the South Esk Fisheries Board was Graham Smart. One autumn night in the late forties, he and his Fisheries superintendent worked out a new approach, and I, being in my late twenties and fit, was asked to assist in their plan. Above all, it was vital to avoid being spotted by the early warning patrols on the highway. This we managed by trespassing onto the railway line just clear of the lights of Montrose station, and crossing the estuary on foot by the two railway bridges. Two miles further south we climbed an embankment and landed in a potato field. We slid down the drills for six hundred yards, coming out at the top of some rough ground which looked down on the river below. There we could just make out a boat with an oarsman in it, keeping his craft static in the centre of the river. It was most likely that he had a net attached to the shore, in which the running salmon and sea trout were being enmeshed.

Before setting out, we had arranged with the local policeman that he should conceal himself somewhere near the end of Ferryden village. If we spotted the poacher, we would warn him by giving a long blast on a whistle. Then we would rush down the bank and hold the poacher until he had time to cycle down the road and arrest him. Being the youngest and fittest, my role was to jump up and run down to the shore on a given word. At the appropriate moment, the whistle went, the word was given, and I clattered down the dark bank onto the shingle. At the same moment, Willie heard all this and made for the shore. We both arrived at the water's edge at the same time, the stern of his boat being attached to the shore by his hang net. Part of the net was in his boat, with the salmon and sea trout still in its meshes.

I knew he would try to make a run for it, so as he reached the shore, I jumped into the boat and knocked him backwards onto the salmon-filled net. We had quite a fight, but I was younger and stronger than he, and after my many fights in H.M.S. Drifter Shower a few years previously, I had become quite skilled at hand-to-hand combat. I got him down in the rowing boat, and each time he struggled I hit his head on the seat. Eventually the panting policeman arrived with Graham Smart.

Willie duly appeared in Forfar Sheriff Court, charged with salmon poaching. Having been found guilty, he was asked whether he had anything to say before sentence was passed upon him. Pointing at me with a glower, he said: "He should be in the dock instead of me, charged with brutal assault and battery!" The sheriff looked me up and down, noting my smart suit, black tie and white collar. "Mr Forsyth-Grant doesn't look that sort of person to me," he remarked briefly.

In the Brechin region, the river poachers were led by Scotland's most famous poacher of the era, Albert Edward McCabe. He had already blown off his hand and forearm with gelignite, but he was cunning in the extreme, and one never knew where he would strike. One day, a local farmer named Salmon, whose farm overlooked a particularly vulnerable stretch of the North Esk, rang me to tell me what a lot fools we were. Poachers, he declared, were having a great time at night beside his farm. When I asked his name, he said I could not expect information for nothing. "What about a salmon for a Salmon?" said he. There and then the deal was fixed. A few nights later, he rang me to say that the poachers had arrived on his farm. This time I simply passed the information on to Superintendent Isaac Wright of the Fishery Board, who, with the local police, made several arrests, including one in which the poacher concerned was intercepted and brought down by means of a rugby tackle, while at full gallop through a turnip field.

In the course of discussing these adventures in the office next day, I said that I would have to give Mr Salmon a salmon for the information he had supplied. My colleagues were horrified; it sounded, they said, like buying information. I, however, insisted that if they would not provide the salmon, I would have to buy one myself. At this, they reluctantly agreed that the company would stand the cost. Thus Mr Salmon became the first of many who were rewarded for supplying information. To the last, my fellow directors never liked the smell of this, although, over a period of many years, I unashamedly claimed my expenses, and the system served us well. After all, such rewards were used for buying information, which was instrumental in getting many a poacher nailed. However, when the chartered accountant asked: "What is Mr Forsyth-Grant's special fund used for?", these colleagues of mine made themselves scarce, and directed the questioning to me!

Gradually, we got the upper hand of the river poachers, but now a new menace erupted. Mono-filament nets were invented, and it was not long before they were being used in half-mile lengths for netting salmon at sea. Suddenly, the whole established system of netting salmon off the shores of Scotland was under threat. Up to this time it had continued almost unchanged for two hundred years, and the conservation policy that had been enforced had been the admiration of the Western World. Now, however, armed with this new type of net, fishing boats that had previously only fished for cod, haddock and whiting, began slaughtering salmon by the thousand. The whole structure of the industry was endangered by these "salmon pirates", who contributed nothing either to conservation in the rivers, or to the policing of them and the enforcement of regulations upon the coastal netters.

In Scotland, the exclusive right of catching salmon is a heritable property right, and covers waters extending three miles out from the shore. As the law stood in 1962, it was a criminal offence to catch salmon within a mile of high water, except for somebody holding such a right, and even then he had to confine himself to certain established methods. In responding to this new threat, and also in enforcing the one mile limit, the Fisheries Authorities in Edinburgh proved hopelessly inadequate. Yet if Joseph Johnston and Sons Ltd. was to survive at all, it was now absolutely vital that the observance of the one- to three- mile limit should be effectively enforced.

The company's own response was to buy a Dowty Turbocraft, a fifteen foot speedboat operated by jet propulsion, and so without a

Private Navy

Poachers Arrested

Salmon War, Press cutting

propeller. This became our new secret weapon, with which to track down the pirates. Sailing it was a most hazardous adventure, for it was not intended to operate at night, nor really in anything but sheltered waters. Yet sometimes, in order to prevent the pirates from making good their escape, we would have to follow them, in their fifty-foot yawls and seiners, out into the North Sea as much as six miles off shore.

Nevertheless, we did intercept and catch a number of them, and it was not long before some were appearing in the Sheriff Courts. Off Montrose Harbour, the skipper of the Silver Fern attempted to ram us, only to catch his propeller well and truly in his own drift-net. Meanwhile we, being jet-propelled, were skating back and forth over that same net without the smallest difficulty. Eventually the Silver Fern was forced to radio for help and had to be towed back twelve miles to Gourdon. All this time, Superintendent MacIntyre and I were following the stricken boat along the coast in my car, and we telephoned the Inverbervie police to say that 'he vessel would shortly be towed into the harbour. We asked them to be at the harbour waiting for her when she got in, in order to preserve the peace and charge the crew of the boat with illegal salmon fishing.

When MacIntyre and I arrived at Gourdon Harbour, the place was deserted. Within half an hour, however, a crowd of two hundred jeering fishermen and their families had arrived. They surrounded my car and started to rock it, obviously with the intention of hurling it, with us inside, straight into the harbour. Meanwhile the two policemen, hopelessly outnumbered and powerless to preserve order, told me to drive off to safety while I could; they would beat back the crowd long enough for me to get started. MacIntyre and I escaped all right, and the crew of the Silver Fern duly appeared in the Sheriff Court.

As time went on, I became used to arresting these fishing boats at sea, and was frequently threatened and spat upon in Arbroath Harbour. By this time, however, the police would be gathered in far greater numbers than they had been in our earlier attempt at Gourdon, and they would be able to hold the crowds back.

Although in the Bervie and Arbroath areas we kept the pirates off, the white fishing fleet between Wick and Berwick was now plundering salmon stocks all down the east coast. I therefore persuaded my colleagues to buy a seventy-foot motor drifter to act as our own North Sea Patrol craft, and the Salmon Boards of the Rivers Don, Dee, Bervie, North Esk, South Esk and Tweed joined forces with us. Together, we waged war against the pirates from Duncansby Head to the Farne Islands.

Our new vessel, named "Souvenir", was just like the Dundarg, which I had commanded twenty-two years before. I recruited a crew for her, and, through the Admiralty Employment Board, was able to secure the services of Lieutenant Commander Brothers R.N. (Retired) as her resident commander. Brothers was a very pleasant fellow, but far too inoffensive, and I found that I had to take to the sea again myself in order to bring my more aggressive spirit to bear, and go out looking for trouble. Trouble I found in plenty, and many were the fights and the arrests that we made. In all this, however, the Inspectorate of Salmon Fisheries in Edinburgh proved useless.

At the time, Jack MacLeay was Secretary of State for Scotland, and fortunately he and his advisors were becoming worried about the state of near-anarchy now raging off the Scottish coast. They feared that if it were allowed to continue, it would not be long before lives were lost.

In the teeth of much Socialist opposition, he pushed a Statutory Instrument through parliament in which a "box" was drawn round the coast of Scotland, and the use of drift-nets within its limits was banned for a period of several years. Meanwhile, the whole question would be more fully investigated. Thus the First Drift-Net, or Salmon War ended uneasily, with both sides licking their wounds.

An uneasy truce followed, lasting nearly fourteen years, during which Lord Hunter and his committee delved into the matter and issued a Report. As it turned out, it was hard to follow, almost every clause of it was disputed on all sides, and in the end it accomplished little. Then in 1977 the war broke out afresh, with larger boats involved, and far more militant skippers at the helm. The ringleaders all came from Dunbar, Port Seton, and the Firth of Forth. The Arbroath fishermen upheld the law, and we experienced little trouble from boats based north of Fife.

When peace had been declared after the First Salmon War, the old Dowty Turbocraft and Souvenir had been sold. By this time, however, Noel Smart, son of Graham, had become a director of Johnstons, and he purchased a Dellquay Dory, powered by twin 65 h.p. outboards, which gave her a speed of over thirty knots. I named her "Trafalgar", and we soon found ourselves back at war. Noel reported a fleet of boats drift-netting in Lunan Bay, and I scrambled to Montrose Harbour, to find a crew for Trafalgar already assembled and waiting there. Alec Coull, our head mechanic and chief engineer had turned up, as had Superintendent MacIntyre. There were also two police constables in full uniform, P.C.s Bell and Powell. Out of Montrose we roared at thirty knots, past Scurdiness and Usan, and into Lunan Bay. Here, just short of Red Head, we saw the enemy line of battle.

I do not believe that either Skipper Thomson or his crew in Rosehaugh were aware of our presence, as I led the boarding party over his bulwarks. Then began a furious confrontation. The crew of Rosehaugh numbered five, and there were four of us, including two police officers, though in circumstances such as those now facing them, these were, in more senses of the phrase than one, completely "at sea". Illegal nets and salmon could be seen lying about everywhere, but Skipper Thomson ignored all orders to stop. We were hijacked out on the high seas!

I shouted to Alec Coull to return ashore and summon assistance, and then asked Police Constables Bell and Powell to arrest and handcuff Thomson, while I took the "prize" to Montrose. Some miles from the coast, however, Thomson, surrounded by his friends of the enemy fleet, stopped and held a pow-wow.

The most militant of the other skippers told Thomson to throw Grant and MacIntyre overboard, and for a time the situation looked quite ugly. While all this was going on, I retired to sit on a coil of rope, and lit a cigar. Suddenly one of the fishermen pointed at me, shouting: "Look at that bastard smoking a cigar! He is enjoying himself!" With this, the atmosphere of extreme hostility seemed to be weakened to some extent, and by this time the police and fishery officers ashore were shouting over the radio. Thomson threw his catch and gear overboard, and made for Montrose, where he and his entire crew were arrested and charged. They received fines of several thousand pounds in the Sheriff Court. P.C. Powell gave evidence that I had obviously enjoyed the whole affair, and had added fuel to the confrontation!

About a week later I set out to attack the seine-netter, Spitfire, from Dunbar. Again, it was off Lunan that she was drift-netting, and launching Trafalgar from a motor trailer on the sands, we roared in to the attack. As we did so, Police Sergeant Bowshire and Police Constable Burnett of Arbroath Police were waiting on the sand dunes; they refused to accompany us.

Spitfire saw us coming and took to her heels, leaving the inshore end of the drift-net for us to inspect. I had my splendid regular crew, Superintendent MacIntyre, always ready for a fight, and that superb and efficient mechanic, Alec. Coull. With our knives, we hacked off about two hundred yards of the drift-net, together with eleven salmon, which was as much as we could manage to stow in the small space available in Trafalgar. Overloaded as we were, now was the time for Spitfire to attack us, and she careered in, looking as if about to ram. I told the skipper to heave to, but he ignored all orders to stop and, having failed to damage us, made off for the Forth and his home port. Back in Montrose, I summoned a meeting of myself, the Arbroath Fishery Officer, and the senior official of Montrose Police. However, when the prosecution was mounted, they made a complete mess of it, as also did the Procurator Fiscal.

It was left to Joseph Johnston and Sons Ltd. to bring a civil action against Spitfire and her skipper, Robert M. Davies of Dunbar. All the evidence against Davies was successfully led and proved, and the Sheriff in Arbroath granted a full interdict against him — the first of its kind ever granted in a Scottish court. This success in the civil courts threw into unmistakable relief the failure of the police, the Fishery Officer, and the Fiscal to uphold the law. After this, however, matters improved greatly. A marked increase in efficiency was apparent on the part both of the police and of the Fiscal.

I had one last great battle off Newtonhill, Aberdeen, when we successfully attacked another Forth drift-netter, capturing both nets and salmon, and landing them at Newtonhill in the presence of police and Fishery officials. The confrontation took place in appalling weather conditions. We had launched Trafalgar at Stonehaven, and suddenly, out of the trough between two huge waves, the drift-netters saw her climbing over a crest and planing down upon them. They could not believe their eyes!

Unfortunately, despite being warned that one of these cases was likely to be appearing shortly, the Fiscal of Stonehaven charged the offenders under another act, with the result that they escaped with the most petty fines. When I proposed to inform the local press, the Fiscal was furious with me and rang me up personally.

By this stage, I was fast becoming an almost full-time anti-drift-net enforcement agent. It was therefore decided to allow me to employ an ex-Royal Navy man again, to do the job full time, while I resumed my more normal duties as managing director of Johnstons. 'an MacCreadie Smith, the man I employed, had no other job, and took this one on immediately. He proved absolutely first-class at it, far surpassing the pleasant Lieut. Cdr. Brothers. In no time, he had the drift-netters on the run.

He worked in complete harmony with Superintendent MacIntyre, and also with Superintendent Crowley of the North Esk Fishery Board. Between the three of them, they virtually drove the drift-netters out of the coastal waters between Stonehaven and Arbroath. Johnstons also hired fast Rig Boats, such as 150 foot, 25 knot Smitt Lloyds, at £3,000 for 24 hours, until at last the inept Department of Agriculture and Fisheries showed a little more spunk, and started to harry the drift-netters themselves.

After some fines of several thousand pounds had been levied, the Second Salmon War collapsed, and apart from the odd clandestine foray, the real fighting was over. As I write this, there can be no doubt that the illegal sea poaching is continuing, and, thanks to the ineptitude of the Department of Agriculture and Fisheries and the Crown Prosecution Service, it is likely to continue. Recently, an Irish skipper was convicted of illegally catching 433 salmon off Barra Head, and was fined £3,500 in Stornoway. The salmon alone were worth £4,000, and a reasonable fine would have been £50,000. It has been said that the law is an ass. On the high seas, at any rate, the point has been amply proven!

A few years before I left the commercial salmon fishing scene, a new form of river poacher appeared, possibly still more dangerous than any of the "pirates" who had preceded him. It was the frogman. Organized gangs of such criminals have grown up in the areas of the Solway, Carlisle, and Dumfries. They have equipped themselves with every relevant device of modern technology: walkie-talkies, eavesdropping devices enabling them to listen to the police radios, and night vision equipment costing £5,000 a set. Armed with these, they have ravaged the East Coast rivers, including the Royal preserves at Balmoral. Today, they constitute a very serious threat.

Within the ranks of the police, a few have even turned poacher themselves. Two such members of the police force actually met their deaths while engaged in poaching at sea in bad weather. One of them was found drowned in his own net, while the body of the other has never been found. However, men of this type are fortunately few and far between.

The war against salmon poaching is unending. At present, indeed, it is intensifying. Unless in the future the Salmon Trust employs people with greater knowledge of the sea, and also of the criminal fraternity, I fear that in this war they will emerge the losers. However, let not any of my readers imagine that I am indulging in self-advertizing here, or promoting myself as a candidate for the job. Lest anyone should receive such an impression, I must state emphatically that I am too old, and that I have most definitely retired!

CHAPTER TWENTY-THREE

Excursion into Politics

As a youth I was fairly retiring and shy, but my initial entry into political debate revealed a completely different side to my character. The occasion was a meeting of the Junior Debating Society at Wellington, where the little boys attending were expected not to speak, but to listen. I was thirteen and a half at the time, and I remember it well, for I astonished everyone who knew me — myself included! In response to a speech by an older boy, I suddenly jumped to my feet, and in no time I was fiercely attacking his politics. From then onwards, I was no longer shy — certainly not where public speaking was involved. While at Wellington, my views were markedly left-wing and anti-establishment. At the age of fifteen, I wrote my first letter to the press. It was to the Daily Mirror, and the subject was the abdication of Edward VIII. I could not see why the act of marrying a divorcee and a commoner should disbar him from the throne, and I argued fiercely against those who wished him to abdicate. Hoping to escape the wrath of the authorities, I signed the letter, "Max Grant, Gardener, Wellesley House, Crowthorne."

The letter was seen and reported all right, and my housemaster was furious, but he could not take any action. At Wellington, in fact, I became notorious for the attitudes I displayed in school debates, and for my anti-establishment views in general. Already, however, I was definitely leaning towards National Socialism, and becoming an admirer of the ideas of Benito Mussolini and Adolph Hitler.

By the time war broke out, I had, of course, already left school. At this time, my dislike of Stalin's Russia far outweighed any hostility I may have felt towards Germany. Indeed, I held that Russia was far more to blame for the outbreak of war than any other power. As hostilities progressed, and despite the appalling bombing which I endured in Southern England, and my later experiences with U Boats, I never really blamed the Germans for the war. When at last Germany and Russia fell out, I strongly supported the position of J.T. Moore-Brabazon, the Minister of Transport, who suggested that we should withdraw from the war and leave them to fight it out between them.

Again, I was disgusted by the behaviour of our own trade unions, whose members, as civilian employees, were paid four or five times as much as our servicemen, yet were forever striking for higher pay. It was they who were the loud-mouthed champions of war against Germany, leaving others to do the fighting. When I was on leave, I was constantly writing to the press to attack the trades unions and the black marketeers, and I admired the way in which the Germans kept such unsavoury people under better control. In 1940 I suppported Oswald Mosley, Admiral Sir Barry Domville, and Captain Maulee Ramsay M.P. , and I held that they were all falsely imprisoned.

Following upon our victory over Germany, the result of the General Election of 1945 disgusted me. It was a victory for the all-powerful trade unions, and for the pro-Russian lobby. By this time, I was hating the Russians more fiercely than ever, and was reinforced in this attitude by what I had seen and heard for myself at Murmansk, during my wartime service.

So it was that in 1948 I was attracted to Mosley's new party, The Union Movement, and impressed by his chief lieutenant, Raven Thomson, who had been imprisoned with him. I saw much of Raven Thomson, and found him sound and persuasive. On several occasions, I also met Oswald Mosley himself. Unfortunately, Raven Thomson died young, and the new leader of the Party was Robert Rowe. As a character he was pleasant enough, but he had no fire in his belly. Within a few years, he had been succeeded by Jeffrey Hamm, but by that time it was too late; the Party had virtually collapsed. Though a splendid character — actually better at writing than public speaking — Jeffrey Hamm could not save it. During the war he had suffered badly for his views, and although he did his best to rally the faithful, the Party lost all impetus and power. I drifted towards the Empire Loyalists and thence towards the National Front.

Our local member of parliament was Colin Thornton Kemsley, and in the early sixties he retired. At the time, I did contemplate, rather half-heartedly, trying to get myself elected as a replacement candidate by the local Unionist Party, but I was too slow, and Thornton Kemsley's shoes were soon filled by Alick Buchanan Smith, a thoroughly hard-working, efficient, and honest young man, who has held the seat since then up to the present day.

While I was milling over my own apathy after losing this chance, I came into contact with Captain James A.L. Duncan, who represented the neighbouring constituency of South Angus. I first met him at Forfar, at a Farmers' meeting which I was attending as Chairman of the Montrose Branch of the National Farmers' Union. At this meeting, Jim Duncan was being fiercely attacked for his politics, and I even more fiercely defended him — the only speaker who did. Thereafter, we became good friends, and shortly afterwards, having been created a baronet, he declared his intention of retiring. About this time, I casually mentioned my own interest in politics.

The chairman of the Unionist Constituency Executive was an old friend of mine, Colonel Ivan Guthrie, and his political views were largely the same as mine. One Saturday morning, having just arrived back from Hamburg, I happened to be in Montrose. I was sitting in a pub with a fisherman friend when the publican told me that there was a telephone call for me. It turned out to be Ivan Guthrie, who had been trying to contact me all week. He told me that there was to be a candidates' election meeting that afternoon at Arbroath, and that he had nominated me! I had already had far too much to drink, and had no notes prepared, yet there I was, due to speak at the meeting in forty-five minutes, and it would take me thirty to get there!

The meeting was due to hear three candidates, of whom I was one. At the start, I was an outsider — completely unknown. By contrast, the other two had been nominated weeks before, and each of them had had his curriculum vitae well circulated. Mine, of course, had not. Perhaps it was the drink (though fortunately no one suspected it!), but, bereft as I was of notes, my speech flowed, and when I sat down I was delighted with my effort. So, in fact, was the committee. I was provisionally elected. However, it was such a shock decision on 'he part of the Selection Committee, that they said they would have to have my election ratified by the whole Executive Committee, and that all three candidates would have to speak again. Before that could take place, the Arbroath fishermen got wind of my candidature, as also did my opponents in the Farmers' Union, whom I had upset by standing up for Jim Duncan. These people were determined that when it came to the meeting before the whole Executive, my candidature should be blocked.

This time I came to the meeting well prepared. I had had absolutely nothing to drink, and had made copious notes for my speech. I was quite uninspired, and the speech itself was rotten. Jock Bruce Gardyne was elected in my place, ultimately becoming M.P.. It was an outcome which pleased Mrs Thatcher. Eventually he was created Lord Bruce Gardyne, and entered the House of

Lords. It was the First Salmon War that had scuppered me, and I returned home to lick my wounds.

During that First Salmon War, the Tory Secretary of State and the Vice-Chairman of the Party in Scotland was Neil Patullo. He had done much on behalf of the established salmon-netting trade in Scotland, and had made every effort to support us. There is no doubt that we owed him a debt. In view of all this, when he asked me whether I would consider opposing Jo Grimond, Leader of the Liberal Party, in his seat in Orkney and Shetland, I felt that I could not refuse. I knew I had no chance of winning, as did the Tory Party itself, but they wanted a standard-bearer, and we in the salmon industry owed them something.

It was therefore arranged that Ian Mowatt, the chief election agent for Scotland, should meet me in Aberdeen and escort me to Orkney and Shetland. There I was billed to meet the local constituency parties, preach to them, and, if thought suitable, be inducted! In Kirkwall, all went entirely smoothly and I was duly elected. Then we went on to Lerwick, a place I had never before visited. Being mid-winter, it was bitterly cold, and the Grand Hotel where we were staying was like a deep freeze! Never in my entire life until then had I experienced the luxury of an electric blanket, but all the beds in the hotel were fitted with them, and — particularly in such circumstances as those — the experience was a very pleasant one.

Ian and I duly appeared at the election meeting, and I was proposed, seconded, and unanimously adopted. After this, the "faithful" invited me to a party — "orgy" would be a better word. How those Shetlanders can drink! Only Russians could have competed with them!

At length Ian and I staggered homewards through the snow and the freezing dark, to what we fondly imagined was the front door of the hotel. It appeared to be locked. We knocked, kicked, and banged for all we were worth. Then I looked up. To my horror, it was not the Grand at all; it was the Commercial Bank of Scotland! Off we scuttled into the night, and at last found our hotel.

I nursed Orkney and Shetland for over a year, and made many good friends all over those far-flung isles. They were remarkably pleasant people, and the locals were always friendly and courteous. Some of those who offered to put us up in isolated hamlets were actually supporters of Jo Grimond.

About this period, I had a fairly serious motor crash, and after being hospitalized for some time, I was told by my doctor that I must take three weeks' holiday. Now I happened to know a young German, Peter Osterchrist, whom I had helped when he first came to England as a penniless youth. His uncle had actually been a State Secretary to Dr Goebbels. This lad was a commercial genius. He had later emigrated to the United States, and, within the space of a few years, had become a millionaire. At this juncture, therefore, I rang him up and asked whether I might stay with him in Baltimore, to which he gladly acceded. That same week, I was on my way. From Peter Osterchrist, I went on to visit Captain James Branscombe of the U.S. Navy, who lived near Washington, and it was while I was there that the Cuban crisis broke out. My next visit was to Victor C. Studley at Kansas City. He was the industrialist who had started the huge Scottish-American industry of Timex at Dundee. He and his wife took me to a cocktail party, where I met a lady who was private secretary to the former President, Harry S. Truman. Hearing of my interest in politics, she asked me whether I would like an interview with President Truman, and on my replying that I would, she booked me one then and there, for 10.30 a.m. the following day, at the Independence Library, Missouri.

This was a time when war seemed imminent. President Kennedy and Kruschev were raving at one another. The Russian and American fleets were due to meet head on at 11 a.m. off Cuba, and it was looking as though a Third World War was about to break out. At 10.30 sharp, I was ushered into the great man's presence — the man who had ordered the dropping of the first atomic bomb on Hiroshima.

Harry S. Truman was very easy to talk to, and to listen to him was fascinating. I had read his biography, and learnt quite a lot about him. He told me that there would be no war. He knew Kruschev, and knew that he was bluffing. Thank God he was right, as we heard on the radio about half an hour later! At the end of my holiday, I was quite glad to be airborne; I had no wish to be caught in the U.S.A. at the beginning of World War III!

Soon after this visit, I returned to Orkney and Shetland. I was trying to achieve as much publicity as I could, and, thinking to improve my political popularity, I bought the champion Aberdeen Angus bull at the much vaunted bull sales at Kirkwall. The Orkney papers showed a photograph of me chatting with President Truman, and underneath it a second one in which I was leading the bull round the Orkney show and sale ring. The caption was truly Liberal in tone. It read, "TORY CANDIDATE — PRIZE BULL".

As I have already said, the senior members of the Tory Party in Orkney were a splendid and loyal crowd. Nevertheless, I had made enemies among the Labour and Liberal Parties, some of whom described me as an under-cover fascist. Then the inevitable opponents appeared within the ranks of the Tories themselves. They were led by a seaweed merchant. For a few months I enjoyed a good running fight, but the dispute was threatening to split, and ultimately destroy, the Tory Party. By this time something approaching real civil war had broken out within the Tory camp in the Islands and, rather than exacerbate the differences, I chose to resign. My opponent within the Party had destroyed it beyond recovery. For my own part, on looking back, I can only feel deeply grateful to all those Islanders who supported me through thick and thin.

In reality, I was positively glad that my efforts to get into Parliament had been thwarted. The life would never have suited me, and I have little faith in the chicanery and time-wasting that are the hall-mark of the House of Commons. At a public meeting at Perth, although not a member, I gave my support to the Scottish Rhodesia Society. Many prominent people manifested their support at that meeting, including the Earl of Southesk, to whom I had given my backing in the past in his opposition to the neo-Communists of Whitehall. As for the meeting itself, it was, to me, unforgettable. I felt a power then which I have never felt before or since. Somehow I seemed to hypnotize the crowd as I had seen Billy Graham do. I got them to cheer when I wanted, and remain silent when I wanted.

A few days after the meeting, the chairman, Colonel Innes, asked me whether I would give a repeat performance in the Marryat Hall at Dundee. I said that it would be packed with left-wingers, who would break up the meeting. I consented to speak only on condition that I could provide some strong-arm stewards. Colonel Innes replied that he would have to do without me. When the meeting was held, the left-wingers, armed with eggs, tomatoes and flour, closed it within ten seconds!

In search of political truth, I have visited many countries, particularly those behind the Iron Curtain, and Cuba has been no exception. I went there in 1985. Throughout the visit, from Havana airport onwards, we were accompanied by a guide/interpreter, who had obviously been well vetted by Castro's secret police. At the time, I happened to be reading a paperback entitled *A Study in Violence*. It was the life story of the notorious Kray twins. The interpreter seemed interested in the book, so I promised to give it to him when I had finished it. This I duly did, remarking that it was a terrible indictment of Western incompetence in enforcing law and order. I admired the absence of graffiti in Cuba. He said that mugging and theft were non-existent. At one hotel, three hundred miles from Havana, we had some very down-to-earth discussions. One day he knocked at my room door and entered in a terrible state. All his clothes had been stolen — from him, the agent of the Party! Gratefully, he accepted my offer of white shirts, under-clothes and so forth, all marked with "St. Michael". They were well named! In fairness to Castro and his people, I must say that I was never molested in any way, and had nothing stolen. That is more than I can say for democratic London!

Now that I am a senior citizen, I have refused to join any political party. I support several, but I will not become a member of any. I believe that one can exercise more power outside the party system than within it.

Envoi

Envoi

The span of time covered by these reminiscences is slightly over sixty years. It begins with the fairly opulent life of a country family owning a large sporting estate in Scotland, and continues through the period of the world slump in the thirties. Next come the years of the Second World War, and finally the social revolution which has followed upon them.

The Industrial Revolution of a hundred and fifty years ago did more to change the face of Britain than anything that had happened in the preceding four hundred years. It was associated with the creation of an Empire (now given away), the like of which had never been known before, and would never be known again.

That major Revolution was followed by a lesser one, based on technical achievements and inventions such as those of the internal combustion engine, radio, and aeroplane. This second Revolution took us up to the Second World War.

During the years 1939-45, when nearly all the major nations of the world were embroiled in fighting one another, public spending on armaments and on advances in technology was immeasurably increased. During that time it reached such a crescendo that, in terms of real money value, it is unlikely to be surpassed in the future. The unforeseen outcome of all this has been a lasting dependence on nuclear power and nuclear bombs, the achievement of flights to the moon and the partial conquest of space, and, with the invention of radar, laser beams, and sophisticated listening devices, the almost total abolition of secrecy and privacy. From all this, a massive social revolution has erupted.

The teeming millions of Africa and Asia, who (apart from the United States), in earlier times, were seen only occasionally outside their own regions, have come flooding into Europe, and this, coupled with the almost universal disappearance of caste systems, has in reality constituted the greatest revolution of all. In seeking to promote world revolution, Marx seized upon the gulf which in his time used to exist between the aristocracy and the toiling masses. Today that is a thing of the past. That revolution has already taken place and has now passed on, a fact which is today borne out by the beginnings of chaos clearly apparent within the Communist states themselves. It is manifesting itself in Russia and China, once so highly organized and disciplined.

Perhaps my personal vision of all this, as I have lived through it, has been more varied than that of most people. That in turn may be due to the conditions of the class and the financial environment into which I was born, and the opportunities for travel which have come my way at a later stage in my life. I remember the years of affluence in the nineteen-twenties, the butlers, housemaids, kitchenmaids chauffeurs and gardeners, governesses and nurse-maids — in all, a miniature version of Buckingham Palace as we see it today. Privacy in the true sense hardly existed. Even I knew that after the older guests had retired for the night, one of my cousins took a parlourmaid to his bed. It was not from prowling around by myself that I knew this, but from gossip emanating from the servants' hall, to which I was sometimes invited as a great privilege when my governess was elsewhere!

The misery of "The Slump" of 1930-31 had its effects upon me. Sixty percent of the staff, both indoor and outdoor, were paid off. To some extent it was a social disaster, and I saw it as a personal one. Yet most of our neighbours and relatives were doing the same. It was a time of adversity indeed.

Probably the greatest crisis I ever suffered in the course of my youthful life was the one which occurred at Wellington during what was to prove my last term there. To every suggestion concerning my future, I was rebellious. I wanted to do this; my father wanted me to do that. Had the state of affairs which then developed lasted much longer, I believe that I would have been expelled. The compromise which was eventually reached between my father and myself seemed to me at the time a personal defeat. As the standard-bearer of a patrician family, I bitterly resented being made to weave fishing nets, or to carry massive loads of timber on my back like a mule labourer, at £1 a week. It seemed worse than a set-back to the glittering future of which I had dreamed. Yet it did me immense good.

On the whole, the outbreak of war did me proud. In spite of some sad and bloody episodes, by December 1943, I was commanding not merely a gunboat, but a group of gunboats. That was in Dover Command at the age of twenty-two. Everything seemed at my feet, and I was my parents' pride and joy.

Then disaster struck. First on Christmas eve, in an operation in which I had foreseen no great excitement, my best friend and second-in-command of my gunboat was killed almost at my feet. At the same time, good friends among the crew were mutilated, and the boat which had been my dream was destroyed. Quickly I recovered from this trauma, only to be faced with another, one which, to me personally, was, if possible, even harder to endure: the wrecking on Shakespeare Cliff at Dover not only of my own motor gunboat, but of the others which I was leading as well. It led to my being court martialled.

At the time, I wished that I had been killed along with, or better still in place of, Ian Galbreath the previous Christmas eve. Such were my thoughts as I left the court martial, with the nightmare of that sword-point staring at me. The nightmare persisted for several months. It was at its worst in June, 1944, while I was undergoing my gunnery course at Devonport Barracks. It was then that I first decided to write a book — more to rid my mind of the nightmare than anything else. I would call it "Courage in Adversity". I hoped that the effort would calm my soul, and carry it away from its morbid forebodings, which at times were nearly suicidal. I had found the title, yet the next step, that of putting pen to paper, was to take me another forty-five years!

The events subsequent to my court martial have already been covered. The further two years which I spent in the Navy were truly marvellous ones.

Certainly, when I became a civilian again, I resented my loss of status. In 1947 I attended an officers' reunion of some sort, and vowed that I would never attend another. All those war heroes were penniless. Those with safe administrative jobs ashore — they were the ones who had prospered! I commiserated with the fallen idols of my own status — but carried on.

My position at home, which at that time was still Ecclesgreig Castle, was also in disarray. When I left for the war, I had been a clean, non-smoking, non-drinking youth of eighteen. When I returned, I was getting through fifty cigarettes and half a bottle of whisky daily. I had turned into a ruthless, loud-mouthed autocrat. No wonder I was a pain to my parents! Yet we struggled on.

I overcame my initial difficulties. My employers were probably more than understanding. I was bursting with energy, and in no time had established a highly profitable sideline to my main job; I had become a timber contractor. By 1948, I had left the war years behind; I was completely rehabilitated. I was now not only a managing director of the same company which I had joined before the war, but also chairman of a Montrose shipyard in my own right. I was on the crest of a wave.

The directors of the firm which had originally employed me, and of which I had myself now become a director, were utterly straight and honest. Forty-eight years on, when I finally retired from them, this was, I will maintain, just as true as on the day when I started. The affairs of the shipyard presented me with a different problem when I was forced into a position in which I had to accept the full responsibility for the overdraft on the yard. The situation which I was facing then was for me as dire as that which I had had to endure in the aftermath of the court martial. My world was collapsing in ruins.

Notwithstanding all this, as my narrative shows, I survived — and, moreover, survived with great joy — the ensuing thirty-six years of life in local business until I retired. Yet that episode with the shipyard could be described as adversity in the truest sense. Indeed, I would count that as an understatement. To survive the pain cost me sore.

Then, after the death of my father, came the struggle to maintain what was left of Ecclesgreig Castle and the estate. It was a major headache. My father was remarkably loyal to his wife, and he had left the estate to me with the express purpose of keeping it on for her sake. My lawyers told me at the time that I was a perfect fool not to sell the estate at once — that it would be an intolerable burden. Burden it was. Yet in a way I enjoyed it. I fulfilled my father's wishes, and it gave great pleasure to my mother.

The cost in money terms was fearful. The annual running of it cost me several times my earned income. The interest on the bank overdraft became quite astronomical, and some years after my mother's death, I decided to sell up eighty percent of the estate, and thereby wipe out the overdraft. Once that was achieved, I was at last in a position to dictate to my bank manager. For the previous thirty-five years it had been the bank which had been dictating to me! I enjoyed the changed status.

Changed status? Yes indeed! I was no longer a Scottish laird of some standing. Instead I was living in a cottage that few people would have preferred to a council house. Yet I was more than happy. This was an end to adversity.

I was independent at last. I could change my bank manager whenever I wished; I could even change banks. I could dictate to those who had previously dictated to me. Maybe I lived in a sub-standard dwelling, but I was free, and I enjoyed it to the full. It was my home, with all my relics of sixty-eight years, and to hell with those which I wished to forget!

I have been more than lucky. In the war, I saw many die vicious and painful deaths, and I have seen others die even more painful deaths of cancer and other diseases. I have no wish to live to an excessive old age, and already I believe I have exceeded the average span. I have seen many ups and downs, but for those of us who are fortunate, as I have been, it is the downs that we forget.

Yet to achieve this, we must survive those awful moments when the end of the world seems to be pressing hard upon us, and that may remind us of one axiom that is always essential to cling to: Courage in Adversity. It has been an unfailing guide to me. May it also be a guide to you.

INDEX

ABEL, Col. Rudolph. Russian Spymaster 173
ACHNASHEEN. Remote Village/ Railhead in Wester Ross. 23
ADAMS. Capt. W.L.G., OBE. RN. (Later Vice Admiral) 106
AGAR. Capt. A.W.S., VC, DSO. RN 79, 176
ALEXANDER, A.V. First Lord of Admiralty 89
ALLEYN Capt. Sir John, Bart. RN. 131
ALLESBROOK. Flight Lieut. DSO. DFC, RAF. 83
ANDERSON, Squadron Leader Gavin 50
ANDES RMS (Troopship) 129
ANDREWS Lieut. H.S. RNVR. 80, 87
ARRAN HMS Isle Class Ocean Trawler 159, 161/2
AULTBEA Village in Wester Ross 23

BARGE Lieut. R. DSC. RNVR. 104
BATHURST Capital of Gambia (Now Banjul) 159
BEATTIE Capt. S.H. VC. RN. 183
BERRY HEAD Sinking of Tanker 56
BERTHON Lieut. Paul DSC. RNVR. 86
BEST-DALLERSON Lieut. RNVR. 141
BINNEY Admiral Sir Thos. Hugh 35, 41, 91, 107
BRIGGS Capt. H.D. RN. N.O.I.C. Loch Ewe. 27, 29, 30, 35
BRITISH POWER BOAT COY. 80
BRIXHAM Devon 69, 71
BROCKLESBY HMS Destroyer 56
BRUCE GARDYNE Jock M.P. (Later Lord Bruce-Gardyne) 213

CAIRD Sir James, Bart. Millionaire Philanthropist 14

CALEDONIAN CANAL 36, 74
CARRINGTON Able Seaman DSM. 99
CHARYBDIS HMS Cruiser Sunk 95
CHESNEY Ronald Naval Officer & Criminal 21
COLEMAN. Petty Officer Engineman 29
COLLINS. Lieut. J. RCNVR 92
COLVILLE OF CULROSS Cmdr. Lord, Naval Officer 23
CONGREVE. Lieut. RNVR. 63
COPINSAY HMS Ocean Trawler 159
CORNWELL Lieut. Cdr. RN. 112, 126
CRABB Commander 'Buster' GC RNVR. Spy Diver 176
CUBA Visit to 217
CUTHBERT Vice Adml. Sir John (Admiral Commanding Reserves) 181

DANIELSON Chief Petty Officer - West African Navy. 149
DARTMOOR PRISON 54
DARTMOUTH 65
DAVEY Lieut. Cdr. RNVR. 126
DAWSON Acting Captain P.F.M. RN 131, 135
DE CRESPIGNY Air Marshal, H.V. Champion 20
DE GAULLE Midshipman Philippe F.F.N. (Later Admiral) 93, 95
DE LOOZE Dutch Naval Officer & Diplomat 80, 81, 179
DE WINTON Capt. F.S.W. DSO RN 151
DEVONPORT 55, 118
DIMBLEBY Richard Broadcaster 44
DOENITZ German Admiral 21
DOLPHIN HMS Submarine Base 83, 85
DOUGLAS Isle of Man 73, 86

DOVER 44
DOWN Brigadier The Viscount (O.C.
  Troops, Sierra Leone) 139
DOWRICK Midshipman Frankm
  RNVR 69, 72
DROTTINGHOLM Red Cross
  Hospital Ship 123
DUFF STILL Lt. Cdr. RNVR. 185
DUKE OF YORK HMS Battleship
  121
DUNDARG H.M. Drifter 33
DUNDAS David Skipper 194

EDDYSTONE ROCK Under Fire 52
ELAND H.M. Naval Base Freetown
  130
EWART BIGGS Christopher.
  Ambassador 11

FAIRLIE Anti Submarine School 86
FEAR Lieut. A.D. DSC RNVR 90
FETTERESSO CASTLE 9
FISHER Rear Admiral R.L. DSO,
  OBE, DSC. 112
FOGARTY Group Capt. F.J. DFC,
  AFC, RAF. (Later Air Chief
  Marshal Sir Francis) 90
FORBES Admiral Sir Charles
  Morton 95
FORRESTER Able Seaman John 90
FORSYTH-GRANT Maurice. Pilot
  Officer/Squadron Leader R.A.F.
  54
FORT WILLIAM 65, 74
FRASER Admiral of the Fleet Lord
  Fraser of North Cape. 174

GAIRLOCH Village in West
  Highlands 30
GALBREATH Sub. Lieut. I.B. (Killed
  in action) 101 - 104
GOSPORT 80, 83
GRADWELL Lieut. Leo. RNVR.
  Naval Officer & Top London
  Magistrate. 32
GRENVILLE HMS Destroyer Sunk
  95
GRIEVE W.R. Lord. Naval Officer &
  Law Lord 27
GRIMOND Jo. Leader of Liberal
  Party (Later Lord Grimond) 214
GUNN Capt. P.L. DSM. RN. 90
GUTHRIE Lieut. G. RNVR. Killed
  88

HAMBURG 183
HENDERSON Able Seaman Alec.
  186
HEWITT Capt. RN. Retd. NOIC
  Detailed 76
HOBBS Joe. Whisky Millionaire 168
HOOD HMS Battle Cruiser 22
HORNET HMS Coastal Force Base
  Gosport 79, 80
HUGHES ONSLOW Lt. Cdr. RN. 33
HUNTER Dr. Medical Practitioner &
  Piper 29
HUSBAND J.I. CBE. 139, 155

INVEREWE World Renowned
  Gardens in West Highlands 30
INVERGORDON 76, 181
INVERNESS 23, 75
IRON DUKE HMS 23, 40
ISLAY Sound of 74

JOHNSTON Joseph & Sons Ltd.,
  Montrose 15
JOHNSTON Provost W. Douglas,
  OBE. 193
JORISSEN, Lieut. H.C. DSC. Royal
  Netherlands Navy. 100, 101

KALE Lieut. Keith. Killed in Action.
  87
KEAY Capt. W.F. OBE, VRD,
  RNVR. 180
KEELING Police Supt. Tony (Later
  Chief of Police Sierra Leone) 142
KEKEWICH Rear Admiral Piers 79,
  86
KENNERLEY, J.E. Senior Civil
  Servant 75, 131, 136, 154
KING ALFRED HMS 21
KING GEORGE V. Battleship 154,
  163
KISSY Suburb of Freetown 130
KITE HMS Sloop. Sunk. 113
KNIGHT Commander RN. 187

LARIVE Lieut. Cdr. Hans. Royal
  Netherlands Navy. 99
LAYE Evelyn. Actress 32
LENNOX BOYD Alan T. M.P. (Later
  Lord Boyd of Merton) 90, 100
LIDDELL, R.B. Civil Service
  Surveyor 136
LIMBOURNE HMS. Destroyer. Sunk
  95

LOCH EWE Remote West Highland Anchorage 28
LONG Brigadier, Hamburg District 185
LUMSDEN Lieut. J. RNVR. 78, 129

McCABE A.E. Salmon Poacher 202
MACDONALD Sir James.
Millionaire Gold 14
McINTYRE Superintendent Donald 206-209
MAIDSTONE HMS Destroyer Depot Ship 40
MALCOLM Sir Ian, Bart. of Poltalloch 67
MALIM F.B. Hedmaster of Wellington College 12
MARS Lt. Cdr. A.C.G. DSO. DSC. RN 175
MASHFORD BROS. Cremyll, Cornwall 69
MENZIES Commodore G.C.P. DSO RN 136/7, 145
MERRITT Donald George (See Chesney)
MIKOYAN Anastas, Russian Kommissar 125
MILFORD HAVEN Mined 56, 57, 73
MILLER Captain Dr. OBE. RNR. 97, 167
MILNE HMS Destroyer Flotilla Leader 116
MILNER Alan, Surgeon Lieut. RNVR 50, 61
ML 292 69, 73
MONTROSE HMS Minesweeper 167, 180, 1
MOORE Vice Admiral Sir Henry 122
MOORE BRABAZON Col. J.T. (Later Lord) 62, 63
MOSSADEG President of Iran 179
MOTOR ANTISUBMARINE BOAT 39 81
MOTOR GUNBOAT 9 87, 89
      ”   ”   6 89
      ”   ”   8 95
      ”   ”   118 98/99/104/ 105,
MOUNTBATTEN OF BURMA Adml. of the Fleet Earl. 41, 57/58
MURMANSK North Russian Port 113, 114, 119
MURRAY Capt. RN (retd) 85

MUSKETEER HMS Destroyer 111, 117, 120

NELSON HMS 18

OXNA HMS Isle Class Ocean Trawler 159

PARIS French Battleship 70
PEARSON Sir Robert, Chairman London Stock Exchange. 14
PETERHEAD 76
PHILOCTETES HMS Depot Ship Freetown 134
PLYMOUTH Blitz on 48, 69, 70
PORTLAND Naval Base 96
PORTREATH Cornwell. RAF Fighter Stn. 60
PORTSMOUTH 41, 43
PRATT Herbert. Oil Tycoon 9
PRIDHAM WHIPPEL Vice Admiral Sir H.D. 107

RAWLINS, Surg. Vice Adml. Sir John 11
REDPOLE HMS Sloop 174
RESOLUTION HMS Battleship 27, 57
RICHARDS Lieut. G.D.K. DSC. RN. 90, 98
RICHARDSON Telegraphist 71, 85
RODNEY HMS Battleship, Russian Convoy 119
ROPER Lieut. R.B. DSC. RN 98
ROTHNIE Sir Alan, Naval Officer and Diplomat 21, 116
ROYAL OAK HMS Battleship 23
ROYAL SOVEREIGN HMS Battleship 123
RUSSELL PONGO Squadron Leader RAF 51

SAMSUVA S.S. Sunk 119
SCAPA FLOW 23, 39, 40, 118, 123
SEA HAWK HMS. Base at Ardrishaig 67
SEAVIEW Isle of Wight 81
SHILLINGTON Cdr. C.A.R. RNVR. 40
SHORE BRUNDELL Lt. Cdr. M. RNVR 78
SHOWER HM Drifter 23
SINCLAIR Police Constable R. 30, 31

SINCLAIR Police Constable W. 30
SLADEN Commander G.M. DSO
   DSC RN 85
SMART G.G.J. Company Director
   201
SOMERS Lieut. D.B. RNVR 23, 36,
   37, 40
SQUIRES Petty Officer 58
ST. CHRISTOPHER HMS Base Ship
   Fort William 60
STEWART Capt. W.R. OBE, VRD,
   RNVR 170
STOGDON Sub. Lieut. E.D. RNVR.
   44
STRENSALL Military Camp near
   York 13
SWAYNE Regional Commissioner,
   Sierra Leone. 142

TAYLOR Paymaster Lieut. A.D.
   RNVR 129 & 145
TELFER SMOLLETT Alastair 11
THOMSON Eric Naval Officer 18, 21
TORQUAY C.I.D. 55
TOUGH BROS. Boatbuilders,
   Teddington 88
TRINIDAD HMS CRUISER 70
TRUMAN President Harry U.S.A.
   215
TUFNELL Lieut Michael RN 56
TULLETT Tom Chief Crime
   Reporter Daily Mirror 22
TUZO General Sir Harryn 11
TWEEDIE Lt. Cdr. H.E.F. DSC RN
   41, 50, 58.
TYNEDALE HMS Hunt Class
   Destroyer Sunk. 38, 63, & 72.

UNICORN HMS Aircraft Carrier 154
UNICORN HMS Drill Ship in
   Dundee 16

VAUX Commander RN 68
VICTORY HMS Base Ship at
   Portsmouth 47
VIVA II HM Armed Yacht Loss of 51
VLISSINGEN (Flushing) 179, 181

WALLACE Sergeant R.A. 143, 151
WARD Police Commissioner, Sierra
   Leone 142
WASP HMS Base at Dover 106
WAUCHOPE Captain RN. NOIC
   Stornoway 34

WAYRE Lieut. Philip W. RNVR.
   Broadcaster and Naturalist. 68, 88,
   101
WEEDON Lieut. John DSC RNVR
   124
WELLINGTON COLLEGE Berks. 7,
   15
WELMAN Capt. DSO. RN. 69
WESTCOTT Sub. Lieut R.L. RNVR
   138, 153, 159
WHEELER Signalman J.J. RNZN. 70
WHITWORTH Vice Admiral Sir
   William 92
WILLIAMS Telegraphist London
   Division RNVR. 34
WINTHROP YOUNG Lieut. J.
   RNVR. 89
WOLLVEN Lieut. D.W.B. RNVR. 104

YOUNG Cmdr. (E) Jimmy RNVR
   183
YOUNG Cmdr. Robert RN. 175